The London Cookbook

The London Cookbook

Written by Jenny Linford
Photography by Chris Windsor
Edited by Abigail Willis
Maps designed by Lesley Gilmour
Book design by Susi Koch and Lesley Gilmour

Published in 2008 by

Metro Publications
PO Box 6336
London
N1 6PY

Printed and bound in India by Replika Press Pvt. Ltd.

British Library Cataloguing in Publication Data.
A catalogue record for this book is available from the
British Library.

ISBN 978-1-902910-29-1

The London Cookbook

Jenny Linford

Photographs by Chris Windsor

Metro Publications

Acknowledgements

Heartfelt thanks, first of all, to Chris for all the time and hard work he put into taking the photographs for this book; they really bring the book to life. Thank you, also, to the many recipe contributors for generously sharing their recipes, the people I interviewed for letting me talk to them and also to all those who helped me find potential recipe contributors. Chris and I would like to thank all those who let us take pictures, including Billingsgate, New Covent Garden and Smithfield markets and Manzes the vintage pie and mash shop, in Tower Bridge Road. My thanks, finally, to my publishers, Andrew, Susi and the team at Metro Publications.

Jenny Linford is a freelance food writer based in London. She is the author of a number of books including Food Lovers' London (Metro Publications), a cosmopolitan guide to London's gastronomic scene including food shops and eating places.

An inveterate food shopper herself, Jenny founded the highly successful Gastro-Soho Tours in 1994, offering personal guided tours around London's food shops, ranging from bustling Chinese supermarkets to vintage Italian delis.

www.jennylinford.co.uk

Chris Windsor is a freelance, professional photographer, based in London. Chris's work has ranged from advertising campaigns and company reports to books including Food Lovers' London.

www.chriswindsor.com

For Chris and Ben, with my love

CONTENTS

Introduction

This book celebrates London's vibrant and diverse food culture, both past and present. For centuries an international trading centre, London has a long, greedy presence as a place of consumption, a tradition continued today in its bustling food markets, superb specialist shops and thriving restaurant scene. The River Thames was central to London's development as a trading hub and its docks and wharves once teemed with shipping bringing in goods and produce from overseas. Today the river runs serenely through the centre of the capital carrying little river traffic other than a few pleasure boats.

London is a city that pulls in people, both from other parts of Britain and from other countries; it is a city that attracts people looking for work and opportunities as well as those fleeing from persecution, war or other hardships. The different communities settling in London have contributed to its food culture. Fish and chips is thought by some to owe its origins to the traditional Jewish dish of fried fish and to have originated in London's East End Jewish community. The practice of smoking salmon with a lighter cure, known as a "London cure", was introduced by Jewish immigrants to London's East End in the late 19th century. At around the same time, Italian immigrants made ice cream and sold it on the streets, helping to popularise this newly affordable, frozen treat. Londoners' appreciation of novelty has long made the city a fruitful ground for new foods and drinks such as coffee and tea. Britain's first ever restaurant specialising in Indian food, for example, was established in London in the early 19th century. Many of London's ethnic communities, such as the Chinese and the Italian, have moved into the catering trade, finding a large audience for their cuisines. Today London's diverse gastronomic scene – with restaurants ranging from Afghani to Singaporean – is celebrated by the British Tourist Board.

Having spent many years writing about London's food scene, charting and mapping its various communities' food shops among other aspects, the chance to work on a cookbook celebrating London was very welcome. The recipes in the book are a mixture of my own and recipes contributed by assorted food-loving Londoners. They include traditional British dishes – such as gooseberry fool and kedgeree – and contemporary recipes for dishes such as purple-sprouting broccoli pasta and Thai green chicken curry, reflecting the reality of how Londoners cook today and the incredible range of ingredients available in the Capital.

Meeting the various Londoners who have so generously contributed recipes to this book proved to be a very hospitable experience. What struck me about the people I talked to was their love of food. Often this was expressed in where they shopped for ingredients – with keenly-held views on where to buy really fresh fish and good meat or find bargain-priced bunches of coriander – and always in the pleasure they took in cooking for family or friends. At a time when the sales of ready-meals are rising inexorably and people are so quickly losing basic food knowledge, it was heartening to find so many people really caring about the food they bought and cooked.

Thinking back over the writing of the book, my most vivid impression is the kaleidoscopic nature of London's food scene. Setting the alarm early to visit the tough, masculine world of Smithfield meat market; walking down Ridley Road Market with its African and Caribbean stalls piled high with bunches of plantains, yams and colourful Scotch bonnet peppers; talking to knowledgeable butchers, fishmongers and grocers who have kept their family businesses alive in the face of substantial competition. With so many food cultures existing side-by-side and so many delicious foods out there to be sampled, London is a great destination for food-lovers – I hope you enjoy exploring it as much as I have.

Jenny Linford

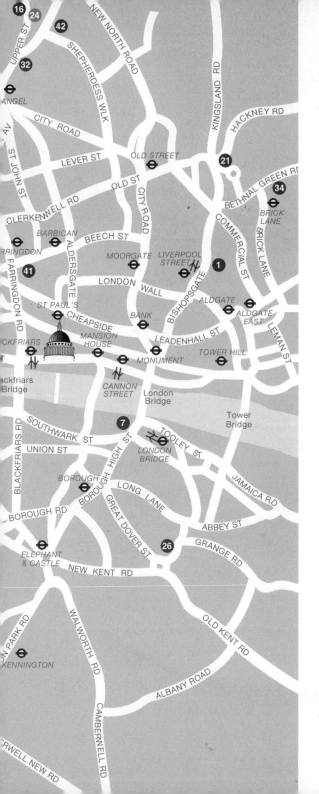

Breakfast

Claire Peasnall's West Indian Marmalade
Makes 2.25kg (5lb)

Claire's marmalade is based on a recipe from Fowler's Black Treacle booklet that Claire sent off for years ago. The West Indian connection appealed to her and she has been making this particular marmalade ever since.

450 g (1 lb) Seville oranges
1 lemon
1.35 kg (3 lb) caster sugar
50 g (2 oz or 2 large tablespoons treacle
2 litres (3 $^1/_2$ pt) water

Equipment:
a square of white muslin or loose-weave cotton or linen, the size of a large handkerchief
1 large jam pan
5-7 clean, dry 450 g (1 lb) jam jars, plus waxed paper discs, labels and rubber bands

Scrub the Seville oranges and lemon thoroughly under the cold tap. Cut the oranges and lemon in half and scrape the pips into a pile in the centre of the muslin square. Fold up the cloth around the pips and tie tightly with a long piece of string.

Squeeze the oranges and lemon, pouring the juice into a large jam pan. Scrape out and discard the remaining pulp from the fruit. Cut the orange and lemon skins into short chunky strips and add to the jam pan, along with the water. Suspend the pips in the pan by using the string to tie the muslin bag to the handle.

Bring the orange and lemon mixture to the boil, then semi-cover and simmer very gently for about 3 hours to soften the fruit skin.

Remove the bag of pips, then add the sugar and treacle and stir until dissolved. Bring to the boil and boil hard, skimming off any scum as it comes to the surface. It usually takes 15-20 minutes to reach setting point. Watch for the moment when the jam rises up the sides of the pan, making loud plopping noises. Test by dropping a teaspoonful onto a cold plate – if the surface wrinkles when you push it remove the pan from the heat.

Warm the clean, dry jam jars in a moderate oven for 5 minutes to sterilise them. Ladle the hot marmalade into the jars and leave until cold to cover and seal.

Claire's Tip: I often put the juice, cut peel and water in a large mixing bowl overnight. This reduces the simmering time and gives you extra marmalade. The texture may be less stiff and the colour paler, but the flavour still dark and bitter-sweet.

> *"We were moving back to London and chose to live here in Newham because we'd fallen in love with Queen's Market, which reminds me of Trinidad. It's a living thing, like a coral reef."*
>
> *Claire Peasnall*

Born in Trinidad, artist Claire Peasnall has vivid memories of her Caribbean childhood: "We had a big house on stilts in the hilly, cool part of Port-of-Spain. We ate sugar apples out of doors, seeing who could spit the shiny black pips furthest, mangoes, sucked off the stone, and sucked on batons of sugar cane during the harvest. Best of all – a treat for the beach – was the green coconut, fetched down from the palm before your eyes. With a flash of the cutlass the top would be opened so wide that when you'd drunk the coconut water inside you could scrape out the pearly jelly. There was a tethered monkey I used to walk by and it had dropped its stone that it used to crack nuts. I adored Monkey so I picked up his stone and gave it to him but he was so angry at being chained that he ignored the chain and bit my arm really badly. I still remember it being stitched up without anaesthetic. I was used to tiny bananas and I remember how disappointing it was to come to England and find only big, dark yellow bananas instead of tiny, child-sized bananas."

Since moving to Newham a few years ago, Claire and her husband John have been actively involved in a campaign to save the market from insensitive development.

Sharon's Cholla French Toast

Makes 6 slices

The traditional Jewish plaited cholla bread, with its sweetness and light texture, makes great French toast. My dear friend Sharon Goldman suggested this recipe to me and it is a favourite Saturday breakfast dish with her two children.

1 large, free-range egg
salt and freshly ground pepper
butter for shallow-frying
6 slices of cholla bread
maple syrup, to serve

Beat the egg in a bowl, seasoning with salt and freshly ground pepper. Heat the butter in a large, non-stick frying pan until it froths. Dip each slice of cholla in the egg, coating it. Fry the egg-coated bread until golden on both sides. Serve at once with maple syrup.

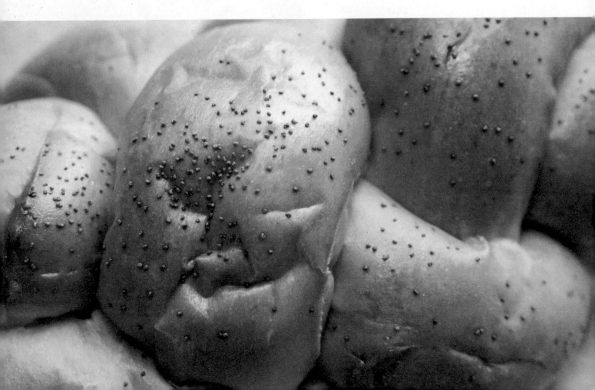

Apricot Cashew Granola
Makes 600g (1 1/4 lb)

Making your own granola is both simple and satisfying. Experiment with different combinations of nuts, seeds and dried fruits until you discover your favourite mix of flavours; this is mine.

250 g (9 oz) oats
115 g (4 oz) sunflower seeds
115 g (4 oz) natural cashew nuts
25 g (1 oz) sesame seeds
100 ml (3$^1/_2$ fl oz) sunflower oil
5 tbsp runny honey
pinch of salt
1 tsp vanilla extract
150 g (5 $^1/_2$ oz) organic dried apricots, chopped

Preheat the oven to Gas 1/140°C/275°F

Mix together the oats, sunflower seeds, cashew nuts and sesame seeds in a shallow roasting tray.

In a small saucepan, gently heat together the sunflower oil and honey for a few minutes, stirring well to mix. Mix in the salt and vanilla extract.

Pour the honey oil over the oat mixture, mixing thoroughly. Bake in the oven for 2-2 $^1/_2$ hours, stirring now and then, until golden-brown and crunchy.

Allow to cool, mix in the chopped dried apricots and store in an airtight container.

Café Stories

Dotted round the capital, London's remaining caffs – warm, bustling, democratic – are a much-loved antidote to the impersonality of 21st-century chain-land. Often family-run, often Italian-run, they serve up freshly cooked food – mushroom omelette and chips, bacon, egg and bubble, golden syrup sponge pudding, jam roll, all washed down with mugs of strong tea. Here food is enjoyed off Formica table tops set with the mandatory squeezy bottles of tomato ketchup and brown sauce, a vinegar shaker, salt and pepper. Meals in these busy cafés are punctuated by characteristic sounds: the sizzle of bacon rashers, the splutter of eggs in oil, and the pressurised hiss of hot water.

"By the time they leave, I know their life story. I'm not nosy, but I take an interest."
Maria Moruzzi

Maria's Market Café

Maria Moruzzi, whose parents set up the legendary Borough Café in 1961, now runs her own café in nearby Borough Market.

"We had wholesalers, Brook Bond Tea, Courage brewery – this is empty compared to what it used to be. The Market used to start at 1pm. In those days every high street had a greengrocer. My parents came over after World War II – there wasn't any work, so they came here in the 1950s. You weren't allowed in the country unless you had a sponsor for work and lodgings. They found it hard, but people used to get on with life. They didn't expect anything from anyone. As a child growing up around here we played in the rubbish tip – took crates and made 'shops' from them, sold rotten fruit. I'd wake up to singing, swearing, laughing – not bird song, the sound of wheelbarrows and bin men; they pushed the rubbish down with their feet in those days. It was safer than

it is now – everyone looked after each other. Then this area sort of died, different customers came – our bubble became trendy, which baffles me! I think it was nostalgia – we'd get people saying 'I haven't had this since I was a child,' it reminds them of home life.

"I like people. I'm interested in people. What I like is that everyone's got a story; in here everyone's equal. The Big Issue seller sitting next to a solicitor, sitting next to an actor. Through the banter everyone gets to know everyone and it's a network. People that have gone through hard times with us, they've become part of the family. If I'm busy they'll help me. I get a lot of customer help – that's how I survive. When someone new comes in I always ask 'Are you working near here?' By the time they leave, I know their life story. I'm not nosy, but I take an interest."

Maria's Market Café , Borough Market, Southwark St, SE1

15

Dory's Café

At Dory's Café in High Barnet, Doreen Cardosi – "Dor" – is never still: bringing plates of freshly cooked food and cups of tea to the formica-topped tables – "Here girls, is that alright? Do you want a drop more milk in it?" – clearing plates and wiping the tables clean. All the time keeping an alert, eagle eye on proceedings: "He's looking for his bread – a couple of slices for Patrick."

"We came here in 1958 – me, Mum and Dad. There was already a café here, don't know how old it was, but we took over it in 1958. The week we opened here the cattle market closed. There was still a market; it was really good then". Today Dory's Café is run by Doreen with her husband Tony and children Giuliano and Angela, open from 6am to 4pm.

Regulars include one couple who've been coming for 43 years, driving from St Albans.

> "Lots of them come in that used to be babies and they come in with their own families now."
>
> Doreen Cardosi

Dory's Café, 3 St Alban's Road, EN5

Lunch & Breakfast

Sausage, Egg, Chips
Egg, Chips & Beans
Egg, Bacon & Chips
Sausage, Egg, Chips & Tomatoes
Egg, Bacon, Sausage & Chips
2 Sausages, Egg, Chips & Beans
2 Eggs, Bacon, Sausage & Tomatoes
Egg, Bacon, Sausage & Mushroom
2 Sausages, Egg, Bacon, Chips & B
2 Beefburgers, Egg, Chips
Ham Egg & Chips
Corned Beef, Chips & Beans
2 Poached Eggs on Toast
Baked Beans on 2 Toast
2 Eggs on 2 Toast
2 Scrambled Eggs on 2 Toast
Egg, Bacon, Sausage, Black Pudding
Extra   Egg, Sausage, Beans, Tom
Extra   Mushrooms, Bacon, Chips,

E Pellicci

Founded in 1900, E Pellicci on Bethnal Green Road is a small but perfect gem of a café, still run by the Pellicci family. Such is its classic caff décor – complete with vintage wooden marquetry panels – that it's been listed by English Heritage. Now in his eighties, Nevio Pellicci, who was born above the café, cuts a spry, elegant figure with his pencil moustache, blue and white striped shirt, tie and tie-pin and white apron tied round his trousers, greeting all Pellicci's customers, whether regulars or newcomers, with courtesy and friendliness. "Good morning young lady," "Ham off the bone, bubble and beans – a good choice, sir." His son, Nevio Junior, has the same warm manner, swapping jokes and banter across the room. A photo album testifies to the list of celebrity customers who've been here – from East Enders soap stars to pop stars. The charm of Pellicci's, however, is that all its customers are made to feel special.

Ham off the bone, bubble and beans – a good choice, sir."

Nevio Pellicci

E Pellicci, 332 Bethnal Green Road, EC!

Classic Fry-Up
(serves 4)

The Great British Breakfast is a national institution. Although the actual cooking is straightforward, attention to timing is required to get everything just right at the same time.

8 rashers of good-quality, dry-cured bacon
1 x 415g tin Heinz baked beans
4 ripe tomatoes, halved
4 free-range eggs
salt and freshly ground pepper
4 slices of white bread, crusts trimmed, quartered into triangles
butter, for frying
sunflower oil, for shallow-frying
HP sauce or brown sauce, to serve
tomato ketchup, to serve

Place the bacon in a large, heavy-based frying pan and set to cook gently on a ring at the back of the stove until cooked to taste (I like it cooked till any fat on the bacon is golden-brown and crunchy).

Pour the baked beans into a heavy-based saucepan and set to simmer gently, stirring now and then.

Preheat the grill and grill the tomatoes until softened and slightly blackened.

Meanwhile, heat a bit of butter and a little sunflower oil in a large frying pan. Add the bread and fry until golden on each side.

On a separate ring heat a bit of butter in a large frying pan. Carefully break in the eggs and fry until cooked to taste, seasoning with salt and freshly ground pepper.

Serve the bacon, baked beans, grilled tomatoes, fried bread and fried eggs at once on warm plates with lashings of brown sauce and ketchup.

The best bacon...

When it comes to what makes really good bacon, pig farmer Peter Gott of Sillfield Farm in Cumbria (whose stall at London's Borough Market does a roaring trade in fresh and cured meat from his own, free-range wild boar and rare breed pigs), has clear ideas.

"*The pig is a wonderful animal – we get three sorts of meat from it, fresh pork, bacon and ham. We use pigs at 26 weeks. An intensively reared pig is killed at 16-18 weeks, when it hasn't really matured into adulthood and the flavour of the bacon is affected. I learn from the Italians and the Spanish – they don't cure young pigs. First your pig, then your cure. Our 20 pounds of pork – dry-cured – turns into 16 pounds of bacon, so we've lost 4 pounds. That concentration of meat means there's a lot of flavour.*"

Peter Gott, Sillfield Farm

Borough Market, Southwark Street, SE1

Dried Fruit Compote
Serves 6

My favourite shop for the dried fruits used in this and the granola recipe on page 13 is Martyns in Muswell Hill. This is an old-fashioned grocer's shop, now over 100 years old, where Mr Martyn still roasts his coffee beans in small batches in the window, sending the scent of coffee wafting out into Muswell Hill Broadway. Inside, the shop's dark wooden shelves are filled with various teas and coffees, packets of biscuits, spices and own-packed, assorted dried fruits.

300 g (10 oz) mixed dried fruit (including prunes, apricots, pears and apple rings)
200 ml (7 fl oz) vin santo or dessert wine
200 ml (7 fl oz) freshly squeezed orange juice
25 g (1 oz) Demerara sugar, or to taste
1 cinnamon stick
1 vanilla pod
3 cardamom pods
natural or Greek yoghurt, to serve

Place the dried fruit, vin santo, orange juice, sugar, cinnamon, vanilla pod and cardamom pods in a heavy-based saucepan. Bring to the boil, reduce the heat, cover and simmer for 30 minutes; cool. Store covered in the fridge. Serve with yoghurt either at room temperature or chilled.

Ben's Ginger Chocolate Muffins
Makes 6

50 g (2 oz) butter
150 g (5 oz) plain flour
2 tsp baking powder
$^1/_2$ tsp salt
3/4 tsp ground ginger
50 g (2 oz) Demerara sugar
150 ml (5 fl oz) milk
1 medium free-range egg
25 g (1 oz) dark chocolate, chopped
2 knobs of stem ginger in syrup,
   finely chopped

Preheat oven to Gas 6/200°C/400°F.

Melt the butter and set aside to cool slightly. Sift the flour, baking powder, salt and ground ginger into a large mixing bowl and then sift again for extra lightness. Mix in the sugar.

In a separate bowl, mix together the milk, egg and melted butter. Add the milk mixture to the sifted dry ingredients. Sprinkle over the chocolate and stem ginger and quickly fold together, taking care not to over-mix.

Spoon the mixture into a greased 6-hole muffin tray. Bake for 25 minutes until risen and golden-brown. Remove from the oven and cool on a wire tray.

My 11-year-old son, Ben Windsor, came up with the idea for these muffins: "I thought it would be a good combination," explains Ben, "as the flavours go together. I like stem ginger and I thought it would be nice to have a sweet ginger dish, but stem ginger on its own would have been too plain."

Sini's Cinnamon Buns

Makes around 20 buns

55 g (2 oz) fresh yeast
500 ml (18 fl oz) warm milk
800 g (1 3/4 lb) plain flour
225 g (8 oz) caster sugar
3 tbsp ground cardamom
1 free-range egg
400 g (14 oz) butter, softened
2 tsp vanilla extract
muscovado sugar, to sprinkle
caster sugar, to sprinkle
ground cinnamon, to sprinkle
beaten egg, to glaze

Add the yeast to the warm milk in a mixing bowl and stir until dissolved. Add the flour, caster sugar and cardamom and break in the egg. Mix together to make a soft dough. Knead vigorously until thoroughly mixed. Mix in 200 g (7 oz) of the butter and knead until the dough no longer sticks to the sides of the bowl.

Cover and leave to rise in a warm place until doubled in size, around 45 minutes. Punch the risen dough down.

Roll the dough evenly into a thin, even sheet about 1-1.5 cm ($^1/_3$-$^1/_2$ in) thick. Mix the vanilla extract into the remaining butter. Spread the vanilla butter evenly over the dough. Sprinkle generously with muscovado sugar, caster sugar and lots of ground cinnamon ("don't be shy", advises Sini). Roll the dough up over the filling to form a tight roll, like a Swiss roll.

Using a large, sharp knife cut slices off the dough roll 5 cm (2 in) thick, slanting the knife so that one side of the slice is longer than the other (say 7-8 cm (3-3$^1/_4$ in) on the long side and 5 cm (2 in) the shorter). Using the handle of a wooden spoon or a broad-handled knife, press down firmly and sharply in the middle of each dough portion, indenting it. Pat the dough portion sharply on each of the 4 sides and set aside on a tray, leaving enough space for it to rise. Repeat the process until all the dough has been portioned and shaped. Cover with a clean tea towel and set aside in a warm place to rise for 10-15 minutes.

Preheat the oven to Gas 3/170°C/325°F. Brush the cinnamon buns with beaten egg, then bake them for 12-15 minutes until risen and golden-brown.

> # "We eat them all day – there's always an excuse for a cinnamon bun."
>
> *Sini Kilalainen*

Austerely stylish, with its high ceilings and uncluttered décor, the Nordic Bakery in Golden Square offers Londoners a rare chance to sample Scandinavian food such as Karelian pies. The choice is limited but the quality is high. Stars of the show, however, are the cinnamon buns, freshly baked downstairs by Finnish chef Sini Kilalainen.

Sini's desire to be a chef was inspired by her uncle, a head chef in a famous Finnish restaurant. "I always looked up to him and thought that's what I want to do" she explains. Her work has taken her to a number of countries, cooking in very different types of restaurants. "Here the thinking behind the food is that it should be made from good ingredients and be very simple, very authentic and very plain. In Sweden their cinnamon buns are a different shape; they cut them. I think that's the lazy way! We eat them all day – there's always an excuse for a cinnamon bun. It's a general, everyday thing – definitely with coffee or with a glass of cold milk, with the buns warm from the oven."

Nordic Bakery, 14 Golden Square, W1

London's Bakeries

Think of bakeries and London's history and of course one particular bakery springs to mind – the bakery on Pudding Lane, near London Bridge. It was here in 1666 that a fire spread out of control, causing a conflagration that burned from Sunday to Thursday, devastating the city.

For centuries, bakeries were a common presence on London's high streets, providing local people with freshly-baked bread, pastries and cakes. These days, however, with bread making increasingly mechanised and industrialised, traditional bakeries (where the bread is made from scratch and baked on the premises) are increasingly hard to find. London's multi-cultural nature, however, does make for a richly diverse bakery scene,

with assorted bakeries serving their own communities. This is a city where, as well as white sliced bread, one can find freshly baked bagels from Jewish bakeries, Portuguese custard tarts, Lebanese flat breads, sesame seed-studded Greek loaves, West Indian bread, flavourful Polish rye bread and crisp baguettes from chic French bakeries. At Yasar Halim, a landmark Turkish foodshop on Green Lanes, industrious bakers work busily behind the scenes, sending out tray after tray of freshly baked, golden-brown loaves of assorted breads and pastries to the bustling bakery. Recent years have also seen the rise of artisan baking in the capital, pioneered by chef Sally Clarke, and a new appetite among consumers for decent bread. Yasar Halim, Green Lanes, N4

Windmills in London

London's bread was once made from flour ground in London's many windmills. Today, Wimbledon Common is still home to .what is believed to be the last example of a hollow-post flour mill in Britain, built in 1817. Street and place names remind us of former mills. Soho's Great Windmill Street, with its Windmill Theatre, was named after a windmill that stood there until the late 18th century, while Windmill Hill in Hampstead gained its name from a windmill that sat on top of the hill from the 14th to the early 18th century. Today G R Wright in Ponders End is Greater London's last remaining working windmill. Formerly known as Ponders End Mill, in the then rural hamlet of Enfield, the mill was taken over by the Wright family in 1867. The family still run the mill today, having modernised its machinery over the decades, enabling it to stay competitive. G R Wright is a major producer of flour and packet bread mixes, supplying both major companies and independent bakeries.

The Baker's Story

Matt Jones of Flour Power City is one of a new generation of craft bakers making their mark on London's bread scene. Flower Power City's eye-catching stalls at Borough Market and numerous farmers' markets – piled high with assorted, good-looking loaves, pastries and cakes – do a roaring trade and the bakery also supplies restaurants and delis: "I've always loved food," explains Matt. "I grew up in a home where we ate proper grub, not ready-meals. My Mum made bread and I was always in the kitchen. After school I worked on a youth training scheme as an apprentice chef. I was always drawn towards pastry-making. Having worked as a chef, I then worked as a baker and set up Mezzo Bakery for Terence Conran.

After that I decided it was time to go out on my own and set up Flour Power City in Hoxton.

"We do artisan baking – it's just flour, water, salt and yeast, no additives. I use Shipton Mill flour and import rye flour from Austria – the Austrians are very good millers. We get through 12 tons of flour a week. The great thing about having my own business is that if there's an ingredient I want to use – say a honey that I like the flavour of, but which is expensive – I can get it.

"For our sourdough we have the mother dough that has to be kept on the go. The whole process of making bread is very precise, involving timing and temperature control. At the bakery we work in three shifts over 24 hours. The 6am-2pm shift do the rye bread and get

all the starters ready, 2pm-8pm do all the brown breads, the sourdoughs and the soft white breads and the 8pm till 4am shift do the 'crusty stuff' like London bloomers. The baguettes are made last; they need to be the freshest. My favourite bread is our Hoxton rye levain, which has a great flavour. Brownies are our biggest selling item. The smell when they come out of the oven is amazing.

"Today there's a good bread scene in London. More and more people are eating good bread. We work as a team. The other bakers have been with me for 4-5 years. I love the bakery environment. It is hard, unrelenting but extremely satisfying work."

Flour Power, Borough Market, Southwark Street, SE1

> *We do artisan baking – it's just flour, water, salt and yeast, no additives. I use Shipton Mill flour and import rye flour from Austria – the Austrians are very good millers."*
>
> Matt Jones

Summer Smoothie
Serves 4

In summertime, when London's street markets are full of abundant, cheap seasonal fresh fruit like strawberries, home-made smoothies make a great breakfast drink.

juice of 2 oranges
400 g (14 oz) strawberries
1 ripe banana
1 tbsp wheatgerm
1 tbsp honey
6 tbsp natural yoghurt

Place the orange juice, strawberries, banana, wheatgerm, honey and yoghurt in a blender. Blend until smooth. Serve at once.

Apple Drop Scones
Makes 14-16

Drop scones are a traditional British dish. Here, a chopped English apple, such as a Cox's Orange Pippin, adds sweetness and spices a touch of fragrance.

15 g (¹/₂ oz) butter
115 g (4 oz) self-raising white flour
pinch of salt
1 tbsp caster sugar
1 free-range egg
150 ml (5 fl oz) milk
1 dessert apple, peeled and finely chopped
1 tsp grated lemon zest
pinch of freshly grated nutmeg
¹/₂ tsp ground cinnamon

Melt the butter and set aside.

Sift the flour and salt into a mixing bowl. Beat in the egg and the milk to form a thick batter. Stir in the chopped apple, lemon zest, nutmeg, cinnamon and melted butter.

Heat a large, non-stick frying pan until hot. Drop in tablespoons of the mixture to form the drop scones, spacing them apart. Cook over a medium heat until set, then turn over to lightly brown on the remaining side. Serve at once.

Street Markets

Markets have always been part of London's life. London's food markets vary enormously in character, from the established wholesale operations, such as Billingsgate or Smithfield, which can trace their histories back for centuries to the local market stalls providing fresh fruit and veg come rain or shine. The pressures of development and changing shopping patterns have seen many street markets struggle. It is, however, still possible to find traditional, down-to-earth street markets, such as Islington's Chapel Street, Hackney's Ridley Road or Notting Hill's Portobello Road, with roadside stalls selling cheap fresh fruit and veg, fresh fish, meat and cheese.

In a city that is constantly changing and in a state of flux, markets, too, are re-inventing themselves. Down by London Bridge, Borough Market, a historic wholesale fruit and veg market, is now home to a thriving weekly retail market on Thursdays, Fridays and Saturdays, showcasing good quality produce from Britain and abroad. Borough Market has become such an important part of London's food landscape that it has its own dedicated section within this book (see page 144). Likewise, Farmers' markets have become an important direct route from food producer to customer and have their own section (see page 337). While many street markets are in decline some have been brought back to life such as Hackney's Broadway Market on Saturdays which is bringing shoppers back from the supermarkets to a slower, more sociable and community-minded way of food shopping. See page 336 for a listing of some of London's best food markets.

In the East End of London, busy Queen's Market on Green Street serves Newham's many diverse communities; here are stalls selling coriander, yams and mangoes side-by-side with ones offering duck eggs, onions and potatoes. Local resident, poet Benjamin Zephaniah, has spoken eloquently of what Queen's market means to him and to the community it serves.

Our culture is not the culture that sells in the West End. All that life in the Market. I came to live here over 20 years ago and I was poor and used to shop in the market. I love the sound of it, with people shouting out their prices. In summer you get these really unusual mangoes – you often see weird or wonderful things on sale. It gives the street a lot of character. There is something very wonderful about a traditional English market with influences from West Indians and Asians. This area has a lot of refugees, a lot of elderly people – it's not just sentimentality, it's practicality – cheap fresh food, job opportunities, a wonderful place in the summer. People need pride of place. We have some valuable things in a community and, once they're gone, they can't be replaced. People who use a market and care about it – that's very difficult to measure isn't it?"

Benjamin Zephania

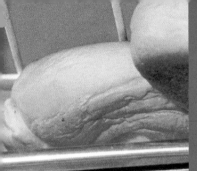

Brunch

Kedgeree
Serves 4

Kedgeree was a mainstay of the Victorian and Edwardian breakfast table, developed from a Hindu dish of rice and lentils, known as khichri. Eliza Acton in her masterly 1845 cookbook *Modern Cookery for Modern Families* gives a recipe for kedgeree without lentils and with flaked fish. Today smoked haddock is regarded as a key ingredient. Look for natural smoked haddock, with its subtle pearly sheen, rather than fluorescent yellow, dyed smoked haddock.

225 g (8 oz) basmati rice
1 cinnamon stick
3-4 cardamom pods
300 ml ($^1/_2$ pt) water
salt and freshly ground pepper
pinch of saffron threads, ground
500 g (1 lb 2 oz) natural smoked haddock fillet
50 g (2 oz) French beans
25 g (1 oz) butter
1 bay leaf

1 leek, finely chopped
1 shallot, finely chopped
1 celery stick, finely chopped
1 tsp Madras curry powder
glug of Amontillado sherry
juice of $^1/_2$ lemon
300 ml double cream
4 hard-boiled free-range eggs, peeled & sliced
finely chopped parsley

Thoroughly wash the basmati rice in cold water to get rid of excess starch. Place the rice, cinnamon stick and cardamom seeds in a medium, heavy-based saucepan.

Add the water and season with salt. Mix the ground saffron with a tablespoon of hot water and add to the rice. Bring to the boil, cover tightly, reduce the heat to very low and cook gently until the water has been absorbed and the rice is tender.

Meanwhile, poach the smoked haddock in a pan of simmering water until opaque. Remove the smoked haddock and flake the flesh, discarding any skin and bones.

Cook the French beans in a small pan of boiling water until just tender; drain and chop into short lengths.

Heat the butter in a large, heavy-based frying pan. Add the leek, shallot and celery and fry gently, stirring now and then, until the leek and shallot are softened. Mix in the curry powder and fry for 1-2 minutes.

Add in the flaked haddock and French beans. Pour over the sherry and allow to bubble briefly. Mix in the lemon juice. Stir in the double cream and cook briefly, stirring.

Transfer the cooked basmati rice to a serving dish. Gently fold in the smoked haddock mixture. Top with sliced hard-boiled egg, sprinkle with parsley, season with freshly ground pepper and serve.

Cheesy Pancakes
Makes 12

This is a Sunday morning brunch favourite in our house: lightly crisped pancake parcels with a melted Cheddar cheese filling, served hot from the frying pan.

115 g (4 oz) plain white flour
pinch of salt
1 free-range egg
300 ml (¹/₂ pt) milk
200 g (7 oz) Cheddar cheese, grated
butter for frying

Sift the flour and salt into a large mixing bowl. Break in the egg. Gradually adding in the milk, whisk together to make a smooth, creamy-textured batter.

Heat a small frying pan until hot, add a small knob of butter and heat until it froths. Pour in half a ladleful of batter, tilting the pan to spread it evenly. Fry until the pancake is set and flecked, then turn it over and fry briefly on the other side.

Turn the pancake over once more and sprinkle a small handful of grated Cheddar in a line down the middle of the pancake. Fold each side over the cheese to form a pancake 'parcel'. Fry for a further 1-2 minutes on each side to melt the cheese and crisp up the pancake. Serve at once direct from the pan. Repeat the process until all the batter and cheese has been used.

A Taste of Jewish London

The Jewish presence in England dates back to the 11th century, when French Jews followed William the Conqueror and settled here, forming a small community. In 1290, however, this community was expelled by Edward I and the practice of Judaism was forbidden for 366 years. In 1656 Oliver Cromwell re-legalised Judaism in England and a small community of Sephardi (Mediterranean Jews) bankers, bullion dealers, merchants and gem importers settled in London, establishing a synagogue in Creechurch Lane.

London's Jewish community grew with the arrival of Ashkenazi Jews from Eastern Europe, who brought with them tailoring, shoemaking and other artisan skills. By 1750 London's Ashkenazim outnumbered the Sephardi community by roughly four to one and in 1760 the London Committee of Deputies of British Jews was established to represent all London Jewry.

Anti-Jewish pogroms and economic hardship in Eastern Europe in the late 19th century resulted in an influx of Ashkenazi Jews into London, who settled predominantly in London's East End, especially the area around Whitechapel. Between World Wars I and II, however, as the community became more prosperous and upwardly social mobile, there was a movement by London's Jewish community away from the East End to the suburbs of Golders Green, Hendon, Edgware and Ilford; areas which to this day retain a large Jewish presence.

Jewish cuisine contains two broad and diverse strands, one influenced by the heritage of the Mediterranean Sephardi and the other by the East European Ashkenazi, with their traditions of preserving and pickling food to last through long, cold winters. Underlying both strands, are the Kashrut, the strict, ancient, dietary laws governing the preparation and consumption of food. Many Jewish food shops, though not all, follow varying degrees of kosherness, often supervised or licensed by Jewish authorities. Kosher butchers, fishmongers, delis and supermarkets are all to be found in London's Jewish areas. Particularly eye-catching are the Jewish bakeries, such as Carmelli's in Golders Green and Daniel's in Temple Fortune, where industrious bakers send out a steady stream of firm-textured bagels, mini-Danish pastries and the symbolic plaited loaves of cholla bread, eaten for Shabbat, the weekly Sabbath.

Platters, 10 Halleswell Parade, Finchley Road, NW11

Sweet Potato Bubble and Squeak

Serves 4

Bubble and Squeak is a traditional English dish, combining leftover cooked potato with cabbage. Adding sweet potato gives the dish a lovely colour and subtle sweetness.

450 g (1 lb) orange-fleshed sweet potato
salt and freshly ground pepper
15 g (1/2 oz) butter
freshly grated nutmeg
450 g (1 lb) potatoes, peeled and chopped
splash of milk
1 small cabbage, shredded
1 tbsp olive oil
1 small onion, chopped

Peel and cube the sweet potato, dropping it at once into cold water to prevent it discolouring. Boil the sweet potato in salted water until tender; drain and mash with half the butter. Season with nutmeg, salt and freshly ground pepper.

Meanwhile, boil the potato in salted water until tender; drain and mash with butter and milk, seasoning with freshly ground pepper.

Steam the cabbage until just tender. Mix together the mashed sweet potato, potato and cabbage.

Heat the olive oil in a heavy-based frying pan. Add the onion and fry until softened. Add in the sweet potato mixture, patting down. Fry until browned on both sides. Serve at once.

Potato Pancakes with Smoked Salmon and Soured Cream

Serves 4

This dish draws on the Eastern European tradition of potato pancakes, combined here with smoked salmon and soured cream.

500 g (1 lb 2 oz) potatoes
2 free-range eggs
25 g (1 oz) plain white flour
salt and freshly ground pepper
sunflower oil for shallow-frying
smoked salmon, to serve
soured cream, to serve

Peel and grate the potatoes. Wrap the grated potato in a clean drying-up cloth and squeeze out the excess moisture. Set aside the cloth-wrapped grated potato while you make the batter.

Break the eggs into a mixing bowl. Whisk in the flour to make a thick batter. Mix in the grated potato and season well with salt and freshly ground pepper.

Heat 1-2 tbsp sunflower oil in a large, heavy-based frying pan over a medium heat. Drop in 3-4 separate tablespoons of the potato mixture, spreading each tablespoon out to form a small pancake. Fry until the pancakes are well set and beginning to brown around the edges, then turn over and fry for a few minutes more until the pancakes are nicely browned on both sides. Set aside to a warm plate and fry the remaining mixture in batches making 12 pancakes in all.

Serve at once with smoked salmon and soured cream.

Salia's Roast Butternut Squash, Mixed Leaves and Tomato Salad

Serves 2

My childhood memories are of people dropping in, coming to eat all the time – very Arabic," says Salia Samia, whose mother was Egyptian and whose father was French. "My mother cooked a lot of tagines, couscous, a lot of vegetables. In my house there was always cooking – it didn't interest me at the time, but now I like to smell cooking in a home – a cake baking – it's comforting. People get so stressed about dinner parties, feeling everything has to be perfect. I like it when friends drop by and you just reach up and get another plate and share what you've got cooking.

I love the food shops on Edgware Road. They're very reasonable and the stuff is so good. I was in Maroush Deli, buying bits and pieces, and the man filled my coat pockets with fresh pistachios and some dates. I felt like a child, being cared for. It reminded me of home; people would always give you something."

1 medium butternut squash, peeled and chopped into 2 cm pieces
extra virgin olive oil
freshly ground sea salt and black pepper
lamb's lettuce
rocket leaves
beetroot leaves
vine-ripened tomatoes, sliced
pine nuts
selection of breads, toasted and un-toasted, to serve

Dressing:
natural yoghurt flavoured with a small quantity of
  freshly chopped mint and salt and pepper to taste

Preheat the oven to Gas 4/180°C/350°F. Place the butternut squash in a roasting dish, toss with olive oil and season with freshly ground salt and pepper. Roast for 25-30 minutes, turning occasionally, until the squash is cooked but not too soft. Set aside to cool to room temperature.

Place the lamb's lettuce, rocket and beetroot leaves in a large bowl. Add the sliced tomatoes and the cooled squash.

Toast the pine nuts over a low heat, stirring often, until golden and sprinkle over the salad. Trickle over the yoghurt dressing and toss just before serving. Serve with a selection of breads, both toasted and un-toasted.

"My childhood memories are of people dropping in, coming to eat all the time – very Arabic."

Salia Samia

MILKING

Dairy London

For centuries life in London retained a rural element. Livestock, such as cattle, pigs and chickens, were kept by many Londoners. Dairy farms, in boroughs such as Islington, Lambeth and Westminster, supplied fresh milk to Londoners and the street selling of milk – usually watered down and notoriously unhygienic – was an everyday reality. Alternatively, people could visit "street cows" for freshly milked milk. By the mid-19th century Henry Mayhew, in his book *London Labour and the London Poor* (1851) could observe that the "principal sale of milk from the cow is in St James's Park" and that syllabubs (traditionally made with milk warm from the udder) were now "unknown". A St James's Park milk-seller interviewed by Mayhew grumbled, "It's not at all a lively sort of life, selling milk from the cows, though some thinks it's a gay time in the Park! I've often been dull enough, and could see nothing to interest one, sitting alongside a cow. People drink new milk for their health, and I've served a good many such. They're mostly young women… Some children come pretty regularly with their nurses to drink new milk. Some bring their town china mugs to drink it out of; nothing less was good enough for them."

The tradition of selling milk from cows in St James Park continued into the 20th century, but the building of Admiralty Arch in 1905 saw the milk ladies being given notice to quit. The milk ladies, however, defended their ancestral rights to sell milk on the site, tracing them back to King Charles II, who reputedly granted their family these rights after their ancestor had given his father King Charles I a cup of milk on his way to his execution. Thanks to their spirited defence the milk ladies moved to a stall near the lake, where they continued selling milk for a further 15 years.

With the rise of the railway system, the 1860s witnessed the beginning of large-scale transportation of milk from the countryside outside London into the city. By 1866, London received 7 million gallons of milk by rail. In 1864, George Barham established the Express Cows Milk Supply Company, later known as the Express Dairy Company, bringing in milk by train. In 1883 Barham took over College Farm at Finchley, running it as a model dairy farm for exhibitions and training. Alongside this mass importation of milk, however, Victorian London retained a number of dairies and the custom of summer grazing cattle on old common lands such as Hackney Marshes continued into the early part of the 20th century.

Today, a few dairy buildings remain dotted around London – among them French's Dairy on Rugby Street, WC1 and The Old Dairy on Crouch Hill – their picturesque, tiled premises turned now into restaurants, bars or shops.

The Old Dairy, Crouch Hill N4

Leila's Eggs Fried With Sage
Serves 4

Tucked away down a sleepy East London side-street is Leila's, Leila McAlister's small, characterful food shop-cum-café. Stock consists solely of a few, simple, good things to eat – rich, dark rye bread, apple juice, muesli. Customers can sit and enjoy an excellent cup of freshly-made coffee or food from the short, to-the-point menu with dishes such as a Polish Platter (Polish sausage, boiled egg, pickles, horseradish and rye bread). Leila's affection for her shop is evident and deep-rooted: "I think we have the nicest customers in the whole world", says Leila, "a real mixture. On Sundays we have people who don't know us peering in and thinking 'What is this? Is it a café or a shop?'"

Leila's feeling for this part of London extends beyond her shop. Just down the street from her shop is Arnold Circus, a long-neglected public gardens and bandstand. Leila is actively involved in the Friends of Arnold Circus and her vision is clear: "We want to make it a beautiful place for the local community to use and enjoy."

The idea for the shop came about by chance: "I used to cycle by here," she explains. "Every shop on the street was boarded up. I noticed this shop and wrote to the council to ask if they'd rent it to me. They wrote back about 4 years later. It used to be a sweetshop a hundred years ago. I did all the work on it myself. I did not play shopkeepers when I was a kid but I have been around food for so long and done a lot of catering. I think this shop is a social enterprise. Food has always been important to me, to my family. My parents used to take me to Leadenhall Market at Christmas to see all the poultry hanging up."

4 free-range eggs
a knob of unsalted butter
slug of olive oil
4 sage leaves
Maldon sea salt and freshly ground pepper

Choose a heavy-based frying pan that will snugly hold the eggs.

Heat the unsalted butter and olive oil in the pan until it foams. Add the sage leaves and sizzle gently until crisp; remove and set aside.

Turn down the temperature, break the eggs into the pan and sprinkle with lots of Maldon sea salt and freshly ground pepper. Put a fried sage leaf on top of each yolk.

Cover the pan with a lid and cook slowly until the whites are set but the yolks are still soft. Serve.

"On Sundays we have people who don't know us peering in and thinking 'What is this? Is it a café or a shop?'"

Leila McAlister

Coffee Stories

London's first coffee house opened in 1652 at the Sign of Pasqua Rosee's Head in St Michael's Alley, Cornhill. Pasqua Rosee's handbills publicising this novel and exotic drink claimed that coffee "is a very good help to digestion, quickens the spirits and is good against sore eyes, dropsy, gout, King's evil &c". Coffee houses quickly took off as places where men could meet and discuss the topics of the day and by the turn of the century there were around 2,000 in the capital. Many of these were known to attract particular trades or professions, with lawyers, clergymen, artists, politicians and military men each gravitating towards different coffee houses. Lloyds coffee house, founded in the 1680s, was frequented by ships' captains, ship-owners and insurers and was the direct ancestor of today's Lloyds, the insurance market. During the 18th century, however, tea became the nation's fashionable drink and coffee's popularity declined. The 1950s, saw another boom in London's coffee consumption with the arrival of the Moka in Soho, London's first coffee bar and the first to use Achilles Gaggia's recently invented espresso machine. Opened by Gina Lollobrigida, the Moka set the trend among young people for drinking in espresso bars and coffee bars sprang up across the capital, offering a place to hang out, meet friends and listen to live music. Today, while coffee once again enjoys a fashionable image, chains rather than individual coffee bars dominate our high streets.

Coffee Price List

	2007	125	250	50C
Blended Coffees				
BREAKFAST BLEND		1.91	3.82	7.64
AFTER DINNER BLEND		1.91	3.82	7.64
CHAGGA BLEND		2.49	4.98	9.96
COFFEE HOUSE BLEND	2.10	4.20	8.40	
CAFE CENTRO BLD		2.82	5.64	11.28
SANTA MOKKA BLEND	2.54	5.08	10.16	
SUMATRA BLEND		2.69	5.38	10.76
Speciality Blends				
MOCHA & MYSORE BD.		2.22	4.44	8.88
VIENNA BLEND		2.49	4.98	9.96
HANOVER BLEND		2.66	5.32	10.64

Higgins Coffee

David Higgins, of H R Higgins, 79 Duke Street, W1, recounts the history of his family's coffee-selling business: "My grandfather, H R Higgins, who was born in 1898, was apprenticed in the grocery trade as a boy. He learnt a lot about coffee as most of it was sold through high-class grocers: he did coffee-blending, coffee-tasting, coffee-wrapping and packing. He had to prepare the coffee for the coffee tasters and he used to taste the samples afterwards and found he could distinguish the flavours. In 1942 he gave up his secure job and started on his own as a coffee wholesaler. He would get up at 5am, start roasting, then grinding – he got a lot of contracts from other roasters in the East End who'd been bombed. He looked for a shop

and set up at 43 South Molton Street, with the roaster in the basement.

"After the war it was hard to get South American coffees. He got a bag of coffee that reminded him of Colombian coffee, not as acidic as most Kenyan coffees, a smooth, good, aromatic coffee – he discovered that it was grown by the Kilimanjaro Native Co-operative Union, African-run by African farmers – and he went to Africa in 1960 to meet the Chagga tribe who grew it. He wanted to promote single origin coffee rather than house blends. He died in 1968. My father, Tony, joined the business when he was 15 in 1952.

"My childhood memories are the smell of roasting coffee in South Molton Street; the coffee grinder was a fantastic-looking thing

with wheels whizzing. I remember sitting on the huge piles of coffee sacks. It was a very busy place, with people queuing out of the door. Most of our customers now buy more and freeze it at home and now they grind their own beans. I joined full-time in 1982 when I was 15, having worked in the holidays before. In 1979 we became coffee suppliers by appointment to the Queen and we moved to this shop in 1986. We have customers who are grandchildren of the original customers who remember coming as children. We've become part of their lives and they've become part of ours."

> "We have customers who are grandchildren of the original customers who remember coming as children. We've become part of their lives and they've become part of ours."
>
> David Higgins

H.R. Higgins, 79 Duke Street, W1

Monmouth Coffee House

Anita Le Roy of Monmouth Coffee House has pioneered quality coffee in London. Her first shop, opened in 1978, is a small, intimate space in Monmouth Street near Covent Garden where customers tuck into tiny, wooden booths in the sampling room to drink her carefully selected coffees, freshly roasted on the premises. Her second, equally characterful shop on Park Street, by Borough Market, is a high-ceilinged, airy space, where customers sit at a large, wooden communal table, eating fresh baguettes and jam with their coffee.

"It was serendipity really," explains Anita. "I was working for friends in Covent Garden – then derelict – and was asked if I'd be interested in importing and roasting coffee. It was a big decision. In those days there were no yellow lines in Covent Garden. The tube station closed at 4pm on Fridays and re-opened on Monday mornings.

"The coffee market was very different then. The City dealers just traded it and sold it on – never visited the growers. Mercanta were the first shippers in the UK to start dealing directly with growers. We'd pay three times more for our coffee to get the quality. It was a fight to get high-quality coffees. Sustainable trading has been the company policy for a long time. Today the quality's better – we can be more precise about who we're buying from.

"There is such a huge variety of flavours in coffee – a complexity of flavour. We don't do such a dark roast that the taste loses its subtleties. We always offer different coffees for tasting; it's a way to open a window to our customers. People in our shops ask for their coffee by farm name, which is what we always wanted."

Monmouth Coffee House, 27 Monmouth Street, WC2

On Neal Street you'd see a cat strolling down the road if you were lucky. There was an armourer's in Neal's Yard; lots of light industry. Setting up Monmouth, with time and money running out, I found the wooden newel posts in a skip outside my shop and just whacked them up on the booths."

Anita Le Roy

Union Hand-Roasted

On an East London industrial estate roastmasters Jeremy Torz and Steven Macatonia of Union Hand-Roasted lovingly produce coffee, hand-roasted on the premises. The roasting takes place in a large hanger, dominated by a formidable 100 kg roaster. A batch of green coffee beans is placed inside a large roasting drum, which begins to rotate over a high heat, tossing the beans inside with a loud rattling noise. Steven – who says simply but firmly "I'm happy with coffee beans. I like concentrating on roasting the coffee" – monitors the process, frequently pulling out samples to check the beans' colour and scent. The first distinctive fragrance is a yeasty one, with the beans now a pale straw colour. The faint popping sound of moisture being driven out of the beans is called "first crack". From now on Steven is intently absorbed by the roasting process, constantly checking the beans which are now turning dark brown and beginning to smell of coffee. He takes the roasting on to "second crack", producing the dark roast which is a Union Coffee characteristic. With split-second timing, the beans are released onto a cooling tray, flooding out with a great clatter – a moment that still thrills Steven and Jeremy.

As their company's name, Union, implies, Jeremy and Steven work closely with the coffee growers, often single family-run estates, visiting them and ensuring an ethical dimension to their buying. "Coffee-blending is a bit of science, a bit of art, a bit of witchcraft, all thrown together," declares Jeremy. "We're trying to get people to look past the packet, forget the milk – to get excited about the coffee itself, what's in the cup."

> *Sometimes I'll get off at West Ham station and get this wonderful smell of freshly-roasted coffee in the air and I float along on it back to the roastery,"*
>
> *Jeremy Torz*

www.unionroasted.com

Baked Duck Eggs

Serves 4

Duck eggs, with their large, rich yolks, make for a luxurious egg-eating experience! Look out for them at market stalls, delicatessens and butchers.

4 duck eggs
4 tbsp double cream
a few snipped chive or tarragon leaves
salt and freshly ground pepper
toast fingers, to serve

Preheat the oven to Gas 4/180°C/350°F.

Butter 4 ramekin dishes and carefully break a duck egg into each ramekin. Spoon a tablespoon of double cream over the top of each egg, sprinkle with chopped chives or tarragon and season with salt and freshly ground pepper.

Place the ramekin dishes in a deep roasting tray and pour in hot water around the ramekins until it reaches up half-way around them. Bake in the oven for 20 minutes and serve at once with toast fingers.

Cheddar Chive Scones

Makes 9 scones

Flavoured with cheese and chives, these savoury scones should be served warm from the oven with lashings of butter.

225 g (8 oz) self-raising white flour
1/2 tsp salt
55 g (2 oz) butter, diced
75 g (3 oz) Cheddar cheese, grated
1 small bunch of chives, finely chopped
approx. 150 ml (1/4 pt) milk

Preheat the oven to Gas 8//230°C/450°F.

Sift the flour and salt into a mixing bowl. Rub in the butter until absorbed. Mix in most of the Cheddar (reserving a little for sprinkling) and the chives. Add the milk and, using a broad-bladed knife, fold it in to form a soft dough.

Pat the dough out on a floured board to about 1 cm (1/2 in) thickness. Cut into 9 evenly sized squares. Place on a greased baking tray and brush with milk and sprinkle with the reserved Cheddar.

Bake for 10-15 minutes until risen and golden-brown. Serve warm from the oven.

Crab Cakes
Makes 12

Crabmeat, with its delicate, sweet flavour, is a great treat. As fresh, picked crabmeat is both hard to find and astronomically expensive, this recipe uses dressed crabs, which can be found in most fishmongers.

2 dressed crabs
100 g (4 oz) fresh breadcrumbs
1 spring onion, finely chopped
zest of 1 lime
1 free-range egg
salt and freshly ground pepper
1 tbsp olive oil
lime wedges, to serve

Scoop out the meat from the dressed crabs into a mixing bowl. Add the breadcrumbs, spring onion and lime zest and break in the egg. Season with salt and freshly ground pepper.

Mix together thoroughly and, using wetted hands, shape into 12 small crab cakes.

Heat the olive oil in a large, heavy-based frying pan. Fry the crab cakes until golden-brown on both sides. Serve at once with lime wedges.

Poached Eggs with Chorizo Sausage
Serves 4

Poached eggs, with their delicate texture and flavour, make a great brunch dish, set off here by the gutsy, robust flavour of chorizo sausage.

4 chorizo sausages
4 fresh, free-range, medium eggs
crusty bread, to serve

Cut the chorizo sausages into fine slices. Heat a medium, heavy-based frying pan until hot. Add the chorizo sausages and fry them in their own fat, turning now and then, until piping hot and lightly browned.

Meanwhile, bring two pans of water to the gentlest of simmers. Break each egg into a cup or small bowl. Slide two eggs per pan into the simmering water. Simmer for three minutes. Carefully remove the eggs with a slotted spoon and drain on kitchen paper.

Place the poached eggs on four serving plates, add a portion of the freshly fried chorizo hot from the pan to each plate and serve at once with crusty bread on the side.

Nibbles, Snacks & Starters

Spiced Roast Nuts
Makes 300 g (10 oz)

Freshly-roasted nuts make a great pre-dinner drinks nibble.

115 g (4 oz) blanched almonds
115 g (4 oz) macadamia nuts
115 g (4 oz) natural cashews
1/4 tsp chilli powder
1/2 tsp salt
1/2 tsp freshly ground pepper
1/2 tsp sugar
1 tsp olive oil

Preheat the oven to Gas 4/180°C/350°F.

Toss together the almonds, macadamia nuts, cashews, chilli powder, salt, pepper, sugar and olive oil.

Spread the nuts out on a roasting tray and roast in the oven for 15-20 minutes, turning now and then, until golden. Remove and cool before serving.

Leek and Ginger Fritters
Makes 8

These light leek fritters are quick and easy to make. Chickpea flour (also known as gram flour) can be found in Indian food shops.

1 large free-range egg
3 tbsp chickpea flour, sifted
pinch of salt
1 tsp melted butter
1 leek, very finely chopped
2.5 cm (1 in) fresh root ginger,
    peeled and finely shredded
1 tbsp sunflower oil

In a large bowl, whisk together the egg, chickpea flour, salt and melted butter. Fold in the leek and ginger.

Heat the oil in a large, non-stick frying pan. Drop in 8 tablespoons of the leek mixture, spacing them well apart to form 8 separate fritters. Fry over medium heat until set and browned, then turn over to brown the other side. Remove and serve at once.

Hummus
Serves 4-6

Hummus is a staple dish in London's Greek Cypriot and Middle Eastern restaurants. Using dried chickpeas, as opposed to tinned, makes a real difference to the flavour and texture. You can find these and tahini (sesame seed paste) in London's Greek Cypriot, Turkish and Lebanese shops.

150 g (5 oz) dried chickpeas, soaked overnight
salt to taste
50 g (2 oz) tahini
1 garlic clove, crushed
juice of 1 lemon
warm pitta bread, to serve

Garnish:
olive oil
paprika
finely chopped parsley

Drain the soaked chickpeas, place in a large saucepan and cover with cold water. Bring to the boil and cook for 1 hour until tender. Drain the chickpeas, reserving the cooking water.

Place the chickpeas in a food processor, adding salt, and blend well. Add in the tahini, garlic and lemon juice and blend again, until well-mixed. Thin the hummus to your taste with the reserved chickpea cooking water.

To serve, place in a shallow serving bowl and pour over a little olive oil, adding a sprinkling of paprika and parsley. Serve with warm pitta bread.

Lebanese Hummus
Serves 4-6

Lebanese hummus is characterised by a generous amount of tahini, which gives a silky texture and rich sesame flavour.

150 g (5 oz) dried chickpeas, soaked overnight
salt to taste
115 g (4 oz) tahini
juice of 1-1 $^1/_2$ lemons
warm khobz Arabi (Middle Eastern flatbread),
*   to serve*

Garnish:
olive oil
paprika
a few reserved, cooked, whole chickpeas

Drain the soaked chickpeas, place in a large saucepan and cover with cold water. Bring to the boil and cook for 1 hour until tender. Drain the chickpeas, reserving the cooking water and setting aside a spoonful of whole chickpeas for garnish.

Place the chickpeas in a food processor, adding salt, and blend well. Add the tahini and a little of the lemon juice. Blend until well-mixed, then taste, adding lemon juice as required.

To serve, place in a shallow serving bowl and pour over a little olive oil, adding a sprinkling of paprika and the reserved whole chickpeas. Serve with warm khobz Arabi.

Stilton Cheese Straws
Makes around 30

Cheese straws make a great, more-ish nibble. This recipe combines two classic British cheeses – Stilton and Cheddar – to tasty effect.

75 g (3 oz) plain flour
1 tsp baking powder
50 g (2 oz) butter, diced
50 g (2 oz) Stilton, finely crumbled
50 g (2 oz) Cheddar, finely grated
1 free-range egg yolk
25 g (1 oz) poppyseeds

Preheat the oven to Gas 7/220°C/425°F.

Place the flour and baking powder in a mixing bowl. Rub in the butter until absorbed. Add the Stilton and Cheddar and mix together.

Add the egg yolk and mix to form a soft, sticky dough. Sprinkle over the poppyseeds and mix in thoroughly.

Roll out the dough on a lightly floured board to ¹/₂ cm (¹/₄ in) thickness. Cut into 1 cm (¹/₂ in) wide strips, then cut into short lengths.

Place the cheese straws on a greased baking sheet and bake for 8-10 minutes until a rich golden colour.

Goat's Cheese and Membrillo Toasties
Makes 12

Membrillo, the sweet, sticky quince paste traditionally eaten with cheese in Spain, can be found in Spanish food shops such as Garcia or P. de la Fuente, located respectively at 248 and 288 Portobello Road.

12 slices from a small baguette
12 thin slices of membrillo
12 slices of soft goat's cheese

Toast the baguette slices under a grill until browned on one side. Top the unbrowned side of each slice with a slice of membrillo, then cover with a slice of goat's cheese. Grill until the goat's cheese is just melted. Serve at once.

Smoked Mackerel Pâté with Melba Toast
Serves 8

2 smoked mackerel fillets
200 g (7 oz) cream cheese
juice of 1/2 lemon
2-3 tbsp creamed horseradish
1 tbsp finely chopped parsley
freshly ground pepper

Melba toast:
8 slices of sandwich loaf bread

First make the Melba toast. Grill the bread until lightly browned on both sides. Trim off the crusts and slice each piece of bread horizontally, forming two thin, evenly sized squares. Place the bread squares on a baking tray and bake in the oven at Gas 4/180°C/350°F for 10 minutes until golden.

Flake the smoked mackerel, discarding the skin and any bones. Place it in a food processor with the cream cheese, lemon juice, horseradish and parsley. Blend until smooth. Season with freshly ground pepper and blend again. Cover and chill until serving.

Serve with Melba toast.

Deep-fried Prawn Wonton Dumplings
Makes 28

These crunchy dumplings were inspired by a visit to Chinatown. Soft, yellow wonton wrappers can be found in the food shops there.

175 g (6 oz) cooked, peeled prawns
2.5 cm (1 in) fresh root ginger, peeled and finely chopped
1 spring onion, finely chopped
2 tsp soy sauce
28 wonton wrappers
1 free-range egg white
sunflower or vegetable oil for deep-frying

Dipping sauce:
2 tbsp chilli sauce
juice of $\frac{1}{2}$ lime

Mince or finely chop the prawns, quickly done in a food processor. Mix together the minced prawns, ginger, spring onion and soy sauce.

Take one wonton wrapper. Place $\frac{1}{2}$ tsp of the prawn mixture in the centre of the wrapper. Lightly brush the edges of the wrapper with egg white. Fold the wrapper over the prawn mixture, forming a triangular parcel, and press the edges together firmly to seal. Repeat the process until all the wrappers have been filled.

Make the dipping sauce by mixing together the chilli sauce and lime juice.

Heat the oil in a wok until very hot. Deep-fry the wonton parcels in batches, frying them so that they puff up and turn a deep golden colour. Turn the parcels over to fry the other side, then remove with a slotted spoon. Drain on kitchen paper.

Serve at once with the chilli dipping sauce.

Thai Salmon Fishcakes
Serves 4-6

Fragrant fresh kaffir lime leaves, which add a characteristic citrus flavour to these dainty fishcakes, can be found in Thai food shops or Chinese supermarkets. The glossy leaves are similar in appearance to bay leaves but broader. They are usually sold in bunches or packets of loose leaves.

450 g (1 lb) salmon fillet, skinned and chopped
1 tsp soy sauce
25 g (1 oz) cornflour
2 tsp Thai red curry paste
1 free-range egg
1 tbsp finely chopped fresh coriander
1 thumb-sized piece of fresh root ginger, peeled and finely chopped
1 shallot, peeled and finely chopped
finely grated zest of 1 lime
2 kaffir lime leaves, finely shredded
50 g (2 oz) French beans, very finely chopped
sunflower oil, for shallow frying

Dipping sauce:
juice of 1 lime
2 tbsp sugar
1 garlic clove, finely chopped
1 small red chilli, deseeded and finely chopped

To make the fishcakes, blend the salmon, soy sauce, cornflour, red curry paste and egg in a food processor to form a smooth paste.

Transfer the salmon mixture to a mixing bowl and mix in the coriander, ginger, shallot, lime zest, kaffir lime leaves and French beans. Cover and chill for 1 hour to firm up the mixture. Meanwhile, prepare the dipping sauce by mixing together the lime juice, sugar, garlic and chilli.

With wetted hands, shape the salmon mixture into 12 evenly sized patties. Heat the sunflower oil in a large, non-stick frying pan. Fry the fishcakes in batches until golden-brown on each side. Remove and drain on kitchen paper. Serve at once with the dipping sauce.

Lydia's Curry Puffs

Born in Singapore, my mother Lydia Linford has vivid memories of the street food she enjoyed as a child. After school she would take out an egg from the house to the kway teow man, who would fry a portion of kway teow noodles for her, adding in the egg she'd given him. Curry puffs are a favourite Singaporean snack.

Curry powder:
1 tsp cumin seeds
1 tsp coriander seeds
1 tsp fennel seeds
1/2 cinnamon stick
2 cloves
1/2 tsp ground turmeric

Puffs:
1 tbsp sunflower oil
1 shallot, finely chopped
2 slices fresh root ginger, very finely chopped
200 g (7 oz) minced lamb
2 tbsp tomato pureé
salt
1 small waxy potato, boiled, peeled and finely diced
500 g (1 lb 2 oz) puff pastry
milk, for glazing

First make the curry powder. Dry-fry the cumin, coriander, fennel, cinnamon and cloves until fragrant. Cool and grind finely. Mix in the turmeric.

Heat the sunflower oil in a frying pan. Add the shallot and ginger and fry briefly. Add the minced lamb and fry until browned. Mix a little water with the curry powder to form a paste, then add it to the lamb. Mix in the tomato pureé, season with salt and fry for 3-5 minutes. Set aside to cool. Mix in the diced potato.

Preheat the oven to Gas 5/190°C/375°F.

Roll out the puff pastry finely. Cut into 7 1/2 cm (3 in) rounds. Place a teaspoon of the mince mixture in the centre of a puff pastry circle. Brush the edges with milk, fold over to form a semi-circle and seal well, pressing together firmly. Repeat the process until all the pastry circles have been filled. Place the curry puffs on roasting sheets and brush them with milk. Bake for 15 minutes until golden and puffy. Serve warm or cold.

Piloo's Coriander Chutney

Makes approx 4 x 300 g (10 oz) jars

The ingredients for this flavourful chutney can be found in most food stores. Piloo uses jaggery in the recipe which is a pale brown sugar made from palm juice or sap, but any kind of sugar can be used as a substitute.

1 tsp cumin seeds
a handful of raw peanuts
3 bunches of coriander
6 garlic cloves, peeled and chopped
6 green chillies, chopped
juice of 1 lemon
1 tsp sugar (Piloo uses jaggery)
1 tsp salt

Pan-roast the cumins in a small pan until fragrant. Set aside to cool, then grind finely. Pan-roast the peanuts until lightly browned. Set aside to cool, then grind finely.

Wash the bunches of coriander thoroughly, making sure that any soil and debris is removed. Chop the coriander finely, including most of the stem, discarding the stem ends up to an inch from the root.

Using a food processor, grind together the garlic and chillies. Add the ground cumin, ground peanuts, sugar, salt, sugar and lemon juice and process to mix.

Add small bunches of the chopped coriander to the base mix until you have a purée. In order to get the coriander to break down into a purée you may need to persist with bursts of grinding. This could depend on the moisture content of the coriander and a few drops of water may help with the grinding. Be careful though not to add too much water, as an excessive amount of moisture may result in a watery chutney! The final texture of the chutney that youíre looking for is very fine and smooth.

Taste the chutney to check that youíve got the balance of flavours right. The coriander is bitter, chillies vary in their piquancy and the strength of garlic depends on taste. The salt sugar and lemon juice needs to be balanced so that none of the individual ingredients overwhelm another.

Spoon into clean, dry jars, cover tightly and refrigerate.

"F ood has no meaning without people," asserts Piloo Patel who cooks the Gujurati food that reminds him of his family. Sent to boarding school in India, where the food was "appalling", home cooking took on an extra significance. "I would go home and eat my grandmother's food and put on a stone in a week. It created a connection to food from desperation." Living in London as a young man, Piloo started cooking by "drawing on memories of what I'd seen. It had all seemed very complicated and elaborate. My mother would wake up at 4am to prepare our meals for the day. In my community people are judged on hospitality; it's the most important thing. For me cooking that kind of food – I only cook Gujurati food, which reminds me of my childhood – provides a sense of connection, as both my parents are dead. What's great about my heritage? I find that it's my food."

The recipe for coriander chutney is one that Piloo watched his mother make. Piloo makes it in batches (buy the coriander on Ealing Road in Wembley, recommends Piloo) and generously distributes it to family and friends. His mother's favourite lunch was wholemeal bread, spread with butter, topped with "really ripe" tomatoes and generous amounts of this vivid green, flavourful chutney. As Piloo rightly points out "this chutney would make the humble baguette magnificent".

Yuka's Chicken Wings Nagoya Style
Serves 4

This simple but flavourful recipe, transforming the humble chicken wing into a delicious snack, is one that Yuka Aoyama learnt from her mother in Japan.

160 ml (5 ¹/₂ fl oz) mirin
20 ml Japanese soy sauce
10 ml sake
5-6 garlic cloves, peeled and sliced
1.5 kg (3 lb) chicken wings
vegetable oil, for deep-frying
salt and pepper
sesame seeds, roasted, for sprinkling

Mix together the mirin, soy sauce, sake and garlic in a large bowl and refrigerate at least overnight. Yuka recommends storing it in the fridge for a few days to increase the depth of flavour. Bring the mirin mixture to room temperature before you start frying the chicken wings.

Heat the oil in a large, deep pan or a deep fat fryer to 150°C/300°F. Add the wings and deep-fry them until lightly browned. Remove the wings and set aside.

Reheat the oil to 180°C/350°F. Return the chicken wings to the oil and deep-fry until golden-brown and crispy. Remove the chicken wings, immerse them in the mirin mixture, then drain immediately.

Season with salt and pepper, sprinkle over the sesame seeds and serve at once.

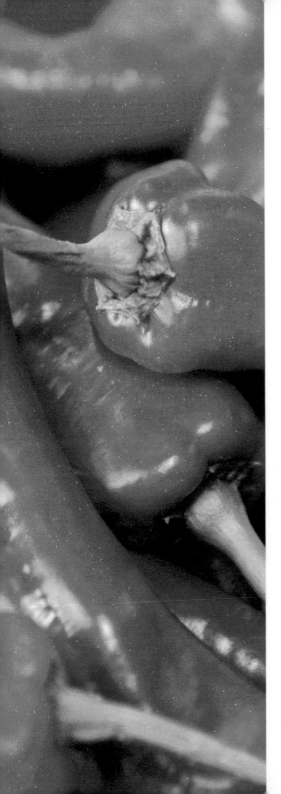

Lily's Hot Peppers with Feta Cheese ('Htepete')

Serves 4-6

"It's a very simple dish," says Lily, "but it tastes good."

2 long, hot, green peppers (alternatively red
peppers can be used with or without the
addition of a red chilli pepper depending
on the spiciness required)
400 g (14 oz) soft feta cheese
50 ml (2 fl oz) olive oil, plus extra for
shallow-frying
a little white wine or cider vinegar
freshly ground pepper
bread or crackers, to serve

Fry the peppers in a little olive oil, or roast them until charred all over. Peel and skin and cut them into little pieces, discarding the top and the seeds.

Mash the feta cheese with a fork and add the chopped peppers, olive oil, vinegar and freshly ground pepper. Serve with fresh bread or crackers as an appetizer.

Lily's Giant Baked Beans (Fasolia Gigantes Plaki)
Serves 6-8

Fasolia gigantes, the large dried white beans traditionally used in this recipe, can be found in Greek or Turkish food shops. Alternatively, substitute butter beans. Lily also suggests adding 1 or 2 long, hot, green peppers to the beans to give a little piquancy to the dish.

500 g (1 lb 2oz) fasolia gigantes or butter beans
2 onions, peeled and chopped
115 ml (4 fl oz) olive oil
3 garlic cloves, peeled and minced
1 kg (2 ¼ lb) fresh tomatoes or 2 tins chopped tomatoes
1 tbsp sugar
salt and freshly ground pepper
1 or 2 long, hot, green peppers, optional
4 tbsp finely chopped flat leafed parsley

Cover the beans with water and soak overnight. Strain the soaked beans, place in a large saucepan, cover with fresh water and bring to the boil then simmer for 1 to 2 hours until the beans are done, but still a little hard; drain.

In a pan, gently sauté the onions in the olive oil until soft, then add the garlic and sauté for another minute. Add the tomatoes and sugar and, if using tinned tomatoes, at least 1 tin of hot water. Bring the sauce to the boil and simmer for 20 minutes. Season with salt and freshly ground pepper.

Put the beans in a shallow baking tray, pour the sauce all over and mix a little. Add the hot peppers, if using. Sprinkle the parsley over the top. Put the tray in the oven and bake at Gas 4/180°C/350°F for about 1 hour. At the end of the cooking time, the sauce should be reduced, but if it looks dry early on, add a little hot water. Serve the beans at room temperature.

> *My generation of Greek women we don't want to spend all day wrapping up vine leaves or frying a lot of appetisers, as my grandmother used to do for my grandfather. It's different times."*
>
> *Lily Perahia*

Born and brought up in Salonika, Greece, Lily Perahia enjoys cooking and loves experimenting with different ingredients. "What's fun is to try things when you're cooking. I love doing different things, when in Rome do as the Romans do. When I lived in America I cooked a lot of American food. When you live abroad you can't always find the right ingredient for a dish, so you try something else and see what happens.

"What I remember from growing up in Greece was that you ate seasonally. I like that. My mother would come back and say 'there are fresh peas in the greengrocer today.'

"I do shop in lots of different places. I can buy big bunches of fresh herbs from my local Turkish shops. People will ask me 'Do you know what to do with that?' And I'll say 'Yes, I'm Greek'. We've got a fantastic farmers' market in Stoke Newington. Steve Hatt (see page 74) – his fish is fantastic. I make a lot of chicken soup – I can order a boiler from Godfrey's in Highbury. Chapel Market is good and so are the Persian shops in Golders Green. I could spend all day shopping in London – you can find so many different foods."

A Taste of Greek London

London's Greek community is predominantly made up of Greek Cypriots, though a small mainland Greek community in the city can be traced back to the 18th century. The 20th century saw the arrival of Greek Cypriots from the island of Cyprus, which had become a British colony in 1925. Poor economic conditions in Cyprus during the 1920s and 1930s meant that many Greek Cypriots came to London seeking work, with Camden Town becoming a focal point for the community. By the 1960s London's Greek Cypriot community was well-established, working as tailors, greengrocers, hairdressers and as restaurateurs and waiters. Greek tavernas, such as Anemos on Charlotte Street, opened in Bloomsbury, Camden Town and Soho, offering a convivial blend of affordable food and warm hospitality. There was also a shift from Camden Town to the borough of Haringey in North London. The Turkish invasion of Cyprus in 1974 saw a further influx of Greek Cypriots, with dispossessed refugees turning to family and friends in London.

London's Greek food shops characteristically combine a greengrocer – bunches of herbs, fresh fruit and vegetables (many imported from Cyprus) – with a grocery element, featuring packets of assorted pulses, bottles of olive oil, olives, round loaves of 'village bread' and feta cheese. On Moscow Road in Bayswater – not far from down the magnificent 19th-century Greek Orthodox Cathedral of Aghia Sophia – the Athenian Grocery is just such a shop, its jaunty blue façade, striped awning and boxes of fresh fruit adding a Mediterranean note to the area.

Athenian Grocery, 16A Moscow Road, W2

Chicken Liver Crostini
Makes 30

Simple to make, this is a traditional Tuscan appetiser.

15 g (¹/₂ oz) butter
1 shallot, peeled and finely diced
400 g (14 oz) chicken livers, trimmed and chopped into evenly sized pieces
4 sage leaves, shredded
generous splash of vin santo or Marsala
salt and freshly ground pepper
1 baguette, finely sliced into 30 slices
3 small gherkins, finely sliced

Heat the butter in a heavy-based frying pan. Add the shallot and fry until softened. Add the chicken livers and sage. Fry gently for 5-7 minutes until the liver is browned on the outside and pale pink inside.

Add the vin santo and cook for 1-2 minutes. Season well with salt and freshly ground pepper. Set aside until cool. Blend until smooth in a food processor.

Meanwhile, preheat the oven to Gas 5/190°C/375°F. Place the baguette slices on a baking sheet and bake for 5-10 minutes until golden. Cool on a wire rack.

Spread the baked baguette slices generously with the liver pâté and top with a gherkin slice. Serve at once.

Samphire, Prawn and Red Pepper Salad

Serves 4

The summer months see sprigs of bright green samphire appear in fishmongers. Marsh samphire grows close to the sea, particularly in estuaries, and has a pronounced salty taste. Historically it was known as "glasswort" because it was used as a source of alkali for glassmaking.

1 red pepper
225 g (8 oz) samphire
500 g (1 lb 2 oz) cooked prawns in their shells
3 tbsp extra-virgin olive oil
1 tbsp balsamic vinegar
squeeze of lemon juice
salt and freshly ground pepper
1 tsp finely chopped chives

Roast the red pepper under a preheated grill, until charred on all sides. Wrap in a plastic bag and set aside until cooled (the resulting steam helps separate the skin from the flesh); peel and chop into short strips.

Rinse the samphire and steam or boil until just tender. Peel the cooked prawns.

Make a dressing by mixing together the olive oil, balsamic vinegar and lemon juice. Season with salt and freshly ground pepper, bearing in mind that samphire is naturally salty.

Toss together the samphire, red pepper strips and prawns with the dressing and the chives. Divide among 4 serving plates and serve.

The Fishmonger's Story

Along the Essex Road in Islington there's a sight to gladden the heart of anyone who enjoys eating fish: an impressive display of gleaming fresh fish on the slab at Steve Hatt's. Fishmonger Steve Hatt is carrying on a family tradition that goes back to the 19th century. "I'm fourth generation," explains Steve. "The shop was set up in 1895 and has always been on this site. My father wanted me to be a solicitor, but I had no interest in being stuck in an office. I joined the business in 1970. He was a hard taskmaster – as is often the way with fathers and sons – but what I got was a thorough training in running a business efficiently. My father had a motto: 'Pay faster than anybody and give no quarter on quality. If a supplier doesn't stick to his agreement be ruthless.' There are very few good fishmongers left in London – 84% of the fish purchases in the UK are in supermarkets. We're known for quality. People have moved out but I still see a lot of my old customers.

"You can generally say that in the days of the old Billingsgate Market – pre-1982 – fish availability was very high. Since I joined the availability of fish, especially finest quality fish, has declined. All wild fish are around 50% less available. Fish has always been an undervalued commodity in the UK.

"We smoke haddock and mackerel on the premises. We haven't used tartrazine colouring for over 20 years. We smoke our fish 25% longer than commercial fisheries – the longer you smoke something the drier it becomes and so the product becomes more expensive. My grandfather used to say about smoking fish: 'If the kitchen doesn't smell of smoke throw the fish away.' The way to smoke a fish is to get the smoke right into the fish. We still have two original pre-1920 smoke chimneys on the premises here. This whole building is dedicated to the handling of fresh fish.

"Handling fish is intensive work. The most important aspect of selling fish is to be totally at ease with the intensity of handling and selling fresh fish. I leave home at 4am and go to Billingsgate. On a Friday and Saturday it's like Wembley Stadium in here – you can't move for people. Christmas is tricky. Between Christmas and New Year everybody is after fish and all the UK ports are closed until 5 January. It's easier to get fish delivered from abroad; that's when all my contacts come into play and I call in the favours. When no one's got large sea bass for New Year's Eve I've got them.

"I'm finding more and more people are asking if we're open on a Sunday or a Monday. Before people would have known that you don't get fresh fish on these days, but we've become a 24/7 society and people have forgotten the fundamental knowledge of the ingredient."

Steve Hatt, 88-90 Essex Road, N1

" I leave home at 4am and go to Billingsgate. On a Friday and Saturday it's like Wembley Stadium in here – you can't move for people."

Steve Hatt

Devilled Whitebait
Serves 4

Whitebait, the small fry of fish such as herring, were once widely fished for in the River Thames. In the 19th century whitebait dinners became a popular tradition at London's riverside taverns, with the Trafalgar Tavern and the Old Ship Inn in Greenwich being particularly noted for their whitebait feasts.

4 tbsp plain flour
2 tsp cayenne pepper
salt and freshly ground pepper
450 g (1 lb) whitebait
sunflower oil, for deep-frying
lemon wedges, to serve

Mix together the flour and cayenne pepper on a plate. Season well with salt and freshly ground pepper. Toss the whitebait in the seasoned flour until well-coated.

Heat the oil until hot in a large, deep pan or wok. Add the whitebait, in batches if necessary, and fry until golden-brown. Remove and drain on kitchen paper. Serve at once with lemon wedges.

ALL PEPPERS
£2.99 KILO

Roasted Red Pepper Bruschetta

Makes 20

Italian-style bruschetta (topped, toasted bread) are a great nibble and roasted red peppers make for colourful topping.

1 small baguette, cut into 20 slices
2 red peppers
8 cherry tomatoes, quartered
1 garlic clove, peeled
$1/_2$ tsp balsamic vinegar
1 tsp olive oil
salt and freshly ground pepper
black olive tapenade, for spreading
small handful of basil leaves, torn

Preheat the oven to Gas 5/190°C/375°F. Place the baguette slices on a baking sheet and bake for 5-10 minutes until golden. Cool on a wire rack.

Roast the red peppers until charred on all sides. Wrap in plastic and set aside to cool. Peel and cut into short strips.

Mix together the red pepper, cherry tomatoes, garlic clove, balsamic vinegar and olive oil. Season with salt and freshly ground pepper.

Spread the baked baguette slices with tapenade. Mix the basil into the red pepper mixture, discarding the garlic clove. Top each baguette slice with the red pepper mixture. Serve at once.

A Trip to Billingsgate Market

Billingsgate fish market can trace its roots back to the Middle Ages, with tolls charged for the market as early as 1016. Initially it was a general market, selling corn, coal, iron, salt and pottery as well as fish. Billingsgate overtook Queenhithe as the popular wharf at which to land fish and a market grew up around at the "hythe" or dock at Billingsgate, with fish and seafood traded from stalls and stands. In 1699 an Act of Parliament made Billingsgate "a free and open market for all sorts of fish whatsoever".

Billingsgate Market, Trafalgar Way, E14

Billingsgate was famous not only for its fish but was also notorious for the bad language heard there. In 1850 a market building was constructed but this was inadequate and was replaced in 1873 by a new purpose-built building, in the French Renaissance style, complete with gilded dolphins. One of the characteristic sights of the market was the porters wearing their leather 'bobbing hats', resembling helmets, which they used to carry the fish on their heads; the name apparently derived from the "bob" (shilling) charged to carry the fish.

In 1982, Billingsgate Market moved to a new site on the then run-down Isle of Dogs. The Billingsgate Market bell was taken from the old market and tolled to mark the beginning of trading in the new premises. Today Billingsgate sits in the heart of Canary Wharf, dwarfed by the gleaming glass and steel skyscrapers of huge international corporations towering above it, and with a few sea gulls sitting hopefully on its roof. Inside, the market bustles satisfyingly – white-coated porters push trolleys deftly over the wet floor, satisfied buyers, laden with black plastic bags of fish, make their way through the aisles and the air is filled with the scent of fish. The Billingsgate soundscape includes the piercing squeak of polystyrene boxes being scraped together, assorted mobile ring tones and the repeated cautionary "Mind your backs, there" from the porters. Billingsgate offers the largest selection of fish and seafood in the U.K. – here are writhing eels, langoustine, crabs, lobsters, scallops in their shells, bundles of razor clams, huge halibut, salmon, tuna, brill, sea bass, cod, all the plunder of the sea.

> **It's my aftershave. It's called 'Kippers by midnight'.**
>
> Billingsgate fish dealer

Fishmongers Alan and Rita
Hammersley visit Billingsgate
every week to buy fish for their stall
at Barnet Market. Rita has vivid
memories of the first time Alan took her to
visit the market, "I remember the first time
I went to Billingsgate Market. I must have
been 19. To see something like that – I didn't
think anyone could work that hard at that
time of the morning and be so lively – and
so friendly, so kind, a great bunch. The first
time we went we parked at the top of Fish
Street Hill by the Monument – there were
these guys pulling trolleys. Those trolleys are
heavy, even without the fish. The porters with
their special hats, carrying loads on their
heads. You'd have loved the old market."

R H Fisheries, Barnet Market, High Barnet

Smoked Fish

Smoked fish in various forms are a characteristic element of British cuisine.

Arbroath smokie: a hot-smoked, headed, gutted and unfilleted haddock, originating from the fishing village of Auchmithie, near Arbroath in East Scotland. The salted haddock were traditionally smoked in barrels with hessian sacking to trap the smoke in.

Bloater: a whole herring lightly salted and then lightly cold-smoked. It was originally known as a "bloat herring". Samuel Pepys refers to bloater in his diary.

Craster kipper: a cold smoked whole herring, split from mouth to tail, from Craster in Northumberland.

Finnan haddock or Finnan haddie: a whole haddock, with the head removed, split, brined and lightly smoked, originating from Scotland.

Kipper: a cured smoked herring. The creation of kipper is credited to a Northumbrian curer called John Woodger, who sent his "Newcastle kipper" to London in 1846.

Smoked haddock: cold smoked haddock fillets.

Smoked mackerel: hot-smoked fillets of mackerel.

Smoked salmon: The rise of salmon farming has made smoked salmon far cheaper and more widely available. Smoked wild salmon remains a luxury. The London cure for smoked salmon developed with the arrival of East European immigrants in London in the late 19th century.

Smokeries:

H Forman & Sons
Stour Road, Fish Island, E3
020 8221 3900
www.formans.co.uk
Founded in 1905, the UK's oldest established salmon curer is currently run by the 4th generation of Formans.

W & F Fish Ltd
56-64 Crogsland Road, NW1
020 7485 6603
Founded by Morris Fulberg in 1936 and specialising in London cured smoked salmon.

Lunch

Asparagus Ham Gratin
Serves 4

Late May and early June see the arrival of flavourful English asparagus in farmers' markets and greengrocers. Asparagus is delicious served simply with melted butter or a poached egg with a runny middle but this recipe, is a good and tasty way of turning it into a more substantial dish.

15 g (¹/₂ oz) butter
15 g (¹/₂ oz) plain flour
300 ml (¹/₂ pt) milk
1-2 tsp grain mustard
salt and freshly ground pepper
freshly grated nutmeg
2 bundles of asparagus, stems trimmed
150 g (5 oz) good quality, finely sliced ham
25 g (1 oz) fresh breadcrumbs
25 g (1 oz) grated Parmesan cheese

Heat the butter in a heavy-based saucepan. Once the butter is melted, mix in the flour. Cook gently for a couple of minutes, then gradually mix in the milk. Stirring, bring to the boil and cook until the white sauce thickens. Stir in the mustard and season with salt, freshly ground pepper and freshly grated nutmeg.

Meanwhile, bring a large pan of salted water to the boil. Add the asparagus and boil until just tender; drain.

Place the asparagus in a buttered heatproof dish, layering with the ham slices. Spoon over the sauce, then top with breadcrumbs and Parmesan.

Preheat the grill and grill the gratin until browned. Serve at once.

Roast Beetroot and Goats' Cheese Salad

Serves 4

Dark purple-fleshed beetroot is well-served by slow roasting, which brings out its natural sweetness.

500 g (1 lb 2 oz) small raw beetroot
2 tbsp olive oil
1 tbsp sherry vinegar
salt and freshly ground pepper
a generous handful of freshly shelled walnuts
1 soft goat's cheese
finely snipped chives, to garnish

Preheat the oven to Gas 2/150°C/300°F.

Place the beetroot in an ovenproof dish, cover with foil and bake for 3 hours. To test if the beetroot is cooked through, rub the skin on one of the beets. If it wrinkles easily the beetroot is cooked. Allow to cool slightly, then peel and chop.

Mix together the olive oil and vinegar, seasoning with salt and freshly ground pepper. Toss the beetroot in the olive oil dressing and place in a serving dish. Mix in the walnuts. roughly crumble over the goat's cheese and garnish with chives. Serve.

Lily's Squid with Spinach
Serves 4

"This squid and spinach dish would usually be made with cuttlefish, which you can't find easily over here," explains Lily Perahia. "But it's also good with squid. If using large squid, chop it into pieces. It's a more unusual dish, one of my favourites. You add a little bit of wine when you cook it and a big bunch of dill – the dill and spinach goes together well."

100 ml (3 ½ fl oz) olive oil
1 large onion chopped
1 kg (2 ¼ lb) squid, washed and cleaned
115 ml (4 fl oz) white wine
salt and freshly ground pepper
1 kg (2 ¼ lb) baby spinach
1 small bunch of dill finely chopped (at least 4 tbsp)
bread or potatoes or rice, to serve

Put most of the oil in a heavy-based pan and sauté the onion until soft. When it starts changing colour add the squid and turn up the heat a bit. Cook until all the water from the squid has evaporated and sauté well.

Pour the wine and cook for a few more minutes. Season with salt and freshly ground pepper, stir, cover and simmer on a lower heat for 15 minutes. Check to see if the squid is tender; if not, add a little water and cook further.

Add the rinsed spinach and the remaining olive oil. Cover the pan and cook, stirring now and then, until the spinach is just wilted. Add the dill, check the seasoning, cover and cook gently until the spinach is really soft and the sauce thick. Serve warm or at room temperature. This dish is usually eaten on its own with bread but goes well with potatoes or rice.

Tuna Teriyaki
Serves 4

A stylish Japanese-inspired fish dish. Rice wine and mirin can be found in Japanese or Chinese food shops.

2 tbsp rice wine
2 tbsp mirin
2 tbsp Japanese soy sauce
1 tsp sugar
4 tuna steaks
sunflower oil, for brushing

In a small pan, heat together the rice wine, mirin, Japanese soy sauce and sugar, stirring until the sugar has melted. Set aside.

Preheat two griddle pans. Brush the tuna steaks with sunflower oil. Cook the tuna steaks on the griddle pans until just cooked to taste, carefully turning over to brown both sides. Spoon over the soy sauce mixture and cook until glazed, again turning over to glaze both sides. Serve at once.

OIL

TERIYAKI SAUCE
*SO TASTY WE RECOMMEND
AS A B.B.Q SAUCE, MARINADE
SAUCE, SALAD DRESSING ETC.

YAKITORI SAUCE

GYOZA NO TARE
SAUCE
FOR
DUMPLING

Gretchen's Okra

Serves 2 as a garnish or side-dish

2-3 handfuls of okra
coarse cornmeal, for coating
a little olive oil, for shallow-frying
a sprinkling of water
salt, to taste

Trim and slice the okra into circles of about $\frac{1}{4}$ -$\frac{1}{3}$ inch thick). Place in a bowl and toss with the cornmeal until well-coated.

Heat the olive oil in a heavy-based frying pan. Add in the okra so that it fries in a single or double layer in the pan but no thicker. You can sprinkle more cornmeal over the top if you like more batter. Using your fingertips, flick in a little water, cover the pan and cook over a low heat. Shake the pan from time to time and cook until the okra turns bright green, uncovering the pan and turning over the okra only once during the process. Cook until just tender. Season with salt and serve at once.

"I want to overcome okra-phobia!"

Gretchen de Soriano

G retchen de Soriano is a woman on a mission; "I want to overcome okra-phobia!" she laughs. Growing up in Southern Virginia, okra was often cooked at home but, in fact, as a child Gretchen "hated it." It was when she was working and living in Japan that Gretchen decided to reclaim okra. "I thought my family like okra, so there must be something to it. In Japan I learnt that food should be fresh and simple. They eat small amounts, cooked beautifully. I'd serve this as a garnish or as a side-dish." The cornmeal coating reflects Gretchen's American roots; "Southern food xyz always has a crust. You need a heavy-based frying pan with a tightly-fitting lid for this. The trick is to get the okra to sweat without burning it. When my mother died, I brought back my mother's cast-iron frying pan from Virginia – it was her mother's pan – and it's perfect for cooking the okra in."

Eel, Pie and Mash

One fish traditionally associated with London is the eel. Eel Pie Island on the River Thames is a reminder of the days when eels were once fished there. By Victorian times, eels had become a popular working class food. In 1851 Henry Mayhew wrote of street stalls selling "hot eels" "greatly relished by the chilled labourers... These dealers are stationary, having stalls or stands in the street, and the savoury odour from them attracts more hungry-looking gazers and loungers than does a cook-shop window... The eels are all purchased at Billingsgate early in the morning. The parties themselves, or their sons or daughters, go to Billingsgate, and the watermen row them to the Dutch eel vessels moored off the market." Billingsgate Market is still the place to go to for live eels and Holland continues to be a major source of eels. Mick Jenrick of Mick's Eel Supply at Billingsgate is a key supplier to the trade, storing his stock of live eels in great water-filled drawers.

The 19th century saw the rise of London's eel, pie and mash shops, which sold stewed or jellied eels (set in their own jelly) and minced beef pies served with mashed potato and liquor (parsley sauce) – hearty food at affordable prices. Today the Cookes and the Manzes, two families still in the eel, pie and mash trade, can trace their roots in the business back to the 19th and early 20th centuries.

F Cooke & Manzes

In 1862 F Cooke began selling pies and eels in London's East End and today his family still run an eel, pie and mash shop in Broadway Market, Hackney. In 1902 Michele Manze, an Italian from Sorrento in southern Italy, bought Robert Cooke's eel, pie and mash shop (founded in 1891) in Tower Bridge Road, Bermondsey. Today, having survived bomb damage during World War II, it is London's oldest eel, pie and mash shop still in business and is still run by the Manze family. Michele's brothers followed in his footsteps and by 1930 there were 14 eel, pie and mash shops bearing the name "Manze."

A perennially popular feature of eel, pie and mash shops were the displays of writhing live eels in the windows, with children pausing eagerly to watch eels being swiftly and efficiently beheaded, then chopped into chunks. 'We're not allowed to have live eels here anymore,' comments Valerie of Manzes. 'It's the pensioners who especially go for eels, especially on Fridays."

Today there are only a handful of traditional eel, pie and mash shops left in London, each with their loyal following of customers. Manzes' Tower Bridge Road shop retains its classic décor of white, cream and green tiles, narrow marble-topped tables and counters and dark wooden benches. Rotating ceiling fans add a welcome coolness and the large sash windows open onto the street. Prices, as is traditional, remain low.

M Manze, 87 Tower Bridge Road, SE1
F Cook, 9 Broadway Market, London, E8

M Manze

A steady stream of customers, many of them regulars, come through: "Two pies, one mash," "Mug of tea, please". Huge platefuls of minced beef pies and mash, swimming in bright green 'liquor,' are consumed with relish.

M Manze

Potato Chorizo Tortilla
Serves 4

A popular tapas nibble, a whole tortilla also makes a great light meal. Adding chorizo to the traditional potato and onion mixture gives an added tastiness. Find good-quality chorizo at Spanish delicatessens such as Brindisa on Exmouth Market or Garcia, on Portobello Road.

4 tbsp olive oil
1 onion, finely sliced
300 g (10 oz) waxy potatoes, peeled and finely sliced
salt and freshly ground pepper
2 chorizo sausages, sliced
4 medium, free-range organic eggs

Heat the olive oil in a 20 cm (8 in), heavy-based frying pan. Add the onion and potato, mixing together gently. Season with salt and cook over a medium to low heat for 15-20 minutes until softened.

Meanwhile, in a separate, small frying pan, fry the chorizo (which will exude its own fat) until cooked, then set aside to cool.

Beat the eggs together in a bowl, seasoning with salt and freshly ground pepper. Add the fried chorizo.

Using a slotted spoon, remove the softened onion and potato, leaving the olive oil in the pan, and add to the egg mixture, gently mixing together. Set aside.

Reheat the olive oil in the frying pan. Pour in the egg mixture and fry over a low to medium heat until set and browned underneath. Carefully place a large plate over the pan and invert the tortilla onto the plate. Gently slide the tortilla back into the frying pan and cook gently until the other side has been browned. Serve warm or at room temperature.

Duck Noodle Broth
Serves 4

A simple but satisfying meal in a bowl, inspired by the hearty soup noodle dishes one can eat in Chinatown's restaurants.

2 duck breast fillets
salt and pepper
$1/2$ tsp Chinese five-spice powder
1 $1/2$ tbsp sunflower oil
250 g (9 oz) fine egg noodles
1 tsp sesame oil
1 onion, sliced lengthways
generous glug of rice wine or medium sherry
1 ltr (1 3/4 pt) fresh chicken stock
1 tbsp soy sauce
115 g (4 oz) bean sprouts
2 heads of bok choy, blanched and quartered
1 spring onion, finely chopped

Dipping sauce:
3 tsp soy sauce
1 tsp rice vinegar
1 small red chilli, finely chopped

Preheat the oven to Gas 6/200°C/400°F.

Season the duck breast fillets with salt and pepper and the five-spice powder. Brush the flesh with half a tablespoon of oil. Place the duck on a rack above a tray and roast for 25 minutes. Slice each breast finely.

Bring a large pan of salted water to the boil. Add the egg noodles and cook until just tender; drain, rinse and toss with the sesame oil.

Heat the remaining oil in a large saucepan. Add the onion and fry until softened. Add the sherry, allow to sizzle, then add the stock and soy sauce. Bring to the boil and simmer for 5 minutes. Taste to check the seasoning, adding salt if necessary. Mix together the ingredients for the dipping sauce.

Divide the noodles among 4 deep soup bowls. Ladle over the hot chicken broth, then top each portion with roast duck slices, bean sprouts, bok choy and a sprinkling of spring onion.

Serve at once with the dipping sauce.

Roast Beef on the Bone with Yorkshire Pudding
Serves 4

Roast beef with Yorkshire pudding is one of the great classics of British cooking. Cooking the meat on the bone gives it a depth of flavour, set off perfectly by the simplicity of the accompanying Yorkshire pudding.

a 3-rib piece of beef on the bone (roughly 2 kg (4 $\frac{1}{2}$ lb)
flour, for sprinkling
mustard powder, for sprinkling
salt and freshly ground pepper
1 tbsp olive oil
home-made gravy, to serve

Yorkshire pudding:
115 g (4 oz) plain white flour
1 tsp salt
2 free-range eggs
300 ml ($\frac{1}{2}$ pt) milk
3 tbsp oil or dripping

Preheat the oven to Gas 8/230°C/450°F.

Sprinkle the beef with flour and mustard on all sides. Season well with salt and freshly ground pepper and rub with the olive oil. Place in a roasting tray.

Roast the beef in the oven for 15 minutes. Reduce the heat to Gas 4/180°C/350°F and roast the meat for a further 1 3/4 hours, basting now and then. Remove and rest, keeping the meat warm, for 30 minutes.

Meanwhile, prepare the Yorkshire pudding. Preheat the oven to Gas 7/220°C/425°F. Heat the oil in a small roasting tin. Sift the flour and salt into a mixing bowl. Break in the eggs and gradually add the milk, whisking to form a thick, smooth batter. Pour the batter into the hot oil in the roasting tin. Bake for 30 minutes until risen and golden. Serve at once with the rested roast beef and gravy.

Beef and Britishness

No other meat is as closely associated with the British as beef, the quintessential red meat. For centuries visitors to Britain were astonished at the quantity of meat eaten by the British and impressed by its quality, with the French nicknaming us "le rosbif". The idea of Britain being a nation of meat-eaters, especially beef, became bound up with national identity and patriotism, with a sturdy, well-fed John Bull, whose favourite food was beef, becoming an iconic image. The Yeoman Warders who guard the Tower of London have long been called "Beefeaters", a nickname thought to derive from the notable amounts of meat they consumed each day as rations. Richard Leveridge's 1735 version of a patriotic song "The roast beef of old England" encapsulates a spirit of cheerfully carnivorous patriotism:

When mighty roast beef was the Englishman's food
It enobl'd our veins and enriched our blood
Our soliders were brave and courtiers were good
Oh the roast beef of old England,
And old England's roast beef!

The 18th-century artist William Hogarth, whose 1748 painting *The Roast Beef of Old England* taps into British patriotism and anti-French sentiment, was a founder member of the Sublime Society of Steaks, who met over a meal of grilled steak.

The sense of beef as a national meat still lingers on, with Britain's rich pastures lending themselves to cattle-rearing. The banning of beef on the bone during the BSE epidemic in the 1980s was deeply resented and many butchers became folk hero figures in their communities by flouting the ban.

One positive aspect of the BSE epidemic was that London's best butchers, those who could source their meat and vouch for its credentials, enjoyed increased business. With a new gastro-patriotism very evident in Britain today, beef continues to enjoy a special place in British cuisine.

Millie's Erachi Dolarthiathu
(Dry Curry of Lamb with Coconut)
Serves 4-6

Just off Oxford Circus, tucked away in Great Castle Street, husband-and-wife team David and Millie Tharakan run the Kerala restaurant, a cosy place, decorated with traditional, colourful Keralan artefacts, offering Londoners a rare chance to sample authentic Keralan dishes. "I love interacting with people," explains Millie, "and so does David, so we love that side of running a restaurant, though it is hard work. We still get people asking for chicken tikka masala – that's what they think of when they think of Indian food – but more and more people have been to Kerala and know about our food. This recipe is a Syrian Christian recipe from Kerala. We do it with lamb – back home it's done with beef. It's very popular with our customers and one of my favourites."

1 kg (2.2 lb) lamb, cut into pieces
4 tsp red chilli powder
6 tsp ground coriander
2 tsp ground turmeric
1 tsp garam masala
2 tsp finely chopped fresh root ginger
1 medium tomato, finely chopped
4 medium onions, peeled and finely sliced
salt
450 ml (3/4 pt) water
2 tsp mustard seeds
3 tbsp vegetable oil
2 garlic cloves, peeled and crushed
a few curry leaves
a few fresh coconut chips, lightly fried in oil (optional)
rice or paratha, to serve

Mix together the lamb, chilli, coriander, turmeric, garam masala, ginger, chopped tomato and half the onion and place in a pan. Season with salt, pour over the water, bring to the boil, reduce the heat and allow the meat to simmer until cooked dry, approximately 45 minutes to 1 hour (depending on the meat).

Heat the oil in a frying pan and add the mustard seeds. Once the mustard seeds begin to splutter add the remaining onion, garlic and curry leaves and fry, stirring often, until the onion is lightly browned. Mix in the cooked meat and coconut chips and fry, stirring often, until the meat browned on all sides. Serve at once with rice or paratha.

"*I love interacting with people,*" explains Millie, "*and so does David, so we love that side of running a restaurant, though it is hard work.*"

Millie Tharakan

Kerala, 15 Great Castle Street, W1

A Taste of Africa & The Caribbean

For centuries, London's black community comprised of largely slaves or servants. By the late 18th century, however, there was also a free black population, including Nigerian-born anti-slavery campaigner Olaudah Equiano, and in 1807 the Abolition of the Slave Trade Act was passed. During the 19th century settlers from Africa and the Caribbean came to London, and Britain, for study or work.

The passing of the 1948 British Nationality Act gave people in the Commonwealth British Citizenship and the right of entry and settlement in Britain. The same year saw around 500 Jamaicans arrive in London on the SS Empire Windrush, to settle mainly in Brixton. Notting Hill became a focal point for London's Trinidadian community and today the Notting Hill Carnival – inspired by Trinidad's spectacular Carnival – has become a major street festival. London today is home to a significant Black British and African population, numbering around 344,000 and over 380,000 in the 2001 census, respectively.

Busy, bustling markets – such as Brixton, Ridley Road, Queen's Market and Shepherd's Bush – are important food shopping centres for London's black communities. Stalls here are piled high with assorted yams, cassava, green and yellow plaintain, knobbly-skinned breadfruit, acid green limes, bright red, ferociously hot Scotch bonnet peppers and bunches of callaloo. Butchers do a brisk business in meat including goat, pig's trotters and cow's feet, fishmongers' slabs feature colourful displays of tropical fish such as parrot fish and snappers, while stalls and shops sell staples such as tinned ackee, pungent saltfish and cornmeal. Dotted around London are a number of Caribbean restaurants, from the long-established Hummingbird, on Stroud Green Road, serving Trinidadian cuisine, to Mr Jerk in Soho, specialising in Jamaican dishes, while African restaurants such as Tobia, Laliblea and Suya Obalende offer a chance to sample Ethiopian, Eritrean, Ghanaian and Nigerian food.

Ridley Road Market. E8

Mussels in Cider

Serves 4

Cooking mussels in cider adds a subtle but delicious sweetness to this dish.

2 kg (4 ¹/₂ lb) mussels
1 tbsp sunflower oil
2 shallots, finely chopped
2 sprigs of tarragon
600 ml (1 pt) dry English cider
salt
chopped parsley, to garnish

Thoroughly scrub the mussels under running water, discarding any that are cracked or open.

Heat the oil in a large, heavy-based saucepan. Add the shallots, mussels, tarragon and cider. Season with salt. Cover and cook for around 10 minutes, until the mussels have opened. Serve at once, discarding any mussels that aren't open.

Courgette and Goat's Cheese Frittata

Serves 4

A fresh-tasting, summery version of a classic Italian egg dish.

2 tbsp olive oil
2 onions, peeled and sliced
3 courgettes, finely sliced into rounds
6 free-range eggs
salt and freshly ground pepper
handful of fresh mint leaves, finely shredded
1 small soft goat's cheese, such as Sussex
  Slipcote, sliced

Heat the olive oil in a 25 cm (10 in) heavy-based frying pan. Add the onion and fry gently for 5 minutes.

Add the courgette slices and fry very gently until softened. Meanwhile, beat together the eggs, season with salt and freshly ground pepper and mix in the mint.

Pour the egg mixture over the fried onion and courgette. Layer over the goat's cheese. Fry very gently for around 10 minutes until set. Preheat the grill and finish off the frittata under the grill to cook the top side.

Pad Thai
Serves 4

Find the ingredients for this popular Thai noodle dish – a classic combination of sour, sweet and hot chilli flavours – in Thai supermarkets or the shops in Chinatown.

250 g (9 oz) broad, flat, dried rice sticks
2 tbsp sunflower oil
3 shallots, peeled and chopped
2 garlic cloves, chopped
200 g (7 oz) pork fillet, cut into strips
2 red chillies, finely chopped
75 ml (3 fl oz) hot water
1 walnut-sized piece of tamarind pulp
juice of $\frac{1}{2}$ lime
2-3 tbsp light soy sauce
1 tsp sugar
generous splash of Thai fish sauce
freshly ground pepper
200 g (7 oz) cooked peeled prawns
200 g (7 oz) bean sprouts
2 tbsp roast peanuts, finely chopped
2 tbsp dried shrimps, finely ground (optional)
coriander sprigs, to garnish
lime wedges, to serve

Soak the rice sticks in warm water for 15-20 minutes, until softened, then drain. Mix the hot water with the tamarind pulp, stirring together thoroughly. Set aside for 15 minutes, then strain, pressing down on the tamarind pulp to extract as much tamarind flavour as possible.

Heat a wok until hot, add the oil and heat through. Add the shallot, garlic and pork and fry for 5 minutes. Add the softened rice sticks and mix well.

Sprinkle over the chilli, tamarind water, lime juice, soy sauce, sugar, and fish sauce, season with freshly ground black pepper and mix well. Add the prawns and bean sprouts and stir-fry for 5 minutes.

Sprinkle over the chopped peanuts and dried shrimp. Garnish with coriander sprigs and serve at once with lime wedges.

Anne's Ackee and Saltfish
Serves 4

400 g (14 oz) saltfish, soaked in
 cold water overnight
vegetable oil, for shallow-frying
4 spring onions, chopped
1 onion, peeled and chopped
1 red pepper, chopped
2-3 red chillies, chopped (optional)
2 garlic cloves, peeled and chopped
2 tomatoes, diced
$\frac{1}{2}$ tsp Tex's Tropical Multi-Purpose Seasoning
$\frac{1}{2}$ tsp ground white pepper
$\frac{1}{3}$ tsp Tex's Aunty Nell's Fish Seasoning
4 tbsp cold water
1 x 540 g (1 $\frac{1}{4}$ lb) tin of ackee, drained

First cook the soaked saltfish. Drain it, place
it in a pan, cover with fresh water, bring it to
the boil and boil for 15-20 minutes until tender.
Drain; remove the skin and de-bone.

Heat the vegetable oil in a large, heavy-based
frying pan. Add the spring onion, onion, red
pepper, chilli, garlic and tomato and fry until
the onion and red pepper are softened.

Sprinkle over the Multi-Purpose Seasoning,
white pepper and Fish Seasoning. Add the
water, taking care not to let the mixture dry
out.

Mix in the saltfish and gently heat through. Add
the ackee and, using a spoon, very gently mix
it in, taking care not to over-mix. Gently heat
through, then serve at once.

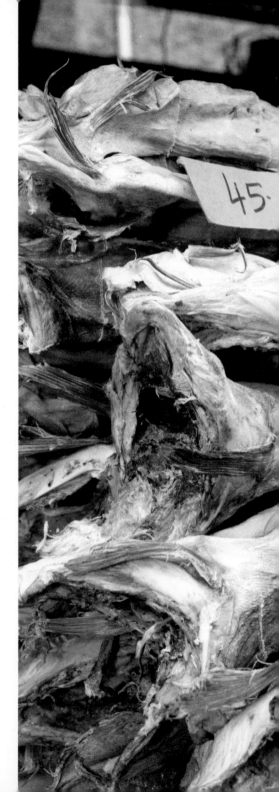

My parents kept to West Indian ingredients, like dasheen and yams. Every Saturday morning my Mum and I would go to Dalston Market to do the shopping. People used to go there to meet and socialise. I do cook Caribbean food now and then."

Anne Grier

"I'm a Londoner," explains Anne Grier, "born in the East End. My family came from Domenica in the Caribbean, they came over in the 1950s. My father was a labourer. He got a job with a Jewish company and stayed with them for 40 years, became a foreman and worked on the QE2.

"In Domenica we just have the saltfish; we wouldn't have the ackee. It was my husband, who's from Jamaica, who introduced me to the ackee. You can eat saltfish and ackee for breakfast, with West Indian bread; for lunch we'd served it with grilled plantains and a salad. To make it more substantial you serve it with provisions – yam, dasheen or sweet potato, baked or boiled."

Smoked Haddock Chowder
Serves 4

Use natural smoked haddock rather than dyed, as its flavour is far more subtle. This substantial fish soup makes a meal in its own right.

450 g (1 lb) natural smoked haddock fillet
1 ltr (1 3/4 pt) milk
1 bay leaf
25 g (1 oz) butter
1 onion, finely sliced
1 leek, finely sliced
400g (14 oz) floury potatoes, peeled and diced
generous glug of sherry
3 tbsp finely chopped parsley
freshly grated nutmeg
salt and freshly ground pepper

Place the smoked haddock, milk and bay leaf in a shallow pan. Bring to the boil, reduce the heat and simmer for 5 minutes or until the haddock becomes opaque.

Using a slotted spoon, remove the smoked haddock and flake, discarding the skin and any bones. Remove and discard the bay leaf and reserve the poaching milk.

Heat the butter in a large, heavy-based saucepan. Add the onion and leek and fry gently for 10 minutes until softened. Mix in the potatoes, then add the sherry and cook for 1-2 minutes. Add the reserved poaching milk and bring to the boil.

Reduce the heat to a simmer, add the flaked haddock and parsley. Season with nutmeg, salt and freshly ground pepper (bearing in mind the saltiness of the smoked haddock). Simmer for 15-20 minutes. Serve.

Lina Stores' Pumpkin Tortelloni with Sage Butter

Serves 4

a small bunch of fresh sage
salt and freshly ground pepper
500 g (1 lb 2 oz) Lina Stores' pumpkin tortelloni
40 g (1 ½ oz) butter
grated Parmesan cheese, to serve

Roughly chop the sage leaves, discarding the tough stalks. Bring a large pan of salted water to the boil. Add the tortelloni, return to the boil, reduce the heat and simmer for 5-8 minutes until cooked through; drain.

Meanwhile, heat the butter in a frying pan. Add the chopped sage and fry briefly until fragrant. Season with salt and freshly ground pepper.

Pour the sage butter over the drained tortelloni. Serve at once with grated Parmesan cheese.

With its pistachio-green façade and wonderful old-fashioned fittings, Italian delicatessen Lina Stores is a Soho institution. Ever since the days of the original "Lina", it has been noted especially for its fresh pasta. Whereas other delis just sold tortellini filled with veal or spinach and ricotta, Lina sold plump cushions of home-made pumpkin tortelloni. The recipe below is a simple but classic Italian combination; "simmer the tortelloni," cautions Gabriella, "if you boil them too hard, they'll burst".

Lina Stores, 18 Brewer Street, W1

Soho Stories

For centuries Soho, in the heart of London's West End, has been known as a cosmopolitan area, home initially to French Huguenots escaping persecution for their religious beliefs during the 16th and 17th centuries, then many other groups of immigrants, who settled in the area, setting up businesses, shops, bars, cafés and restaurants. Today, rising rents are implacably driving out the small, family-run businesses, many of whom have been in the area for decades.

Angelucci's

Alma and Andy Angelucci run the coffee business founded by their father in 1929 with a gentle courtesy and charm. Angelucci's became a Soho institution and was even referred to in a Dire Straits song. But times have changed and rents have gradually driven smaller retailers from the West End. In 2008, after nearly 80 years of trading from its Soho store, Angelucci's upped sticks and moved to East Finchley. Frith Street will be very much the poorer for Angelucci's absence. Customers can visit the store in Finchley or order online (www. angeluccicoffee.co.uk).

"The war was very hard for my mother; she made her way down here from Muswell Hill in the dark because of the blackout. The prostitutes used to get coffee to send to their families in France; the troops would send it back for them. I can remember I was waiting outside one evening when this prostitute came along and said to me, 'You're standing on my patch', but I said, 'I'm standing outside my father's shop!'

"I've always enjoyed being in a broad-minded atmosphere; I believe in live and let live. I could tell you lots of stories about the customers we've had. This area was like a theatre – out there was the stage. In the 1950s there were lots of characters – crime fighters too. They only killed among themselves; never touched us. We didn't pay protection. In the 1970s there used to be lots of little shops around here. I wish they'd bring it back or give small shops a chance to stay open. It's the rents that cripple everyone. London – now it's for the wealthy."

Alma Angelucci

Alma Angelucci of Angelucci's coffee shop, Frith Street, W1
After 79 years in Soho, Angelucci coffee has moved to East Finchley,
472 Long Lane, East Finchley, N2

I Camisa

Stepping into this small, narrow shop, the first thing that strikes you is the wonderful, savoury smell, the accumulated aroma of Parmesan cheese, hams, salamis and dried mushrooms. There's a sprinkling of sawdust on the floor, glass-fronted wooden drawers and shelves filled with packets of dried pasta, polenta, risotto rice and lentils, while the glass-fronted counter houses cheese, salamis, salsicce, home-made fresh pasta and olives. On the counter there are punnets of Sicilian cherry tomatoes, packets of rocket and bunches of basil, while dangling overhead are packets of sugared almonds, pine nuts, dried porcini, plus, at Easter, columbe (dove-shaped cakes) and, at Christmas, panettone.

Gabriele Pierotti of I Camisa, Old Compton Street, known by staff and customers alike as Gaby, has presided genially over this shop for many years – exchanging football banter with delivery men ("That's what I'd expect from a Tottenham supporter"), catching up on news with old customers, taking telephone orders from the restaurants he supplies, instructing his staff to give a packet of sugared almonds to my son.

"This shop's been here since 1961. I've been working here for 28 years now. It's a hard life. I work six-and-a-half days a week and I wake up every morning at 5.30am. Even though I live nearby I don't get home before 7.30pm. I haven't had a holiday in the summer for 28 years now. It's much the same as it used to be, but it's got a bit more specialised. We didn't have things like truffle oil; there was no demand for it. My Parmesan..." he pauses thoughtfully, "now I am proud of my Parmesan – it is good."

I Camisa & Son, 61 Old Compton Street, W1

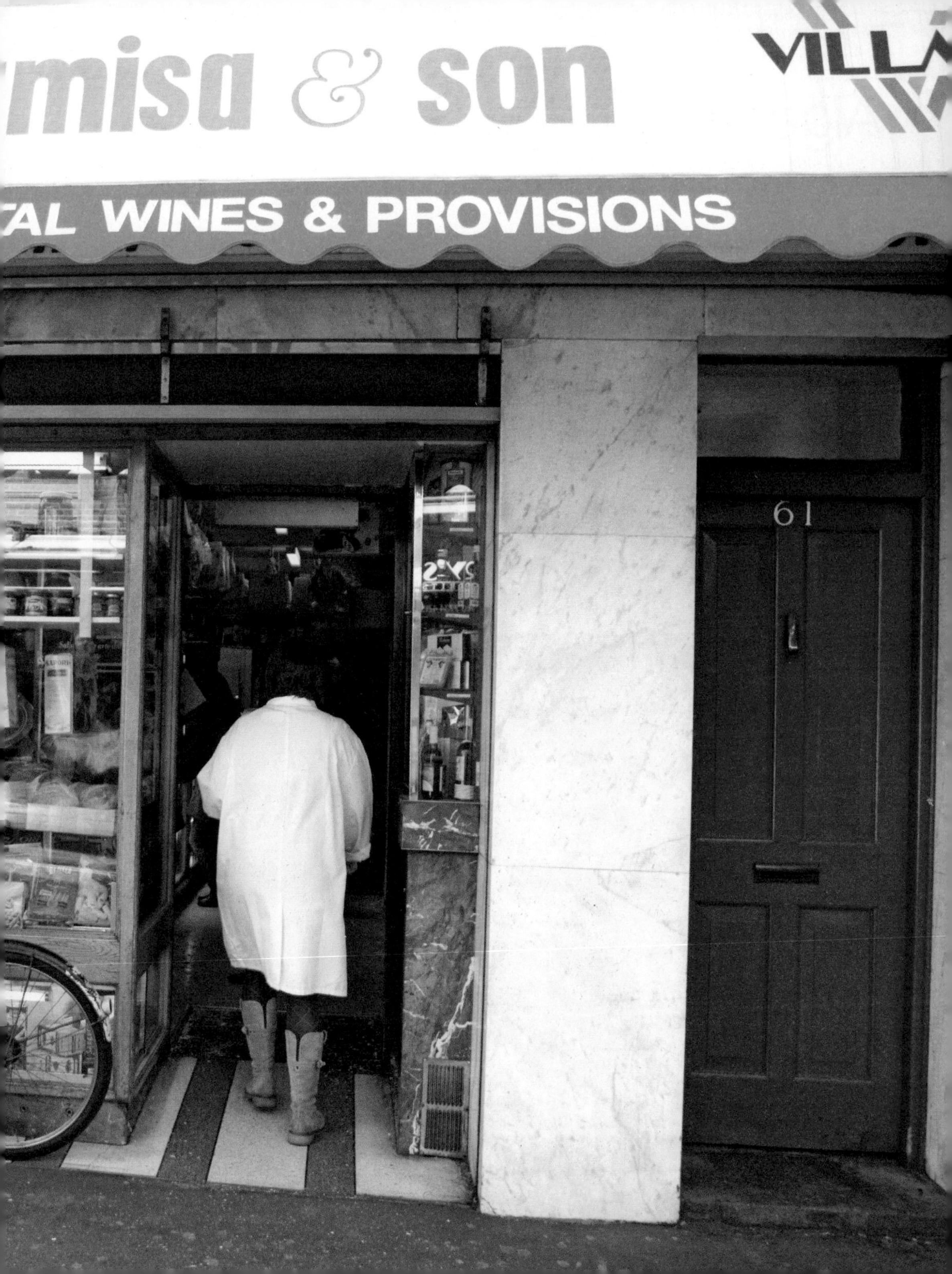
misa & son
VILL
AL WINES & PROVISIONS
61

Algerian Coffee Stores

With its bright red shopfront, the Algerian Coffee Stores is a Soho institution, founded in 1887 by an Algerian businessman called Mr Hassan. Today the shop is run by Paul Crocetta, who joined the business in 1972, working with his father-in-law John Jones, who'd taken over the shop in 1948. "There were lots of Italians in Soho then," reminisces Paul, "and lots of small shops – everyone would come on a Saturday to do their shopping, they'd visit the Italian shops: Bifulco the butcher, the fishmongers, Ortega for Spanish foods, Hamburger for smoked foods. At Rupert Street market the prices were higher but the quality better, though Berwick Street was good."

"There was a stall selling chicken and rabbits. The rabbits were hanging up – I remember if you bought a rabbit he skinned it by pulling the skin down and off it before your eyes."

"Our stock was very traditional when I joined – about 12 blends of coffee and 20 teas. Nowadays more English people are drinking coffee, they know what they want and are more choosy, more willing to try different things too. Bestsellers include Velluto Nero – strong and smooth – and Formula Rossa. I've extended the range. We've got such a variety of teas – the in-thing now is white tea and those artistic teas. I'm trying to get them direct from Shanghai. You've got to keep offering people new things, keep them happy. We've got customers who've been coming here for 40-50 years. Some of our mail-order customers tell us 'I used to come here when I was a child,' I've seen a lot of changes in the area. The rents just kill you; it gets harder and harder. I used to carry 3 tonnes of coffee without thinking, but now my back cricks!"

Paul Crocetta

Algerian Coffee Stores, 52 Old Compton Street, W1

Lina Stores

"The original Lina – her shop was down the road where the Piccola Bar was – used to make the pasta in the window of her shop. There used to be lots of Italian delis in this area: Parmigiani, Vinorio, Torino, the Camisa on Berwick Street, as well as the Camisa on Old Compton Street. We are famous for our pumpkin tortelloni, made with pumpkin and amaretti, which is a Northern Italian recipe. I don't like the rubbery texture that supermarket fresh pasta has."

We've seen our customers get married, have kids, their kids come in – we watch the toddlers growing up, they bring them in here and they get to taste all the good things."

Gabriella Filippi

Lina Stores, 18 Brewer Street, W1

Maison Bertaux

"Maison Bertaux was founded in 1871 by a member of the Communards, Frédéric Bertaux. At that time this area had refugees from all over Europe: Hungarians, Belgians, Jewish. It was the first French patisserie in London. The family lived upstairs and baked downstairs. I first came here when I was 14 to work as a Saturday girl. I was so frightened when I came in for the job interview – I thought it was so posh. I remember trying to hide my scruffy shoes under the table. I got the job and served a few querulous coffees. I went off to RADA and made some money and bought the business in 1988. When it comes to our pastries no-one takes short cuts; I've never bought mixers. I can tell if the choux pastry is fresh with my eyes shut; I love that. I always remember customers and what they like."

Someone came in after 20 years and I said, 'Coffee éclair for you.' He was amazed that I remembered. I love the shop at night when it's closed – the atmosphere, the history. It's like my home."

Michelle Ward

Maison Bertaux, 28 Greek Street, W1

> *It's a very traditional spring and summer dish – very well-known throughout Iran – if people travel to Iran they want to try this dish."*
>
> *Harry Dasht*

Harry Dasht was born in Iran: "I grew up by the Caspian Sea – I know all about fish as my father was a fisherman and we had a hotel and a restaurant. I like cooking and fish." Having come over to England to study engineering, Harry then ran B & M Seafood in Kentish Town, selling both fish and organic meat. "I liked being in the shop much more than engineering; it was more social." His latest enterprise is as a restaurateur, having recently set up R E D, a smart but relaxed and friendly eatery, up the road from B & M Seafood.

This dish is one that Hary remembers with great affection from his childhood in Iran; it is something that his mother would often cook for the family. "It's a very traditional spring and summer dish – very well-known throughout Iran – if people travel to Iran they want to try this dish. In my family we ate it with rice and smoked sea bass, steamed and crumbled over rice. There are only two main ingredients, but honestly the finished dish is delicious. You mustn't hurry," emphasises Harry, "cook it slowly. It's really nice hot or cold."

Harry's Mirza Ghasemi (Aubergine with Eggs)
Serves 2

This dish is one that Harry remembers with great affection from his childhood in Iran; it is something that his mother would often cook for the family.

3 aubergines
3 tomatoes
olive oil or sunflower oil, for shallow-frying
1/2 head of garlic, cloves peeled and chopped or crushed
salt and freshly ground pepper
pinch of turmeric
2 free-range eggs

Over a gas flame or on a charcoal barbecue, grill the aubergines and tomatoes until their skins are charred on all sides. Set aside to cool.

Heat the olive oil in a heavy-based frying pan. Add the garlic and fry very gently until browned. Season with salt, freshly ground pepper and turmeric.

Meanwhile, skin the aubergines and tomatoes and press down on them with your hands to crush them. Add the crushed aubergines and tomatoes to the fried garlic. Cook very gently, stirring now and then, and adding more oil if needed, until all the aubergine and tomatoes are soft and smooth.

Crack the eggs on top of the aubergine mixture. Turn off the heat and cover the pan with a lid, poaching the eggs. Serve at once.

Donato's Orecchiette with Rocket
Serves 4

olive oil, for shallow-frying
2 garlic cloves, peeled, left whole
300 g (10 oz) cherry tomatoes, chopped
a few sprigs of parsley, torn
a few sprigs of basil, torn
500 ml (17 fl oz) tomato passata
1 kg (2 ¼ lb) rocket
500 g (1 lb 2 oz) orecchiette pasta
cacioricotta cheese, diced or shaved, to serve

Heat the olive oil in a heavy-based frying pan. Add the garlic and fry until browned. Add the cherry tomatoes, parsley and basil and cook, stirring now and then, for 10 minutes. Add the tomato passata and cook very gently for 15 minutes.

Meanwhile, bring a large pan of salted water to the boil. Add the rocket (reserving a little for garnish) and cook briefly until softened. Using a slotted spoon, remove the rocket, reserving the cooking water. Bring the reserved rocket water to the boil. Add in the orecchiette, bring back to the boil and cook until al dente. Add the cooked rocket to the orecchiette, then drain. Mix in the tomato sauce,

Serve each portion garnished with diced or shaved caccio or ricotta and the reserved rocket.

> ❝
> # We'd be given a lamb for Easter and sheep's milk. I remember my father making mozzarella."
>
> *Donato Colasanto*

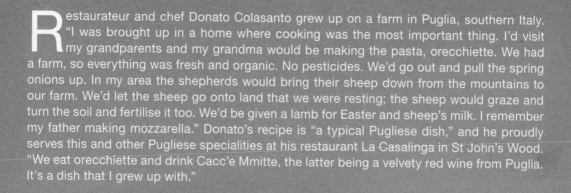

Restaurateur and chef Donato Colasanto grew up on a farm in Puglia, southern Italy. "I was brought up in a home where cooking was the most important thing. I'd visit my grandparents and my grandma would be making the pasta, orecchiette. We had a farm, so everything was fresh and organic. No pesticides. We'd go out and pull the spring onions up. In my area the shepherds would bring their sheep down from the mountains to our farm. We'd let the sheep go onto land that we were resting; the sheep would graze and turn the soil and fertilise it too. We'd be given a lamb for Easter and sheep's milk. I remember my father making mozzarella." Donato's recipe is "a typical Pugliese dish," and he proudly serves this and other Pugliese specialities at his restaurant La Casalinga in St John's Wood. "We eat orecchiette and drink Cacc'e Mmitte, the latter being a velvety red wine from Puglia. It's a dish that I grew up with."

La Casalinga, 64 St John's Wood High St, NW8

Singapore Garden, 83A Fairfax Road, WN6

Mrs Lim's Singapore Laksa
Serves 4

Down a peaceful side road in ‘Swiss Cottage, the well-established Singapore Garden restaurant has a loyal following, with regulars returning for authentic Malaysian and Singaporean dishes such as beef satay, ho jien (oyster omelette) or chilli crab. Having set up the Singapore Garden in 1984 (following in the footsteps of her mother who set up a Singaporean restaurant in London during the 1960s). Mrs Lim presided over the kitchen there for many years. Today Mrs Lim has retired and her daughter Lin, together with her husband, are now running this popular restaurant. Laksa – a traditional hawker dish from Singapore – is one of the restaurant's signature dishes. The specialist ingredients – candlenuts, blachan and fishcakes – can be found in Chinese or South-East Asian food shops.

225 g (8 oz) raw prawns
225 g (8 oz) fresh beansprouts
350 g (12 oz) rice vermicelli
1 Chinese fishcake, sliced
3 candlenuts
115 g (4 oz) dried shrimps
1 tbsp shrimp paste (blachan)
1 onion, peeled and chopped

100 ml (4 fl oz) vegetable oil
1 tbsp ground turmeric
$1/2$ tbsp chilli powder
2 lemon grass stalks, bruised
350 ml (12 fl oz) fish stock
300 ml (10 fl oz) canned coconut milk
salt
4 cubes of deep-fried tofu, halved
fresh coriander leaves, to garnish
finely sliced spring onion, to garnish

Soak the rice vermicelli in warm water for 10 minutes or until soft; drain and set aside.

Meanwhile, blanch the beansprouts in a pan of boiling water; drain and set aside.

Cook the prawns in boiling water until they turn pink and opaque. Drain, cool and peel, discarding the heads.

Divide the rice noodles, beansprouts, peeled prawns and fishcake among four deep serving bowls.

In a food processor, finely grind the candlenuts and the dried shrimps. Add the shrimp paste, onion and a little water and grind into a paste.

Heat the oil in a wok and fry the paste for three minutes, stirring as you do so. Mix in the turmeric and chilli powder and add the lemon grass. Fry the mixture, stirring often, until it smells fragrant and the oil comes to the surface.

Add the fish stock and bring to the boil. Reduce the heat and simmer for 10 minutes. Mix in the coconut milk and, stirring, bring to the boil once more. Season with salt. Add the tofu and cook for 1 minute.

Ladle the laksa soup into the bowls containing the noodles. Garnish with coriander and spring onion and serve at once.

Simple Suppers

Spiced Mince
Serves 4

It was during my time as a perpetually hungry student that I discovered Madhur Jaffrey's cookbooks and the way that spices could transform humble ingredients into delicious meals. This is a favourite with my son Ben – my version of a classic Indian mince dish called keema.

1 tbsp sunflower oil
1 onion, peeled and chopped
2.5 cm (1 in) fresh root ginger, peeled and chopped
1 garlic clove, peeled and chopped
2 cardamom pods
1 cinnamon stick
500 g (1 lb 2 oz) minced lamb
3 tsp ground coriander
2 tsp ground cumin
$1/2$ tsp ground turmeric
salt and freshly ground pepper
3 tbsp tomato purée-
200 ml ($1/3$ pt) hot water
2 carrots, peeled, boiled and diced
3 waxy potatoes, boiled, peeled and diced
115 g (4 oz) frozen peas, cooked and drained
steamed basmati rice, to serve
natural yoghurt, to serve

Heat the oil in a heavy-based frying pan. Add the onion, ginger, garlic, cardamom pods and cinnamon stick. Fry, stirring now and then, until the onion is softened and fragrant. Add the minced lamb and fry until browned on all sides.

Sprinkle over the coriander, cumin and turmeric and mix in. Season with salt and freshly ground pepper. Stir the tomato purée into the hot water, then add to the mince mixture, mixing well.

Cover and simmer for 10 minutes, stirring now and then. Add the carrot, potato and peas, mixing well. Cook for 10 more minutes, stirring often. Serve with basmati rice and natural yoghurt.

Meatballs in Tomato Sauce
Serves 4

There's something very satisfying about home-made meatballs. Serve them with rice or mashed potato for a hearty meal.

500 g (1 lb 2oz) minced beef
50 g (2 oz) fresh breadcrumbs
1 tsp finely chopped fresh oregano
1 tbsp finely chopped parsley
1 garlic clove, finely chopped
1 free-range egg
salt and freshly ground pepper
1 tbsp olive oil
1 bay leaf
1 onion, chopped
1 celery stick, chopped
glug of Amontillado sherry
1 x 400 g (14 oz) tin chopped tomatoes
2 tbsp tomato purée
300 ml (¹/₂ pt) hot water

Place the beef, breadcrumbs, oregano, parsley and garlic in a large bowl. Break in the egg, season generously with salt and freshly ground pepper and mix together thoroughly. Using wetted hands, shape the mince mixture into meatballs the size of large marbles.

To make the sauce heat the olive oil in a large, heavy-based frying pan. Add the bay leaf, onion and celery and fry gently until the onion is softened. Add the sherry and allow to bubble for 1-2 minutes.

Mix in the chopped tomatoes. Stir the tomato purée into the hot water and stir into the tomato mixture. Season with salt and freshly ground pepper. Bring to the boil, reduce the heat and and simmer for 5 minutes. Add the meatballs, bring to the boil once more, cover the pan and simmer for 15 minutes, gently turning the meatballs now and then. Serve.

Purple-sprouting Broccoli Pasta
Serves 4

Purple-sprouting broccoli, with its striking dark purple florets, is a seasonal treat in the late winter months. It goes very well with pasta – for this recipe I would recommend orecchiette, but you could substitute other pasta shapes.

450 g (1 lb) purple-sprouting broccoli
salt and freshly ground pepper
400g (14 oz) orecchiette
2 tbsp olive oil
2 garlic cloves, peeled and chopped
150 g (5 oz) cherry tomatoes, halved
300 ml ($^1/_2$ pt) double cream
3 tbsp pine nuts, dry-fried until golden
freshly grated Parmesan, to serve

First prepare the purple-sprouting broccoli. Trim off the florets, cutting any large ones down to the same size as the small ones. Shred the leaves and cut the stalks into short lengths.

Bring a large pan of salted water to the boil. Add in the orecchiette, bring to the boil and cook until al dente, around 10-11 minutes.

Meanwhile, heat the olive oil in a heavy-based frying pan. Add the garlic and fry for 1-2 minutes until fragrant. Rinse the sprouting broccoli and add to the garlic, mixing well to coat it in the oil. Add the cherry tomatoes and season with salt and plenty of freshly ground pepper. Cover and cook until the broccoli is tender, stirring often to prevent burning. Stir in the cream and the pine nuts.

Drain the cooked orecchiette, mix with the broccoli sauce and serve at once with Parmesan.

Linguine with Walnut Sauce
Serves 4

Freshly ground walnuts are the base for this quickly-made but luxurious pasta sauce.

150 g (5 oz) walnut halves
1 garlic clove, peeled and chopped
4 tbsp olive oil
50 g (2 oz) grated Parmesan cheese
150 ml ($^1/_4$ pt) double cream
freshly grated nutmeg
salt and freshly ground pepper
400 g (14 oz) linguine, fresh or dried

Finely grind the walnuts in a food processor. Add the garlic and olive oil and blend until well-mixed. Stir in the Parmesan and double cream. Season with nutmeg, salt and freshly ground pepper.

Bring a large pan of salted water to the boil. Add the linguine and cook until al dente; drain. Toss the freshly-drained linguine in the walnut sauce and serve at once.

Daddy's Spaghetti A O P

Serves 4

Every time my father, John Linford, visits us from Tuscany, where he now lives, we ask him to cook this dish for us as it always tastes particularly delicious when he makes it. It's a classic southern Italian pasta dish, properly called Spaghetti con Aglio, Olio e Peperoncino – that is Spaghetti with Garlic, Oil and Dried Chilli Pepper – but known in our family simply as "Spaghetti A O P".

450 g (1 lb) spaghetti
salt and freshly ground pepper
125 ml (4 fl oz) extra-virgin olive oil
3 garlic cloves, peeled and sliced
1 peperoncino (small, dried chilli pepper),
  crumbled or finely chopped ("careful not to
  touch your eyes afterwards," cautions
Daddy)
2 whole peperoncini (small, dried chilli
peppers)
finely chopped flat-leafed parsley, for garnish
grated Parmesan cheese, to serve

Cook the spaghetti until al dente in a large pan of salted water; drain.

Meanwhile, heat the olive oil in a small frying pan over a low heat with the garlic and peperoncino. Cook gently until the garlic takes on a golden colour. Set the oil aside to infuse while the spaghetti cooks, heating through again gently once the spaghetti has been cooked.

Place the freshly drained spaghetti in a warmed serving dish. Pour over the seasoned olive oil discarding the whole peperoncini. Sprinkle with parsley and serve at once with Parmesan cheese.

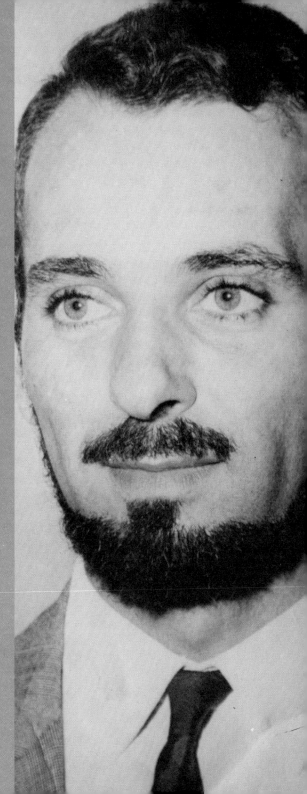

The Grocer's Story

In the days before supermarkets, tea was one of the items bought at grocers. Stepping into Martyns on Muswell Hill Broadway – a rare vintage grocer's shop complete with handsome, purpose-built wooden shelving and counters – is an evocative experience. Today the business is run by William Martyn, following in his family's footsteps.

"The shop was founded by my great-grandfather W Martyn in 1897 and has been in the same family all the way through. When great-grandfather opened the shop he lived above it with his family and members of staff too. One of his daughters had her appendix out on the kitchen table. We would have had tea and coffee in those days – but not the range we have now. It was in the 1920s that we started roasting the coffee. The shop would have sold sugar, flour and our own brand of tea; we would have had one or two teas. We used to have three shops, this one, one in Finchley and one in Golders Green. They both closed in the 1960s and kept the best one, this one, going. When I joined the firm in 1964 we were selling everyday items like Andrex toilet paper and cornflakes.

"It was father who kept the firm going; he joined in 1948. We used to do a lot of deliveries, before the supermarkets thought of it. I remember as a child that we'd stop off and do deliveries on the way home. When I was a child Grandfather was very much around and the business was not a place for children. Things have changed since then. We've always closed on Sundays. I think it's important for families to have time to be together.

"One of our customers is 102 years old. We've got customers whose parents used to shop here or who've moved away and come back and are amazed to see us still here. We believe in service – our customers are important to us. We also have a keen pricing policy. Lots of the things I sell are cheaper than the supermarkets. That's why we're here; our customers know us. When I came in 1984 there were four butchers here, now there isn't one.

"Our tea – it's about quality. When people try our tea, they love it. We're looking for the small producers, that don't over-package their products. We do more flavoured teas now – a Christmas tea we did was so popular that we sell it all year and call it Winter tea. You can buy a quarter of fine tea from us for £1.50. We don't want to be a fancy, expensive shop. We want to be somewhere an old lady can come in and buy a quarter of dates for 40p – we want to be run-of-the-mill."

Martyn's, 135 Muswell Hill Broadway, N10

Risotto Verde
Serves 4

Risotto rice, once found only in Italian delis, is now widely available. Risottos can be flavoured in many different and delicious ways. This recipe uses assorted vegetables to make a tasty green risotto.

1.2 ltr (2 pt) chicken stock, ideally home-made
25 g (1 oz) butter
3 tbsp olive oil
1 shallot, peeled and chopped
1 garlic clove, peeled and chopped
1 handful of French beans, chopped into short lengths
1 bunch of asparagus, chopped into short lengths
1 handful of broccoli, finely chopped
1 courgette, finely diced
300g (10 oz) risotto rice
1 small glass of dry white wine
salt and freshly ground pepper
freshly grated nutmeg
a handful of basil leaves
a handful of pine-nuts, dry-fried until golden
grated Parmesan, to serve

Bring the chicken stock to a rolling simmer in a pan. Heat the butter and olive oil in a large, heavy-based saucepan. Add the shallot and garlic and fry until fragrant. Add the green beans, asparagus, broccoli and courgette and fry, stirring, for 2 minutes. Add the risotto rice, mixing well.

Pour in the wine and cook, stirring for 2 minutes. Season well with salt, freshly ground pepper and freshly grated nutmeg. Add a generous ladleful of the simmering chicken stock. Cook, stirring, until the stock is nearly totally absorbed. Repeat the process until most or all of the stock has been used up and the rice is tender, but retains a little bite. Mix in the basil and pine nuts. Serve at once with grated Parmesan.

Smoked Haddock Fishcakes with Cherry Tomato Sauce

Serves 4

Fishcakes are a great British dish. Using smoked haddock makes for particularly tasty results, with the sweetness of the cherry tomato sauce providing a nice contrast to the saltiness of the haddock.

500 g (1 lb 2 oz) natural smoked haddock fillet
500 g (1 lb 2 oz) floury potatoes, peeled
    and chopped
salt and freshly ground pepper
3 tbsp milk
pinch of saffron threads, finely ground
15 g (1/2 oz) butter
1 tbsp finely chopped parsley
1 shallot, finely chopped
beaten egg, for coating
matzo meal, for coating
sunflower oil, for shallow-frying

Cherry Tomato Sauce:
1 tbsp olive oil
1 small onion, chopped
1 garlic clove, chopped
250 g (9 oz) cherry tomatoes, halved
1 tsp balsamic vinegar
a handful of basil leaves
salt and freshly ground pepper

First, prepare the fishcakes. Poach the smoked haddock in a pan of simmering water until the fish turns opaque. Remove the smoked haddock with a slotted spoon and flake the flesh, discarding any skin and bone.

Boil the potatoes in a pan of salted water until tender; drain. Meanwhile, gently heat the milk then mix in the saffron. Add the saffron milk and butter to the drained potatoes and mash thoroughly, seasoning with salt and freshly ground pepper. Mix together the flaked smoked haddock, saffron mash, parsley and shallot. Shape the mixture into 8 evenly sized fishcakes and chill in the refrigerator for 30 minutes, to firm them up.

Dip each fishcake in beaten egg, then coat thoroughly in matzo meal. Heat the sunflower oil in a large, heavy-based frying pan. Fry the fishcakes until golden on all sides and thoroughly heated through.

Meanwhile, make the cherry tomato sauce. Heat the olive oil in a small frying pan. Add in the onion and garlic and fry until softened and fragrant. Add the cherry tomatoes, balsamic vinegar and basil leaves. Season with salt and freshly ground pepper.

Serve the fishcakes with the cherry tomato sauce on the side.

Fish and Chips

A large piece of crispy golden, battered cod fillet and a portion of chips, sodden with pungent malt vinegar and sprinkled with salt – fish and chips, a British gastronomic institution. Quite when the combination of fish with chips came about is a culinary mystery. In Oliver Twist, published between 1837-38, Dickens refers to a "fried fish warehouse". While the Victorian journalist Henry Mayhew, interviewed a fried fish seller, publishing his account in 1851: "I served the public-houses and soon got known. With some landlords I had the privilege of the parlour, and tap-room, and bar, when other tradesmen have been kept out. The landlords will say to me still: 'You can go in, Fishy.' Somehow, I got the name of 'Fishy' then, and I've kept it ever since."

Toff's, Muswell Hill

Although the exact origins of fish and chips are unknown, the great industrial cities in Lancashire and Yorkshire are often credited with the dish's creation. With fried fish a traditional Jewish dish, others point to East London's large Jewish community in the 19th century as a likely area of origin. Certainly by the early 20th century fish and chips were a popular working class food: cheap, tasty and convenient as, wrapped in newspaper, they could be taken home or simply eaten in the street. Fish and chips still often tops the polls as the nation's favourite dish. A regional divide sees haddock as the preferred fish in the North, with cod more popular in the South.

London offers a number of down-to-earth, traditional fish and chip shops – such as Fryer's Delight on Theobald's Road, where the chips are fried in dripping – and also, increasingly, a number of upmarket fish and chip restaurants.

One much-loved fish and chip shop is Toffs, in Muswell Hill in North London. Established in 1986, Andreas Toffalli put it on the map, winning industry awards and much acclaim before retiring to Cyprus in 1999. Today Toffs is run by two brothers, Costa and George Georgiou, both committed to keeping Toffs a great fish and chip shop.

Toff's, 38 Muswell Hill Broadway, N10

Mr Toffalli comes back now and then to see how the shop is going," says Costa. "Our fresh fish gets delivered here from Grimsby docks daily. We treat the customers as friends – they come as customers and leave as friends. We do a special lunch offer for the pensioners. The school run is around 1pm, for chip butties, and we've won an award as a family-friendly restaurant.

"Our batter is traditional, but we also offer grilled fish and fish in egg and matzo for the Jewish community. When it's a Jewish holiday like Passover we get inundated with orders for fried fish – we cook it and leave it to get cold. We have to do a lot. We don't just do chips – we also do boiled or mashed potatoes and salads. The biggest problem is the lack of cod – the price has shot up really fast. Cod is still the most popular fish, but people do eat haddock as well. Haddock has a firmer texture and more of a fish taste. We do 12 fish on our menu, including Dover sole, sea-bass.

"There are three things about our chips that make them so good," explains George. "We filter our oil every day and change it. We use Maris Piper potatoes, which are good potatoes for chips. We cut them thickly and we wash the starch off them. We've got a person – Charles – who does the chips all day long; he peels, cuts the eyes out, puts them through the chip cutting machine, rinses the starch out. Then you've got expert fryers. The ideal chip should be golden and crispy on the outside, then with a soft centre inside. You've got to fry them gently then turn the heat up. We get loads of celebrities. We've got a regular customer from Northampton and someone who lives in Marylebone – with Seashell round the corner – comes all the way to Muswell Hill to have skate – now that's the best accolade."

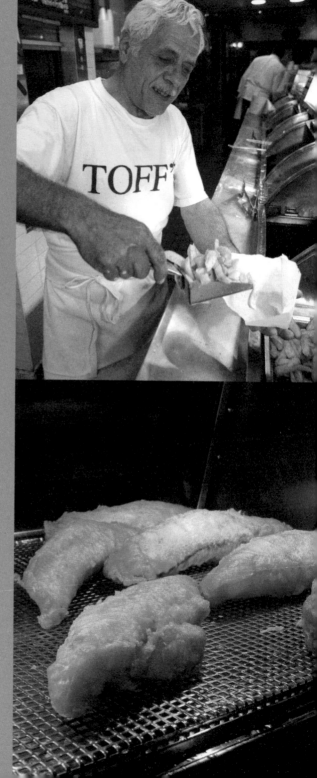

Rosalind's Bobotee
Serves 4

Mince mixture:
1 onion, peeled and chopped
2 tbsp sunflower oil
1 thick slice white bread, soaked
* in 125 ml (4 fl oz) milk*
450 g (1 lb) minced lamb
1 free-range egg, well-beaten
12 almonds, chopped
1 tbsp ground almonds
1 tbsp raisins
5 dried apricots, chopped
1 tbsp apricot jam
juice of 1 lemon
zest from 1/2 lemon, cut into strips
salt and freshly ground pepper
1 tbsp curry powder
3 bay leaves or fresh lemon leaves
steamed rice, to serve

Custard:
1 free-range egg
pinch of curry powder
pinch of salt
250 ml (8 fl oz) milk

Fry the onion in the oil until golden-brown; set aside to cool.

Preheat the oven to Gas 3/170°C/325°F.

In a large bowl, place the soaked bread, mince, egg, almonds, ground almonds, raisins, dried apricots, apricot jam, lemon juice and zest, salt, freshly ground pepper and curry powder and mix together well.

Pat the mince mixture into a small casserole dish, placing the bay leaves in the mixture. The mince should be about 8 cm (3 in) deep.

To make the custard, beat together the egg, curry powder, salt and milk. Pour the custard mixture over the mince.

Bake in the oven for 30-40 minutes. Do not over-bake as the bobotee must be moist. Serve hot from the oven with steamed rice.

> *"It was a cheap dish to cook while my husband was a student and we were on a tight budget and my husband loves it. I must make it for him again."*
>
> *Rosalind Rathouse*

Born in Johannesburg, South Africa, Rosalind and her husband came over to London in 1966. "Growing up in the colonies we had romantic expectations," she laughs, "we thought there'd be lovely old English food, cream teas, clotted cream on every corner. The reality was margarine everywhere and chips deep-fried in lard. The shopping was terrible. I never bought fresh produce in a supermarket. I shopped at Berwick Street Market, which was fantastic in the Sixties. The stall-holders were very strict – you couldn't touch or take anything."

Today Rosalind feels that London's food-scene is "fantastic." She has achieved a long-held dream of hers to run a cookery school – called simply Cookery School – on Little Portland Street. Her recipe for bobotee, a classic Cape Malay dish, comes from her mother ("a fantastic cook") and is one Rosalind often cooked during those early years in London. "It was a cheap dish to cook while my husband was a student and we were on a tight budget and my husband loves it. I must make it for him again."

Cookery School, 15b Little Portland Street, W1

Tony's Spaghetti with Asparagus and Peas

Serves 4

400 g (14 oz) spaghetti
salt and freshly ground pepper
250 g (9 oz) freshly podded peas (around
 500 g (1 lb 2 oz) unpodded)
1 tbsp olive oil
1 onion, finely chopped
1 bunch of asparagus, chopped into
 3.5 cm (1 $^1/_2$ in) lengths
115 g (4 oz) mascarpone cheese

Cook the spaghetti in a large pan of salted water until al dente; drain.

Meanwhile, boil the peas until just tender in a separate pan of boiling water; drain.

Heat the olive oil in a heavy-based frying pan. Add the onion and fry gently until softened and fragrant. Rinse the chopped asparagus and add to the pan, together with the peas. Fry gently, stirring, until the asparagus is just tender. Add the drained spaghetti to the pan together with the mascarpone and cook gently over a low heat until the mascarpone has melted. Serve at once.

I was taken to Spitalfield Market when I was seven years old to get me out of the way. I can remember washing beetroot in a bath, scrubbing it with a brush, in my Dad's Crouch End shop on a Saturday morning."

Tony Booth

Tony Booth's stall, with its colourful display of seasonal fruit and vegetables, is one of the sights of Borough Market. Depending on the time of year, one's eyes might be caught by red-blushed blood oranges, exquisite young artichokes or the wild mushrooms for which Booth's is particularly known. The chances are that you'll also see Tony busy at work, putting out a new delivery, pausing only to patiently answer queries. "That's barba de frate, monk's beard," explains Tony to a passer-by curious to know what the bunches of green shoots are.

As a third-generation greengrocer, Tony has spent his life surrounded by fresh produce; "I was taken to Spitalfields Market when I was seven years old to get me out of the way. I can remember washing beetroot in a bath, scrubbing it with a brush, in my Dad's Crouch End shop on a Saturday morning."

When he moved into wholesale, Tony kept an eye out for new things to stock; "I've always liked to look at cookery books and see what was being used, see if there's a market for it. I was one of the first people to bring fresh limes in from Brazil. We're known for our mushrooms and fresh herbs. Nobody wanted to eat wild mushrooms. Antonio Carluccio brought them to life in the 1980s. They fascinated me. They weren't sold in England and it was hard to find suppliers. I had to try and try; bought them in France at first. I can remember the first avocados and the first kiwis; they used to cost 5 shillings each. It makes me laugh; they were ever so expensive. You've got to keep on finding things; it brings a lot of interest." Tony pauses, then says reflectively, 'It's the people that give me a buzz. I think it's nice that people want to know and try."

A Trip to Borough Market

On the south bank of the River Thames, Borough Market traces its history back several centuries and is thought to be London's oldest fruit and vegetable market. Its prime position first on, then by London Bridge has been a key element of its existence. The first recorded mention of the market is in 1276 as the cause of inconvenient congestion on London Bridge. Since then the market has been moved a number of times, though always staying close to southern end of London Bridge, and has been trading from its present site in 1756. Access to the River Thames then the later coming of the railway, with the construction of London Bridge station, were both important factors in the market's survival, allowing fresh fruit and vegetables to be brought to it in bulk. Over time the market developed into a wholesale fruit and vegetable market, operating in the early hours of the morning and little-known to the general public.

In recent years, however, Borough Market has transformed itself, hosting a weekly retail food market open to the public which has become a gastronomic destination, eagerly flocked to by food-lovers. An imaginative initial partnership between the existing wholesalers at Borough and invited producers and suppliers has resulted in a unique food market where one can find both down-to-earth fundamentals such as decent bacon or farmhouse cheese and rare and exotic luxuries. What makes Borough stand out is the diversity and quality of its producers. Stalls range from specialists offering simply one foodstuff – chunks of excellent Parmesan, bread or hand-made fudge– to those with an impressive range to choose from, whether of fresh fruit and vegetables, fish and seafood or poultry. While many of the stalls showcase fine British foods, such as mutton from the Lake District or Colchester native oysters, there's also a cosmopolitan element. Here one can find Italian olive oils, delicate Japanese teas, Moroccan argan oil, Polish sausages, Swiss mountain cheeses and fine Spanish foodstuffs such as jamon Iberico, the meltingly flavourful ham from acorn-fed, black-footed pigs imported by wholesaler Brindisa.

The characterful setting, tucked away beneath the railway arches and looked over by Southwark Cathedral and the central location – a short stroll from Tate Modern and the reconstructed Shakespeare's Globe – have helped put it firmly on the map, popular with both Londoners and visitors alike. Today the market throngs with devoted food shoppers and curious tourists while the side-streets around it are now filled with food shops, restaurants, bars and cafés, a tribute to the capital's appetite for good food.

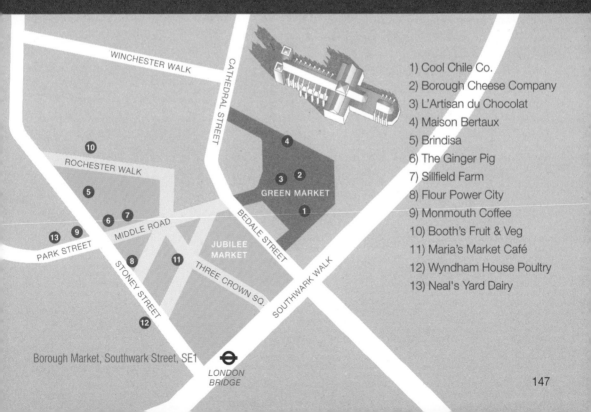

1) Cool Chile Co.
2) Borough Cheese Company
3) L'Artisan du Chocolat
4) Maison Bertaux
5) Brindisa
6) The Ginger Pig
7) Sillfield Farm
8) Flour Power City
9) Monmouth Coffee
10) Booth's Fruit & Veg
11) Maria's Market Café
12) Wyndham House Poultry
13) Neal's Yard Dairy

WINCHESTER WALK
CATHEDRAL STREET
ROCHESTER WALK
GREEN MARKET
BEDALE STREET
MIDDLE ROAD
PARK STREET
JUBILEE MARKET
STONEY STREET
THREE CROWN SQ.
SOUTHWARK WALK

Borough Market, Southwark Street, SE1

LONDON BRIDGE

Yuka's Miso Katsu
Serves 4

Ever since she was a child, Japanese chef Yuka Aoyama, has been fascinated by food; "I love cooking, so that's why I learnt to cook," she says simply. "It's the greatest compliment I can have if someone enjoys my cooking." Her mother's cooking is a great source of inspiration. As Head Chef at Loungelover in Hoxton, Yuka has enjoyed introducing her mother's recipes, taking great pleasure from the fact that these dishes from home have proved the most popular. "I love London," says Yuka warmly, "because I can just be myself – and I can try foods from all over the world." Her recipe here uses dark red, richly flavourful hatcho miso for which her area of Japan is famous, with Yuka recommending the Japan Centre food shop at 212 Piccadilly as a place to buy it and the other Japanese ingredients.

4 tbsp hatcho miso paste
3 tbsp mirin
2 tbsp sake (Japanese rice wine)
2 tbsp sugar
3 tbsp water
4 pork loin steaks
salt and freshly ground pepper
flour, for coating
beaten free-range egg, for coating
panko (Japanese breadcrumbs), for coating
sunflower oil, for deep-frying
chopped spring onion, for garnish
finely shredded white cabbage, to serve

Place the miso paste, mirin, sake, sugar and water in a small, heavy-based pan. Cook gently, stirring with a wooden spoon, until the mixture is thick and smooth. Set aside.

Season the pork with salt and pepper. Coat the steaks in flour, then dip in beaten egg and coat in panko breadcrumbs.

Heat the sunflower oil in a deep-fat fryer, wok or large, deep pan until it reaches 180°C/350°F. Add the coated pork steaks and fry until golden-brown. Remove and drain on paper towels.

Spoon the miso sauce over the cutlets and sprinkle over the spring onion. Serve at once with shredded white cabbage.

"I love London because I can just be myself – and I can try foods from all over the world."

Yuka Aoyama

A Taste of Japan

London's Japanese community developed largely during the late 20th century. Reflecting the growth of the Japanese economy in the years following the end of World War II the community here was originally composed primarily of Japanese business people working in London. Today London's Japanese population is thought to number over 19,000, with the majority visiting either for work or study rather than settling here permanently. Particularly popular residential areas for the Japanese community are the boroughs of Barnet and Ealing, in London's leafy outer suburbs. The latter is home to two Japanese schools and both offer access to golf courses, another important factor.

Dotted around the city, particularly in North and West London, are a number of specialist Japanese food shops, such as the mini-chain Atari-ya. Here one can find essential specialist Japanese ingredients, from the freshest cuts of fish for sashimi to flavourings such as mirin or wasabi. In the heart of London, on bustling Piccadilly, the Japan Centre, in addition to having a travel agent and a Japanese bookshop, features a basement food shop, which does a roaring lunchtime trade in take-away sushi.

Not so long ago, Japanese restaurants in London were the exclusive preserve of predominantly Japanese businessmen entertaining clients on expense accounts. Today, London's Japanese eateries are both far more numerous and diverse, ranging from small, homely sushi bars to stylishly contemporary restaurants. Diners can sample Japanese cuisine in a variety of forms, with dishes ranging from okonomiyaki (griddle-cooked cabbage batter pancakes) to sticky-glazed yakitori (grilled skewered chicken). Sushi itself has become so mainstream that sandwich chains and supermarkets sell it as a lunchtime snack.

Henning's Spanish Chick Pea and Chorizo Stew
Serves 4

250 g (9 oz) cooking chorizo, chopped into small chunks
200 g (7 oz) Spanish smoked pancetta, chopped into small chunks
1 medium red onion, peeled and finely chopped
2 x 200 g (7 oz) jars fritada sauce (Spanish tomato & red bell pepper sauce)
150 ml (5 fl oz) red wine
4 large garlic cloves, peeled and crushed or chopped
4 tsp wild Spanish oregano or any good oregano
freshly ground black pepper to taste. No need for salt.
2 x 660 g (1 ½ lb) jars Navarrico chick peas (from Brindisa)
chopped flat-leafed parsley, to garnish
wholemeal or crusty bread, to serve

Fry the chorizo, pancetta and onion all together over a medium heat in a thick-based saucepan, stirring occasionally, until the onion has reduced a little and the chorizo and pancetta are just slightly browned. No need for oil as the chorizo and pancetta will produce their own fat when frying.

Now add the jars of fritada sauce plus 1 equal-size jar of water and the red wine. Then add the garlic, oregano and black pepper.

Bring to the boil and then set to simmer on a low heat for 15 minutes.

Add the chick peas. Do not drain the brine from the chick peas as it will give the dish just enough saltiness. Bring back to the boil, then simmer for a further 10 minutes.

Garnish with fresh chopped flat leaf parsley and serve with your favourite wholemeal or crusty bread.

> *My Dad was always experimenting. I remember him making Bolognese sauce out of snails, the small ones you find in Spain, more like winkles."*
>
> *Henning Marstrand*

Having grown up in a household where good food was important, Henning Marstrand has fond memories of "Danish open sandwiches, pickled herrings – nothing like rollmops, much more subtle and delicious. My Dad was always experimenting. I remember him making Bolognese sauce out of snails, the small ones you find in Spain, more like winkles." While particularly fond of Indian food, since working for Spanish food importer and retailer Brindisa, Henning has learnt a lot about Spanish food. "Before I worked here I only knew a bit about Spanish food. Brindisa's products are the pick of the crop of Spain. The thing that stands out for me is the rustic style of Spanish cooking – the stews, the beans, the pulses. Pulses here were traditionally a poor man's food, but are produced in a very refined way, grown in particular soil, almost like grapes. The Navarra chickpeas are really large and very tender." For the recipe below, Henning has drawn on ingredients stocked at Brindisa, including jarred chick peas and Spanish tomato sauce. "This is a nice easy dinner to make," he says. "The word stew is a bit misleading as it doesn't simmer slowly for 2-3 hours; it's a quick stew!"

Brindisa, 32 Exmouth Market, EC1

Carl's Teriyaki Chicken and King Prawn Noodles
Serves 4

As a child, Carl used to help his mother cook at home and he enjoys cooking for his wife and friends. "We go to a lot of restaurants and I try to create the sort of food we enjoy eating out in restaurants. I don't have that much time for cooking; it has to be done when I get back in from work. If there's a specific ingredient that's essential to a recipe, some people wouldn't bother to go and get it – but I would – things like lemon grass, fresh chillies, limes. I cook lots of seafood and salads. What I like is the freshness of ingredients and bringing that to the plate."

2 medium-sized chicken breast fillets
3 tsp peeled and finely chopped fresh root ginger
2 tbsp teriyaki sauce, for marinating
sunflower or vegetable oil
250 g (9 oz) medium thread egg noodles
half a clove of garlic, peeled and finely chopped
1 red chilli, finely chopped
1 green chilli, finely chopped
1 small bunch of spring onions, finely chopped
150 g (5 oz) fresh tiger or king prawns, de-shelled and de-veined
light soy sauce
freshly squeezed juice of 1 lime
200 g (7 oz) bean sprouts

Using a sharp knife, cut slashes in the chicken breast fillets. Place the chicken breasts in a shallow dish. Sprinkle over 1 teaspoon of chopped ginger, then pour over the teriyaki sauce. Cover and marinate in the refrigerator for 3-4 hours.

Mix a little sunflower oil into the sauce and coat the chicken breasts evenly with it. Preheat the grill on high. Grill the chicken breasts until cooked, continually coating them with the marinade as they cook and taking care not to let the chicken dry out. Cool and slice diagonally.

Bring a large pan of water to the boil. Add the noodles and cook for 3-4 minutes until the noodles are reasonably soft. Drain and rinse in cold water to stop them clumping.

Heat some sunflower oil in a wok. Add the remaining chopped ginger, garlic, red and green chilli and stir-fry until fragrant. Add the chopped spring onions and prawns. Sprinkle over the lime juice and stir-fry.

Once the prawns are nearly cooked – a matter of minutes – add the drained noodles, stirring thoroughly. Mix in a little light soy sauce, then add the teriyaki chicken. Add the bean sprouts. Toss the noodles to mix well and stir-fry briefly, making sure that the bean sprouts stay crunchy. Serve immediately.

Jean and Mirella's Dolma (Stuffed Aubergines)

Serves 4-6

500 g (1 lb 2 oz) lean ground beef
225 g (8 oz) long grain white rice, washed and drained
2 medium onions, finely chopped
3 tbsp chopped flat-leafed parsley
1 tbsp finely chopped mint
2 medium tomatoes, skinned, seeded and finely
    chopped or 1 x 400 g (14 oz) tin chopped tomatoes
salt and freshly ground pepper
8 medium aubergines
1 tbsp tomato purée
600 ml (1 pt) water
1 tbsp freshly squeezed lemon juice
2 tbsp vegetable oil
1 tsp sugar
2 tbsp water
natural yoghurt, to serve

Combine the beef, rice, 2 chopped onions, parsley, mint and chopped tomato in a large bowl. Season well with salt and freshly ground pepper. Knead together thoroughly until the mixture is well-blended and smooth.

Cut off about 1 cm (½ in) from the stem ends of the aubergines and scoop out, chop and reserve the aubergine pulp, leaving a 1 cm (½ in) thick shell all around. Spoon the meat stuffing into the aubergine shells.

Place the stuffed aubergines side-by-side in a heavy casserole dish, large enough to hold them comfortably. Add in the tomato purée, water, lemon juice and salt.

Bring to the boil and cover, lower the heat and cook for around 1 hour, until the aubergines are tender, adding more water if necessary.

About half-way through the cooking time, heat the oil in a heavy-based frying pan. Add the remaining onion and fry gently until softened. Add the reserved aubergine pulp, sprinkle over the sugar and water and season with salt and freshly ground pepper and cook gently, stirring often for 20-30 minutes.

Transfer the aubergines to a serving dish, spooning over some of the cooking liquid. Serve with natural yoghurt and the fried aubergine as a side-dish.

"We enjoy our food," laughs Jean Keheyan. Born in Cyprus to an Armenian family, Jean came to London 50 years ago. His Italian-born wife, Mirella, learnt many Armenian dishes from Jean's mother, who was a wonderful cook. Since retiring, Jean has found that he too enjoys cooking; "It became a hobby. I cook Italian, French, English food. What a cookbook says is good, but you can always do it differently. My daughters say 'We are your guinea pigs!' They like my cooking." The stuffed aubergines are a family favourite, very popular with Jean's daughters and grandchildren.

CYPRUS RED AUBERGINE £2.99 Kilo

"My daughters say 'We are your guinea pigs!' They like my cooking." Jean Keheyan

Farmers' Markets

London's first Farmers' Market opened in 1999 in Islington and since then farmers' markets have been springing up around the capital. Venues such as school playgrounds become transformed at the weekend, filled with stalls selling everything from wild game sausages to fresh vegetables. London's Farmers' Markets (www.lfm.org.uk) organised London's first farmers' market and the markets they run follow strict guidelines. All the produce at their markets must be grown, reared, raised, baked, caught or produced by the seller within a 100 miles of the M25. From its pioneering start they now run around 15 markets across London, working with around 180 farmers.

Cheryl Cohen of London Farmers' Markets is very clear why farmers' markets appeal to food shoppers. "People enjoy the contact with the producers, the way they can ask questions or get advice on how to cook an ingredient. They like getting to know the traders. Farmers' markets also offer the experience of seasonality. At the moment we've got blackberries, sweetcorn and pears in the markets. People can look forward to something becoming available and everything is fresh as it's direct from the producer.

"When people shop at a farmers' market they come with an open mind rather than a shopping list and see what looks good. It's not just adults who like shopping at farmers' markets; it's children too. I talk to them and ask what they like eating and it's not the obvious things like strawberries or fruit juices, they'll say 'I love crab'. They try things. Markets make such a difference to a community. They have a vibrancy that you'll never get in a shopping mall. Londoners are really enjoying farmers' markets."

"People enjoy the contact with the producers, the way they can ask questions about how something's made or grown or get advice on how to cook an ingredient."

ROCKET
Spicy little
£1.00 pack

CORN SALAD
£1.00 pack

PARSLEY
£1.00 pack

PARSLEY FLAT
£1.00 pack

COOKED BEETROOT
£1.00 pack

BEETROOT
£1.60 kg

CORN BEETROOT
£1.60 KG

BLACK RADISH
£2.00 ea

RUSSIAN KALE
£2.00 ea

CURLY KALE
£2.40 kg

HAMBURG PARSLEY
2.40 KG

JUICE PACKS

£1.50 bag

YELLOW
CARROTS
£1.00 kg

RED
CARROTS
£1.00 kg

BABY TITAN

TITAN

KINGCUP FARM
BUCKS
ALL PRODUCE GROWN ON
FARM 16 MILES
THIS MARKET

Nick's Pan-fried Mackerel with Gooseberry Relish
Serves 4

4 fresh mackerel, filleted
6 tbsp plain flour
1 tbsp polenta
salt and freshly ground pepper
2 tbsp olive oil
2 knobs of butter
fennel salad, dressed with lots of lemon and parsley, to serve

Gooseberry relish:
125 ml (4 fl oz) water
75 g (3 oz) unrefined granulated sugar, or to taste
1 tbsp white wine vinegar
1 small chilli, deseeded and chopped
1/2 cinnamon stick
2 star anise
4 strips of lemon zest
350 g (11 oz) green gooseberries topped and tailed
salt and freshly ground pepper

Make the gooseberry relish first. Heat the water, sugar, vinegar, chilli, cinnamon, star anise and lemon zest. When the mixture has come to the boil, add the gooseberries and stir gently.

Return to the heat and slowly cook until the fruit starts to split slightly and looks transparent, then take off at once. Be careful not to overcook it. Carefully remove the gooseberries, using a slotted spoon, and set them to one side. Boil the liquid until it reduces to a thick syrup, strain out the chilli, cinnamon, star anise and lemon zest and spoon the spiced liquid onto the gooseberries. Season with salt and freshly ground pepper and allow to cool.

Score the mackerel fillets on the skin side with a sharp knife to stop them curling in the pan.

Season the flour and polenta with salt and freshly ground pepper. Sprinkle the seasoned flour onto a large serving plate. Lay the fillets onto the flour mixture and lightly coat with the flour.

Now heat a large, non-stick frying pan to a moderate heat with the half the olive oil and butter. Lay the 4 fillets skin-side down first and fry for 3 minutes then flip and fry the flesh side for a further 3 minutes. Cook until golden-brown on both sides. Depending on the thickness of the fillet, the cooking time should be between 5-8 minutes.

Serve at once with a fresh fennel salad dressed with lots of lemon and parsley.

> "By the age of ten I was cooking full Sunday lunch for everyone – I wouldn't let anyone come in and help."
>
> *Nick Selby*

Inspired by a love of cooking and good food, Nick Selby, together with his partner Ian James, set up Melrose and Morgan, a stylish delicatessen-cum-eaterie in leafy Primrose Hill named after their mothers' maiden names. An open-plan kitchen offers a chance to see the chefs hard at work – carefully filling savoury flans or clarifying stock. Nick's love of good food stems back to his childhood in Dorset. "I just grew up baking – my mother would make Victoria sponge and melting moments. We had a veg patch in the garden and looked after a sheep in the back garden. Mum was a good cook and she insisted we helped in the kitchen. I got the bug for baking. By the age of ten I was cooking full Sunday lunch for everyone – I wouldn't let anyone come in and help. I have a fond memory of eating this dish this time last year. I was in Ireland by the sea and I threw the line out and caught the mackerel. It was caught and put in the pan in less than one hour, just floured, then butter in the pan – phenomenal. Simple cooking –food from sea to plate."

A Trip to New Covent Garden Market

Covent Garden was for centuries London's most famous fruit and vegetable market. Its setting was the elegant Italianate piazza commissioned by the Earl of Bedford, and built during the 1630s by the architect Inigo Jones. Very soon this striking new public space attracted market traders and in 1670 the Earl and his heirs were granted a Royal charter to hold a market for flowers, fruits, roots and herbs. By the 1760s the market occupied much of the piazza and in 1830 a new permanent market was built on the site: a splendid construction, complete with avenues and colonnades. The market, with its flower sellers and fruit and vegetable stalls became a picturesque attraction as well as a lively place of commerce.

Much of the fresh fruit and vegetables sold at Covent Garden came from market gardens both within London and on its edges. Mortlake was noted for asparagus, Deptford was famous for its onions, potatoes came from Barking and Leyton, while Brentford, Isleworth and Twickenham were renowned for their strawberries and Plumstead for its cherry orchards.

Exotic produce, too, was available. "There is more certainty of purchasing a pineapple here, every day in the year, than in Jamaica and Calcutta, where pines are indigenous," boasted John Timbs in *Curiosities of London*, 1855.

Writing in 1851, Henry Mayhew gave a vivid description of Covent Garden: "About six o-clock in the morning is the best time for viewing the wonderful restlessness of the place, for then not only is the 'Garden' itself all bustle and activity, but the buyers and sellers stream to and from it in all directions, filling every street in the vicinity. Along each approach to the market, too, nothing is to be seen, on all sides, but vegetables; the pavement is covered with heaps of them, waiting to be carted; the flag-stones are stained green with the leaves trodden under foot; sieves and sacks full of apples and potatoes, and bundles of broccoli and rhubarb, are left unwatched upon almost every door-step; the steps of Covent Garden Theatre are covered with fruit and vegetables; the road is blocked up with mountains of cabbages and turnips; and men and women push past with their arms bowed out by the cauliflowers under them, or the red tips of carrots pointing out from their crammed aprons, or else their faces are red with the weight of the loaded head-basket."

In 1973 Covent Garden was moved to an industrial estate in Vauxhall, from where it still operates. Today, New Covent Garden Market, as it is now known, is a very different place from the market that Mayhew described. This is a market run on an industrial scale: from the huge refrigerated lorries delivering their loads to the fork-lift trucks moving slowly around the high warehouse units. The range of produce, most of it neatly packed in crates, is immense: grapefruit, broccoli, kiwis, grapes, plums, spring

onions, asparagus, lettuces, strawberries, tomatoes, leeks, salad leaves and sacks and sacks of potatoes. The global nature of greengrocery is apparent: apples from New Zealand, fennel from Israel, pears from Chile, oranges from Spain. The traders stand waiting, with their ledgers before them and cups of coffee handy. This is an orderly, businesslike place – quiet on the whole, with the silence broken most often by mobile ring tones. "Only thing I can think of that still has a season is cherries," remarks one trader. "Everything else we can get round the year now."

New Covent Garden, Nine Elms, SW8

Only thing I can think of that still has a season is cherries," remarks one trader. "Everything else we can get round the year now."

Comfort Food

Spring Greens and Potato Soup with Chorizo
Serves 4

Potatoes, onion and shredded spring greens combine to make a hearty, warming soup. Spanish smoked pimenton, sold in dainty, pretty tins, and cooking chorizo can be found in Spanish delicatessens and add a particular smoky flavour to the recipe.

2 tbsp olive oil
1 onion, peeled and chopped
450 g (1 lb) floury potatoes, peeled and diced
1 garlic clove, peeled and chopped
½ tsp Spanish smoked pimenton
a glug of Amontillado sherry
1 ltr (1 3/4 pt) chicken or vegetable stock, ideally home-made
2 tbsp chopped parsley
salt and freshly ground pepper
450 g (1 lb) spring greens
2 cooking chorizo sausages, sliced

Heat the olive oil in a large, heavy-based saucepan. Add the onion and fry gently till softened. Add the potato and the garlic, mixing well, and fry for 1-2 minutes until the garlic is fragrant.

Sprinkle over the pimenton and pour over the sherry, letting it sizzle for a minute or so. Add the stock and parsley and season with salt and freshly ground pepper. Bring to the boil, reduce the heat, cover and simmer for 30 minutes.

Trim the tough stalks off the spring greens, roll up the leaves and shred as finely as possible.

Heat a small, heavy frying pan, add the chorizo slices and fry them in their own oil until cooked.

Meanwhile, add the shredded spring greens to the soup and cook until just tender – a matter of minutes.

Spoon the soup into serving bowls, top each portion with a few slices of fried chorizo and serve.

Sausages, Mash and Onion Sauce

Serves 4

"Bangers and mash" always go down well, set off here by a traditional, creamy onion sauce.

700 g (1 ¹/₂ lb) potatoes, peeled and chopped
salt and freshly ground pepper
knob of butter
2-3 tbsp milk
freshly grated nutmeg
8 good quality sausages

Onion sauce:
50 g (2 oz) butter
2 onions, finely chopped
2 tbsp plain flour
300 ml (¹/₂ pt) milk
2 tbsp double cream
salt and freshly ground pepper
freshly grated nutmeg

First, prepare the onion sauce. Heat the butter in a small, heavy-based saucepan. Add the onion and sweat it very gently over a low heat for 10 minutes until softened. Stir in the flour, cook gently for a few minutes, then gradually mix in the milk. Cook, stirring, until the sauce thickens. Stir in the cream along with salt, freshly ground pepper and a generous amount of freshly grated nutmeg.

Meanwhile, cook the potatoes in a pan of boiling, salted water until tender; drain. Mash the potatoes with the butter and milk, season with freshly ground pepper and freshly grated nutmeg.

While the potatoes are cooking, grill or pan-fry the sausages, turning them often, until cooked through and browned on all sides.

Serve the sausages and mash with the onion sauce.

The Sausage Maker's Story

Biggles, in Marylebone Lane, specialises simply in sausages. The shop is the brainchild of Colin Bailey, who makes the sausages himself fresh every day. "I was working abroad in Saudi Arabia, but wanted a change of direction," explains Colin. "I'm pretty well-travelled and I'd always enjoyed sausages all over the show. Had collected a few recipes – so that was the starting point. Biggles has been here 19 years now."

"I put 100% meat in my sausages, like the Germans do. A lot of my seasonings come from Germany. I've taken English recipes and adapted them to make gluten-free sausages. The fact my sausages are gluten-free is very important too; a lot of my customers are coeliacs. I've reduced the fat content in all my sausages; I'm next to Harley Street don't forget. Toulouse is far and away the bestselling sausage, followed by good old traditional Cumberland. The meat comes into the shop every morning and I make it all into sausages. I'm very hands-on; I suppose you could call me a control freak, but that's the way to guarantee consistency. It's great when people come in and tell you 'they're the best sausages' – that happens all the time."

Biggles. 66 Marylebone Lane, W1

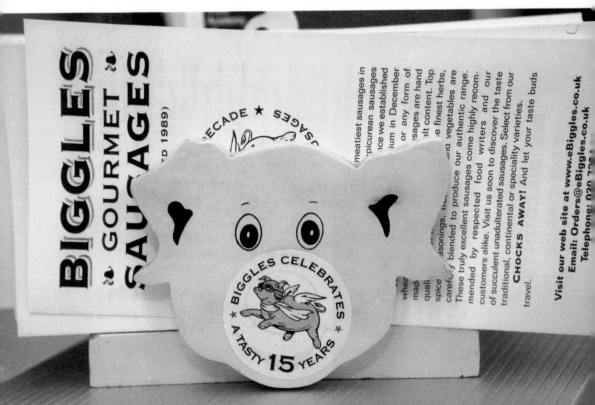

Sausages

There is a huge range of sausages from around the world to be found in London. Many good butchers, too, offer decent, own-made sausages, with flavourings ranging from herbs and spices to fruits, such as prune or apple.

Black pudding: a British blood sausage, made from blood and cereal (often oats), traditionally eaten at breakfast.

Bratwurst: German grilling sausages, made from pork or pork and veal.

Chorizo: a Spanish sausage, flavoured with sweet or hot paprika which gives the sausage an eye-catching orange-red colour, available both fresh for cooking or cured for eating.

Cumberland sausage: a British sausage, historically from Cumbria, long, unlinked, made from highly spiced fresh pork, often flavoured with sage.

Kielbasa: a Polish fresh pork and beef sausage, flavoured with garlic.

Lap cheong: Chinese cured pork or pork and liver sausages, the former a dark pink, noticeably studded with white fat, the latter a dark brown, which must be cooked before eating.

Lincolnshire: a British fresh pork sausage, flavoured with sage.

Loukanika: Greek beef sausages, flavoured with red wine, herbs and spices.

Luganega: a long, unlinked Italian fresh pork sausage, flavoured with cloves and cinnamon.

Merguez: a North African fresh beef sausage, flavoured with harissa which gives a piquancy and distinctive dark red colour to the sausage.

Toulouse: a French fresh pork sausage flavoured with garlic.

Fiona's Chicken Soup

Serves 8-10

Platters Deli in Temple Fortune is a North London Jewish institution, set up in 1980 and still going strong. Customers return time and time again for the freshly prepared, hand-made classic deli dishes, such as dangerously more-ish potato latkes, chopped liver and the smoked salmon, finely sliced by Len, now in his eighties. As one Platters' customer remarked, watching Len skilfully hand-carve wafer fine slices of smoked salmon, "What would Sunday be like without you, Len?"

Among the popular dishes is Fiona Platter's chicken soup. "Chicken soup – it's like a religion among Jewish people all over the world," exclaims Fiona. "Every Jewish community, wherever they are, has a chicken soup recipe. So delicious. They call it the Jewish penicillin. A lot of people won't give their recipes away. I don't add celery – it's basically chicken, carrot and onion. You must use a boiling fowl as it gives more flavour and my secret touch is the ginger. Chicken soup keeps us together."

1 boiling fowl, cleaned thoroughly
1 medium onion, washed but unpeeled
2 carrots, chopped
2.8 ltr (5 pt) water
½ tsp ground ginger or a couple of small slices of fresh ginger
salt and freshly ground pepper
1 chicken stock cube
4 nests of vermicelli noodles

Place the boiling fowl, onion, carrot and water in a large saucepan. Bring to the boil and skim off any scum that forms on the surface.

Add the ginger, salt and freshly ground pepper and the stock cube. Bring to the boil once more, reduce the heat, cover and simmer for 3 hours over a very low heat. Remove the boiling fowl and the onion.

Crumble the vermicelli into a heatproof dish and grill until slightly golden. Cook the vermicelli in a pan of boiling water until tender; drain and rinse.

Add some cooked vermicelli to each portion of chicken soup.

"Chicken soup – it's like a religion among Jewish people all over the world."

Fiona

Platters, 10 Halleswell Parade, Finchley Road, NW11

Fish Pie
Serves 4-6

This is an old-fashioned, homely dish that makes a substantial meal. Vary the mixture of fish as you wish or according to what's available.

900 g (2 lb) potatoes, peeled and chopped
salt and freshly ground pepper
15 g (¹/₂ oz) butter
3-4 tbsp double cream
250 g (9 oz) spinach
300 g (10 oz) natural smoked haddock fillet,
    skinned and cubed
300 g (10 oz) salmon fillet, skinned and cubed
300 g (10 oz) white fish, such as haddock,
    skinned and cubed
250 g (9 oz) cooked peeled prawns
grated Cheddar, for sprinkling

Béchamel sauce:
600 ml (1 pt) milk
1 slice of onion
1 bay leaf
25 g (1 oz) butter
25 g (1 oz) flour
salt and freshly ground pepper
freshly grated nutmeg
2 tblsp finely chopped parsley
1 tsp finely chopped lemon zest

First, prepare the béchamel sauce. Place the milk, onion slice and bay leaf in a saucepan. Heat until the milk comes to just below boiling point. Remove from the heat, cover and set aside to infuse for 20-30 minutes.

Heat the butter in a heavy-based saucepan. Stir in the flour and cook gently, stirring, for 2-3 minutes. Strain the infused milk and gradually add to the flour. Cook, stirring, until the sauce thickens. Season with salt, freshly ground pepper and freshly grated nutmeg. Stir in the parsley and lemon zest.

Preheat the oven to Gas 5/190°C/375°F.

Cook the potatoes in a pan of salted, boiling water until tender; drain. Mash the potatoes with the butter and cream. Season with freshly ground pepper.

Rinse the spinach and cook, covered, in a heavy-based saucepan until just wilted. Drain the spinach, squeeze out excess moisture and chop.

Place the smoked haddock, salmon, white fish and prawns in a pie dish. Mix in the spinach, then pour over the béchamel sauce. Top with the mashed potato, forming a thick, even layer. Sprinkle with the Cheddar cheese and bake for 30-40 minutes until golden. Serve hot from the oven.

Salsicce with Lentils
Serves 4

Italian sausages ("salsicce") are very different from traditional British sausages. My favourite salsicce come from I Camisa – a vintage Italian delicatessen in Soho – and are flavoured with fennel.

2 tbsp olive oil
1 shallot, peeled and chopped
1 celery stick, chopped
1 carrot, peeled and finely chopped
300g Italian brown lentils
900 ml (1 ½ pt) cold water
200 ml (7 fl oz) red wine
salt and freshly ground pepper
2 onions, peeled and sliced
1 garlic clove, peeled and chopped
1 bay leaf
4 fresh Italian sausages
1 x 400 g (14 oz) tin chopped tomatoes
200 ml (7 fl oz) hot water
chopped flat-leafed parsley, for sprinkling

Heat 1 tbsp of olive oil in a heavy-based saucepan. Add the shallot, celery and carrot and fry gently for 1-2 minutes until fragrant. Add the lentils, cold water and red wine. Bring to the boil, reduce the heat and simmer for 30-40 minutes until the lentils are tender. Season with salt and freshly ground pepper; drain and keep warm until serving.

While the lentils are cooking, heat the remaining olive oil in a heavy-based frying pan. Add the onion, garlic and bay leaf. Fry for 2-3 minutes until fragrant. Add the Italian sausages and brown on all sides.

Add the chopped tomatoes and the hot water. Season with salt and freshly ground pepper. Bring to the boil, reduce the heat, cover and simmer for 15 minutes.

Uncover and cook for a further 10 minutes, stirring now and then. Sprinkle with chopped parsley.

Serve the sausages with the lentils on the side.

A Taste of Italy

London's first Italian quarter was in Clerkenwell, known in Victorian times as "Little Italy" with Soho later becoming home to a large Italian population. Today many of Clerkenwell's Italian food shops and small businesses, which represented the area's Italian roots have gone, driven out by high rents. St Peter's church on Clerkenwell Road, however, remains a focal point for London's Italian community. Every July, on the first Sunday on or after July 16th, the church celebrates the Festival of Our Lady of Mount Carmel with a religious procession through the narrow steep streets around St Peter's, an event attended by many Italian families from around Britain.

London's Italian restaurants have moved far away from the days of waiters wielding priapic pepperpots and serving indifferent spaghetti Bolognese to diners at tables bearing wax-coated Chianti bottles. Today many of London's most fashionable restaurants are Italian, offering a chance to sample authentic Italian food made from the finest ingredients.

Many Italian delicatessens still retain their roots as neighbourhood shops, serving a community and offering the everyday basics of Italian cuisine rather than going upmarket and offering attractively packaged luxuries. In these shops one can find fresh pasta (infinitely better than the pre-packed, so-called "fresh pasta" sold in supermarkets), Italian brands of dried pasta, freshly sliced hams and salamis, Italian cheeses, olive oil, olives and many other simple but good things to eat.

Bartek's Bigos (Huntsman's Stew)
Serves 4-6

2 small handfuls of dried, sliced wild mushrooms, such as porcini
1 tbsp vegetable oil
300 g (10 oz) Polish smoked pork belly (bochek) or
 good quality streaky bacon, chopped into lardons
2 medium onions, peeled and chopped
700 g (1 ½ lb) Polish kielbasa sausages
1 x 900 g (2 lb) jar of sauerkraut
1 small white cabbage, finely sliced
half a tube of tomato purée
4-5 tbsp tomato ketchup
5-6 bay leaves
a small handful of marjoram or oregano
generous amount of cracked black pepper
500 ml (18 fl oz) boiling water
good bread, to serve

Set the dried mushrooms to soak in a small bowl of hot water for 10-15 minutes.

Heat the oil in a large frying pan until hot, add the smoked pork belly lardons and fry until they crisp up. Add the chopped onions and fry, stirring often, until well browned. Transfer the smoked pork belly and onion to a large casserole dish.

Cut the kielbasa sausages into half-moon slices and fry in the same frying pan until browned. Add these to the casserole dish.

Also add the soaked mushrooms and their soaking water, the sauerkraut, white cabbage, tomato purée, ketchup and bay leaves. Sprinkle in the marjoram and black pepper. Pour in the boiling water and mix well.

Bring to the boil over medium heat, then cover and simmer over a low heat for 1 1/2 hours, stirring occasionally to make sure the ingredients aren't sticking to the base of the pan and adding in a little hot water if it appears to be drying out. Once cooked, set aside covered for a few hours and re-heat before serving. Bigos improves with keeping and can be stored in an airtight container and kept refrigerated for up to 2 weeks.

> *My family all lived in the kitchen; we had a big table in the kitchen and there were always people around it"*
>
> *Bartek Fabinaski*

Friendly and welcoming, Bartek Fabinaski presides over Beetroot, a cosy Hampstead-based Polish deli-cum-café, complete with beetroot-coloured walls. Customers sit down at the communal table for coffee and a slice of Polish poppyseed cake or to buy take-away portions of marinated herrings, pausing for a chat with Bartek. "Lots of my customers say it feels like a living room. I know a lot of people around here; it's nice to be part of a community."

Brought up in Poland, Bartek grew up in a food-loving household. "My family all lived in the kitchen; we had a big table and there were always people around it. The whole family would go mushroom-picking in the woods; we'd bring them home and cook them straight away. Because we lived in Gdansk we'd go to the fishermen and get smoked fish. My father would get half a pig and bring it home – some for the freezer, some for eating fresh. It taught me about food. My grandmother who lives in London is a very good cook. She cooks wonderful pierogi, makes them so quickly. I'd always wanted to have a Polish deli, to introduce Polish food to Londoners."

"Bigos, for me, it's one of those dishes that every family has a different recipe for; one person will add prunes, another red wine. You always make it the way your household does. You must use Polish smoked sausage; English sausages would just fall apart. You need smoked pork belly to give it that smoky flavour. In my family, we always cook it for Christmas. It tastes better the day after it's made and can keep for 2 weeks, so you make it and store it in the fridge and when it's chilly outside you can heat it up and enjoy it. It's winter food."

Beetroot Deli, 92 Fleet Road, NW3

Thai Green Chicken Curry
Serves 4

This popular coconut milk-based curry is a great Thai classic, flavoured with piquant chillies, aromatic galingal and fragrant, citrus-flavoured lemon grass and kaffir lime leaves. Galingal is a brown-skinned rhizome, similar in appearance to ginger. Kaffir lime leaves look like bay leaves and can usually be bought in bunches or packets of loose leaves from Chinese or Thai food shops.

1 tbsp oil
500 g (1 lb 2 oz) skinned, boneless chicken,
   cut into small chunks
2-3 tbsp green curry paste (see below)
1 x 400 ml (14 fl oz) tin coconut milk
2 tbsp fish sauce
8 kaffir lime leaves
1 x 227 g (8 oz) tin sliced bamboo
   shoots, drained
55 g (2 oz) pea aubergines
1 tbsp palm or dark brown sugar
2 red chillies
generous handful of Thai basil or basil leaves
a few sprigs of coriander
steamed rice, to serve

For the green curry paste:
1 tsp cumin seeds
1 tsp coriander seeds
8 black peppercorns
1 nutmeg
2 cloves
2 lemon grass stalks
2 shallots, peeled and chopped
4 garlic cloves, peeled and chopped
1 thumb-size piece of galingal, peeled and
   chopped
8 green chillies, chopped
1 tsp shrimp paste (kapee or blachan)
2 tbsp sunflower oil
75 g (3 oz) fresh coriander (including roots
   and stalks)
grated zest of 1 lime
1 tsp salt

First prepare the green curry paste. Dry-fry the cumin and coriander seeds until fragrant; allow to cool. Finely grind together the cumin, coriander, peppercorns, nutmeg and cloves.

Peel and discard the tough outer covering from the lemon grass stalks. Finely chop the lower, white bulbous part of the stalks, discarding the rest of the lemon grass.

In a food processor, blend together the ground spices, lemon grass, shallots, garlic, galingal, chillies, shrimp paste, oil, coriander, lime zest and salt to form a thick paste. Transfer to clean, dry container, cover and store in the fridge for up to 2 months.

To make the curry, heat the oil in a casserole dish. Add the chicken and fry until whitened. Mix in the green curry paste and fry until fragrant.

Stir in the coconut milk and cook, stirring, until it comes to the boil. Reduce the heat to a simmer and add in the fish sauce, lime leaves and drained bamboo shoots.

Cook gently for 10 minutes, stirring now and then. Add the pea aubergines and simmer for a further 10 minutes. Mix in the palm sugar, chillies, basil and coriander and serve with steamed rice.

Chinese Five-spice Spare Ribs
Serves 4

There's something very satisfying about spare ribs – the simple pleasures of picking them up in your hands, nibbling at the meat close to the bone, licking sticky fingers afterwards. This recipe draws on the ingredients found in Chinatown, from abundant root ginger to packets of aromatic star anise.

1 tsp Chinese five-spice powder
$1/2$ tsp white pepper
1 $1/2$ tsp salt
1 kg (2 $1/4$ lb) spare ribs
2 tbsp sunflower oil
1 onion, peeled and roughly chopped
4 garlic cloves, peeled and chopped
1 thumb-sized piece fresh root ginger, peeled and sliced
2 tbsp rice wine or Amontillado sherry
1 tbsp tomato purée
3 tbsp dark soy sauce
2 star anise
200 ml (7 fl oz) hot water

Preheat the oven to Gas 5/190°C/375°F.

Sprinkle the five-spice powder, white pepper and salt over the spare ribs and rub in.

Heat 1 tbsp of oil in a heavy-based roasting tin in the oven. Add the ribs to the hot oil and roast them in the oven for 20 minutes.

Meanwhile, heat the remaining oil in a saucepan. Fry the onion, garlic and ginger for 3-4 minutes, until softened and fragrant. Add the rice wine and sizzle briefly. Mix in the tomato purée, then add the soy sauce, star anise and hot water.

Pour the soy sauce mixture over the ribs. Cover the ribs with foil and roast for 30 minutes. Uncover and roast for a further 20 minutes. Serve.

A Taste of China

Today London's Chinatown occupies a prime site in Soho in the middle of the bustling West End. London's first Chinese community, however, grew up in Limehouse, near the docks, and consisted primarily of Chinese seamen recruited by the East India Company and other shipping firms to take advantage of the Chinese ports opened up to Britain after China's defeat in the Opium Wars (1842-60).

The early 20th century saw the Chinese community move into the laundry business as a way of making a living, with London's first Chinese laundry opening in Poplar in 1901. The laundry trade, however, declined with the development of automated washing machines and chain laundrettes. The devastation to London's docklands caused by the Blitz in World War II prompted London's Chinese community to move from Limehouse to Soho after the war, Soho then being distinctly run down with consequently affordable rents. Here, following a trend begun in Manchester, the Chinese community began opening restaurants offering Chinese food aimed at English consumers. Today, Gerrard Street and Lisle Street – the two main arteries of Chinatown – are lined with Chinese, predominantly Cantonese restaurants. The air as one strolls through Chinatown smells appetisingly of steamed rice and dumplings, roasted meats and the occasional waft of frying garlic.

Chinatown, too, is home to a number of Chinese food shops. Visit in the morning and the air is filled with the beeps of reversing lorries, getting into position to unload substantial quantities of goods, which are then swiftly wheeled on trolleys into the shops. The sheer range of ingredients that even a small Chinese food shop will stock is always impressive, from bundles of fresh green vegetables, such as gaai laan or bok choy, and fruit such as pink-skinned lychees or tiny orange kumquats to dried lotus leaves, strong-smelling dried black shiitake mushrooms and tiny dried shrimps.

Alongside the shops and restaurants there are a web of Chinese businesses including banks, herbalists, lawyers and hairdressers, while the Chinese Chamber of Comwwerce in Soho houses a large Chinese language school. Soho is where the Chinese community celebrate their major festivals: Chinese New Year, which falls between late January and mid-February and the autumnal Moon Festival, events which see the streets festooned with bright red lanterns and coloured flags.

Hazel's Braised Sheep's Hearts

Serves 4

4 sheep's hearts
flour, for coating
115 g (4 oz) butter
350 g (12 oz) tomatoes, skinned and chopped
2 large onions, peeled and finely chopped
7 level tbsp fresh breadcrumbs
2 handfuls of fresh sage or 2 tbsp dried sage
salt and freshly ground pepper
1 bay leaf
juice of ½ lemon

The butcher will not fully prepare the hearts for you. You need to soak them for a minute or two in 3 or 4 changes of salted water to free them of blood. Then take some sharp scissors and cut out the gristle in the middle and the large vein.

Preheat the oven to Gas 3/170°C/325°F.

Dry the hearts, roll them in flour and brown gently in 75 g (3 oz) butter in a casserole dish large enough for the hearts to sit comfortably in with a little room to spare. Set the hearts aside and adding a tablespoon or two of water to the casserole dish, stir into the residue from the bottom of the pan. Remove the casserole dish from direct heat and add in the tomatoes.

Mix together the onions, breadcrumbs, sage and the remaining butter and season with salt and freshly ground pepper. Push this stuffing into the cooled hearts without worrying about some of the stuffing spilling out.

Return the hearts to the casserole, then gently warm the casserole on the hob. Cover with foil, tucking it lightly around the dish, allowing some steam to escape, and bake in the oven, turning the hearts once or twice during cooking. Medium-sized hearts need 3 ½ hours; larger hearts need 4 hours. Half an hour before the end of the cooking time add the bay leaf to the dish. At the end of the cooking time, add the lemon juice to the hearts and serve warm from the oven, with boiled potatoes and spinach.

> ## "Hearts are still amazingly cheap to buy. They need some initial preparation but no special skill or good luck on the part of the cook."
>
> *Hazel Richardson*

Hazel Richardson grew up in more frugal, thriftier times; "I was five years old when war broke out. Housewives had to be so inventive. I remember my mother making the most of every little scrap of meat. We ate a lot of offal and I admired my mother for not turning a hair at skinning a rabbit."

Sheep's hearts are a dish which Hazel remembers her mother cooking and which she rediscovered when married. "My recipe draws heavily from Jocasta Innes's *A Pauper's Cookbook*, which appeared in 1971 – so fortunate as we were dreadfully short of money at the time – and I was so pleased to find a recipe for sheep's hearts. My mother would have stuffed them and Jocasta Innes recommends stuffing them and then sewing them up, but I think they're just as good with stuffing oozing out, so I let it ooze out. Hearts are still amazingly cheap to buy. They need some initial preparation but no special skill or good luck on the part of the cook, and once you have them in the oven you know you will have a delicious dish in four hours' time." Hazel recommends going to a "good quality butcher for offal of any kind," – with the Ginger Pig at Borough Market her favourite – and cooking the offal on the same day or at the latest on the following day.

The Butcher's Story

In an age when any butchers, let alone a good one, is increasingly hard to find, C. Lidgate's at Holland Park is a butcher's shop to treasure. Founded in the mid-nineteenth century, this establishment radiates self-confidence and pride – from the mouth-watering display of meat in the window to the admirably spic-and-span, traditionally tiled interior, complete with numerous framed awards on the walls and a quote from Ruskin above the cash desk. Lidgate's offers only free-range or organic meat, carefully sourced from suppliers, including the Prince of Wales' Highgrove estate. As well as the prime meat, the shop does a roaring trade in its famous, award-winning meat pies. The business is run by David Lidgate, a much-respected figure among his peers, – a thoughtful man, whose conversation sparkles with ideas and enthusiasm.

> "My great-grandfather started the business in 1850; became a butcher's boy and worked his way up. I'm the fourth generation."
>
> David Lidgate

"My great-grandfather started the business in 1850; became a butcher's boy and worked his way up. I'm the fourth generation. My sons work hard here; they're the fifth generation. I often think back to my father and his father and how they would have thought about what we do; looking back to go forward. My father died when I was nineteen. It was hard to make a decision quickly, as there seemed to be no future in being a butcher at that time. We had two other shops, which we closed, and I was able to specialise. I wanted to make things in the shop. In the 1960s we started to make things, particularly pies. The most important part of a meat pie is the meat, so it makes sense that butchers should make them. Our first pie was a steak and kidney pie, but we've expanded the range. They're all made in the old-fashioned way – the meat is cooked on the hob and we use good wine. Making things, that's been the driving force."

"We're selling meat and all the things made from meat and we're also selling our knowledge. We know the meat's good – we've enough experience. We have a tasting panel and do blind tastings of our meat – very important that as we don't want to be influenced

We have traceability here – we know where all our meat comes from. I want to see the farmers, see how the meat is raised, how it's fed. After BSE people want to shop with people they feel they can trust. We actually sold more beef during the time of the BSE. crisis. I'm looking to improve all the time."

C Lidgate, 110 Holland Park Avenue. W11

& Organic Meat

"We have traceability here – we know where all our meat comes from. I want to see the farmers, see how the meat is raised, how it's fed."

Baked Cannellini Beans
Serves 6-8

Dried cannellini beans and pancetta (Italian bacon) can be found in Italian delicatessens. This is a robust dish – ideal comfort food on a cold, grey day.

350 g (12 oz) cannellini beans, soaked in cold water overnight
2-3 sage leaves
2 tbsp olive oil
1 bay leaf
a strip of pancetta, rind trimmed, chopped into small chunks
1 onion, peeled and chopped
2 garlic cloves, peeled and chopped
1 celery stick, chopped
1 x 450 g (14 oz) can chopped tomatoes
3 tbsp tomato purée
400ml (14 fl oz) hot water
a handful of parsley, finely chopped
½ tsp sugar
salt and freshly ground pepper

Drain the soaked cannellini beans and place in a large saucepan. Add the sage leaves and enough cold water to generously cover. Bring to the boil. Boil for 1 hour, checking now and then in case the water needs topping up, until the beans are tender; drain, discarding the sage leaves.

Preheat the oven to Gas 4/350°C/180°F. Heat the olive oil in a large, heavy-based casserole dish. Add the bay leaf, pancetta, onion, garlic and celery. Fry, stirring, over a medium heat until the onion is softened. Add the chopped tomatoes, mixing well.

Stir the tomato purée into the hot water and add to the casserole, along with parsley and sugar. Season generously with salt and freshly ground pepper. Mix in the cannellini beans and bring to the boil.

Cover the casserole and cook in the oven for 30 minutes. Serve.

Beef and Ale Stew with Herbed Dumplings
serves 4-6

London porter adds a particular flavour and sweetness to this substantial dish of stew and dumplings.

50 g (2 oz) butter
1 onion, halved, then finely sliced
2 leeks, finely sliced
1 tbsp Demerara sugar
900 g (2 lb) shin of beef, cubed
flour, seasoned with salt and freshly
   ground pepper, for coating
300 ml (1/2 pt) London porter or dark ale
600 ml (1 pt) beef stock or water
1 parsnip, peeled and chopped
salt and freshly ground pepper

Herbed dumplings:
175 g (6 oz) self-raising flour
75 g (3 oz) suet or vegetable suet
4 tbsp finely chopped chives
2 tbsp finely chopped parsley
salt
cold water, to mix
vegetable stock or water, for poaching

Heat the butter in a large, heavy-based casserole dish. Add the onion and leek and fry very gently for 10 minutes, stirring now and then. Sprinkle over the sugar and fry gently for 5 more minutes, stirring often.

Coat the beef in the seasoned flour and add to the onion mixture. Fry until browned on all sides.

Add the London porter, stock and parsnip. Season with salt and freshly ground pepper. Bring to the boil, cover, reduce the heat and simmer for 1 1/2 hours, stirring now and then.

After the beef has been simmering for 45 minutes, prepare the dumplings. Place the flour, suet, chives and parsley in a mixing bowl. Season generously with salt and gradually add enough cold water to form a soft dough. With wetted hands, shape into 12 evenly sized balls. Bring a large pan of salted stock or water to a rolling boil. Add the dumplings and poach for 30 minutes.

Serve the stew with the dumplings.

Siobhan's Bacon 'n' Cabbage
Serves 4

1 shoulder joint of green back bacon
1 dark green cabbage, such as Savoy
floury potatoes
salt
Irish butter
Daddy's sauce or mustard, to serve

Put the bacon into a large, heavy-based pan and completely cover with cold water.

Bring the water to the boil, reduce the heat and simmer for 30 minutes. Wash and tear the cabbage and put into the pot with the bacon after the 30 minutes. Simmer together for another 30 minutes, topping up the water if required.

Meanwhile, boil the potatoes in their jackets in salted water until tender; drain.

Drain the bacon and cabbage together, keeping a small jug of the cabbage water for any extra 'cabbage juice' required during the meal. Lift the bacon out and slice whilst steaming.

Serve the sliced bacon with the drained cabbage and the potatoes with "a lovely slab of butter".

> *The smell of bacon and cabbage cooking – a sweet, salty smell – wafted out from our house"*
>
> *Siobhan Dunne*

Siobhan Dunne has fond childhood memories of this traditional Irish dish. "My Mum cooked this. We would have it for Sunday dinner, a special meal and we always had it when we went to Ireland. There's nothing like the smell of bacon and cabbage cooking in the same pot; it's unique. So simple. Has to be green cabbage – you need one that holds its texture. My memory of it is the smell. We were the only Irish family on an English road, a crescent, with very little traffic so all the children played on the street. The smell of bacon and cabbage cooking – a sweet, salty smell – wafted out from our house. I don't remember smelling anyone else's food! Green back bacon was very hard to find. My Mum would go to a lot of trouble trying to find a good piece of green bacon and floury potatoes. There was an Irish butcher in Leytonstone that she used. You've got to have brown or Daddy's sauce or mustard with it. The potatoes were always in their skin. Learning to peel a hot potato – you'd pick it up with your hands – was part of the meal."

Safia's Coddle

A London take on an Irish Coddle.

*4 thick slices of really good ham (such as Alderton, Ginger Pig or Woodall's),
   cut into 5 cm (2 in) strips*
6 chunky pork sausages (Sillfield rare breed pork are excellent)
800 g (1 3/4 lb) potatoes, peeled and sliced
2 large onions, peeled and sliced
300 ml (¹/₂ pt) water
lots of fresh chopped parsley
salt and freshly ground black pepper
rustic bread, to serve
Pitfield London Porter, to accompany

In a heavy-based saucepan with a close-fitting lid, mix together the ham, sausages, potatoes and onions. Add half of the chopped parsley and season with salt and freshly ground pepper, using the salt sparingly.

Pour on the water and slowly bring to the boil. Cover tightly (using a tea-towel to tie around the lid, if it's not very tight-fitting), reduce the heat and simmer for around 1 hour.

> ❝*Our customers range from City people, who buy ingredients for their breakfasts here, to Japanese tourists, who seem to think we're a living museum and take a lot of pictures.*❞
>
> Safia Thomas

I n a peaceful side-street just by Spitalfields Market, A Gold, Safia and Ian Thomas's appealing food shop, is handsomely housed in a wood-panelled Georgian house. The couple, who appreciate the property's character and heritage, chose to name their shop after one of its former inhabitants, a French milliner called Amelia Gold. The shop's discriminatingly chosen stock of good things to eat, from sticky Chelsea buns to Cornish crab, reflects their interest in and enthusiasm for British food. Safia and Ian gave up jobs in TV journalism to set up the shop in 2000. "We wanted to work with something we were interested in," explains Safia. "We're down-to-earth foodies and we were tired of being told how bad British food was. I grew up in the country. I knew how good English food could be.

"The shop is much harder work than we ever thought it would be. Our customers range from City people, who buy ingredients for their breakfasts here, to Japanese tourists, who seem to think we're a living museum and take a lot of pictures. It's a very personal space, like our living room. We want to be a useful shop, so we have bread, eggs, jam, cheese, bacon and ham off the bone. Running the shop has made us feel reassured by our food heritage. I don't think it's merely a fad, I think, little by little, people are selling more good food. Farmers and producers like Peter Gott of Sillfield Farm are the real champions of British food.

"You've got to have good quality ingredients for this recipe, for the flavour and because of the long cooking time – it is slow food. More I more, I find myself cooking comfort food for friends, rather than something fancy. I think it's what people really enjoy eating."

Green London

London's urban nature is an undisputed reality. Yet, the city, too, is home to green spaces: from people's gardens to the many parks. There are also over 36,000 allotments, pieces of land rented to individuals for the purposes of growing fruit and vegetables. During World War II, with food in short supply, Londoners were exhorted to 'Dig for Victory' and grow their own fruit and vegetables, which they did, digging over gardens, parks and open ground. Today the demand for allotments in London has never been higher, with many people on waiting lists, but the pressure on land for building and roads means that some allotment sites are under threat.

London is also home to the Chelsea Physic Garden (founded in 1673) and the Royal Botanical Gardens, Kew (founded in 1759), both places of valuable botanic research into the cultivation and uses of plants for food, drink, and medicine. The Museum of Garden History was established in 1977 as the world's first museum dedicated to garden history and is situated on the site of the churchyard containing the family tomb of the John Tradescants, two notable 17th century plant hunters.

Useful addresses:

National Society of Allotments & Leisure Gardeners
www.nsalg.org.uk
The nationally recognised body for the allotment movement.

London City Farms
www.farmgarden.org.uk
London has 17 city farms and over 100 community gardens. Each autumn these take part in a City Harvest Festival.

Royal Botanic Gardens
Kew, Richmond,
Surrey, TW9
020 8332 5655
World-famous botanical gardens, established in 1759.

Chelsea Physic Garden
66 Royal Hospital Road,
London, SW3
020 7352 5646
Founded in 1673 by the Society of Apothocaries, this is the England's second oldest botanic garden.

The Garden Museum
Lambeth Palace Road,
London, SW1
020 7401 8865
A museum dedicated to the history of gardens and gardening.

Michael's Allotment Gooseberry Fool
Serves 4

700 g (1 ½ lb) gooseberries, topped and tailed
75-115 g (3-4 oz) castor sugar
1-2 tbsp water
3-4 tbsp elderflower cordial, ideally home-made
1 large tub of Greek yoghurt

For the elderflower cordial:
1.5 kg (3 lb) castor sugar
1.7 ltr (3 pt) water
25 heads of elderflower
55 g (2 oz) tartaric acid (from chemist)
5 oranges, squeezed and then sliced

Heat the sugar and 0water together, stirring until the sugar has dissolved. Bring to the boil and cook until the mixture thickens into a syrup. Place elderflower heads, tartaric acid and orange slices in a large bowl and pour over the boiling syrup. Cover and infuse for 24 hours, then strain carefully and bottle in clean, dry bottles. Store in the fridge.

To make the gooseberry fool, gently cook the gooseberries with the sugar and water for a few minutes until the gooseberries are softened. Cool and mash with a fork. Gently fold together the cooked gooseberries, elderflower cordial and yoghurt, checking that the sweetness is to your taste. Cover and chill until serving.

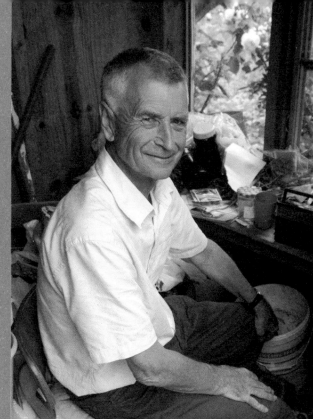

> *I remember as a child that we would have gooseberry fool always on a Sunday evening – the elderflower adds something to it."*
>
> *Michael Wale*

A man of many talents and considerable energy, Michael Wale has a particular fondness for gardening and for allotments. As a writer and presenter, Michael is an articulate campaigner on behalf of allotments. "There's huge pressure on them from developers," he explains. "I hope that the new green thinking will help." Michael himself has an allotment on a plot in East Acton where he particularly likes to sit in his shed and think. Here, tucked away, surrounded by busy roads, is a small, green world with that characteristic allotment mix of the orderly (neatly weeded strawberries beds, trellises) – and the random (bolted salad leaves, stray brambles). A blackbird sings in the trees overhead and there's the background cackling of the chickens kept by one allotmenteer whose fresh eggs the others can buy. "We have a real mix of nationalities on our allotment: Italians, Croatians... Once you could visit allotments and see particular crops growing and know where the people who were gardening came from – fresh coriander, must be Indian. Today I've noticed you can't tell anymore; people are trying all sorts of different crops."

Michael's recipe is for a dish that he remembers as a child. "I was brought up by my father on a farm. I had a rural upbringing; our food was off the farm. My father was a great gardener. I remember as a child that we would have gooseberry fool always on a Sunday evening – the elderflower adds something to it."

A Trip to Smithfield Meat Market

S till proudly located in the heart of the metropolis, Smithfield, London's largest meat market, has a long history at its current site. Its name derives from "smooth field", as it was indeed originally a grassy plain just outside the old City walls. For centuries Smithfield has been a place of trading, chronicled in 1174 as the site of a weekly horse market as well as a place where sheep, cattle and pigs were bought and sold. During medieval times public entertainments such as jousts and tournaments were held at Smithfield and it was here that the famous Bartholomew Fair first took place in 1123. Originally a cloth fair, this had developed by the 16th century into a raucous festival, finally suppressed for causing public disorder by the City authorities in 1855.

Smithfield has many bloody and violent associations, not merely as a place where animals were slaughtered. It was at Smithfield that Wat Tyler, leader of the Peasants' Revolt, was stabbed by the Mayor of London before King Richard II, and was then executed in front of St Bartholomew's Hospital. For over 400 years Smithfield was a place of public execution and it was here, during Queen Mary I's reign, that over 200 Protestant martyrs were burned to death.

In 1638 a cattle market was formally established on the site under Royal Charter. Live cattle were driven to the market, often causing much disruption en route, and slaughtered there, athough in 1852 the live cattle market was relocated to Copenhagen Fields in Islington.

The impressive main building of the Central Meat Market that exists today was built in 1868 by Horace Jones. With characteristic Victorian flair and ingenuity, the building came complete with an underground railway and hydraulic lifts to bring up the meat. The extensive use of wrought iron allowed cooling air to flow through the market. Following an extensive refurbishment during the 1990s, however, today's market traders work in temperature controlled units. Today around 100,000 tons of meat pass through the market each year, roughly 8% of the UK's meat trade. In the early hours of the morning huge refrigerated lorries pull up outside the market to deliver carcasses and the air is filled with the beeping of reversing vehicles.

Smithfield has long been a self-contained world, complete with its own police and

hierarchy of allotted roles: pitchers, shopmen and bummarees (self-employed porters who carried the meat from the market to the purchaser's transport). Walking through Smithfield Market the air smells of meat and blood. All around are men – and this is still very much a man's world – in blood-stained white overalls and hard hats handling meat, moving pallet trucks of meat through the market or chopping up carcasses. It's a carnivore's paradise. Meat on sale ranges from huge sides of beef, lamb and whole suckling pigs to offal – in demand once more – and pigs' tails and ears, particularly popular with the Portuguese and Chinese.

Gregg Harrison of H & C Meats, his father's business, has seen the market change since he was first brought here when he was five years old.

"Fifty-two years I've been here. We were always laughing and dancing. They used to say it was better up here than the London Palladium. Things have changed a lot. We used to give away breast of lamb to the fat man – Lardie, the soap man – to use in soap. Now breast of lamb – it's gold-dust."

Terry, a Smithfield porter

"My first memories of Smithfield are of learning – you had to watch your toes because of the porters pulling the big, heavy barrows. They don't have them here anymore. One of the porters – called Disney – was only a little bloke but he was nearly 80 when he retired. He used to take part in the barrow races. I liked it then; the characters we had then aren't here anymore.

"Look at this old photo of the market. The guys at the back in their smocks were the cutters, the porters, then you get the clerks and the salesmen, all smartly dressed in suits and ties. They had standards then.

"People's eating habits have changed – now there's television telling them what to eat. Three to four years ago lamb shanks were all the rage. I used to start at 4am, now I get here at 1.30am. The congestion charge has put a kibosh on the market; by 7am everyone's gone. We supply restaurants, butchers, pubs and the general public. Years ago they wouldn't entertain the general public here. If someone asked for something they'd say 'On your bike'. When you supplied a butcher you supplied all his shops – 10 or 15 of them – they were busy then. Today you've got to go out and find your business. You can't wait for clients to come here. In the old day's people traded with people. Technology's come along; logistics have changed."

Smithfield Market, Charterhouse St, E11

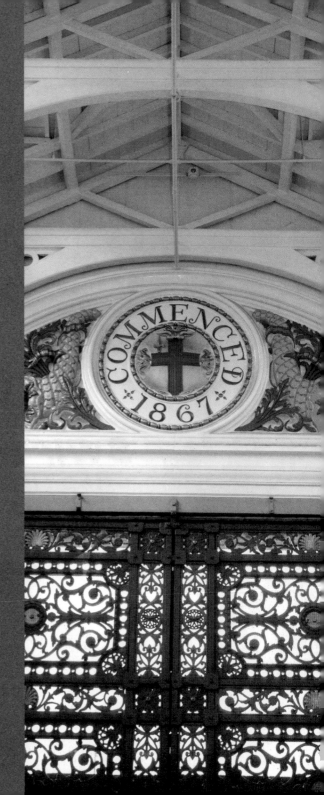

"Boiling hot the meat used to be then, freshly killed from the market up Caledonian Road. They'd herd them to the cattle market, slaughter them. We had pitchers (to pitch the meat), – puller backs (to pull it back) and bummarees (porters). Everything was carried in those days. It was quicker than it is now."

Alan, Smithfield porter

Roast Pork Belly
Serves 4

Once dismissed as a cheap and fatty, pork belly is now valued as a rich, flavourful cut of meat. Avoid pork from intensively reared pigs and instead buy your pork belly from a good butcher or a reputable farmer such as Peter Gott of Sillfield Farm at Borough Market. Unwrap any plastic from the pork belly and allow the meat to dry out in the fridge before cooking.

1 3/4 kg (4 lb) piece pork belly
2 garlic cloves, peeled and crushed
4-6 rosemary sprigs, torn into small sprigs
salt and freshly ground pepper

Preheat the oven to Gas 7/220°C/425°F.

First make sure the pork is dry. Using a very sharp knife, cut slashes into the skin of the pork. Rub the garlic over the meaty side of the pork belly and insert the rosemary sprigs into nooks and crevices. Season with salt and pepper, generously rubbing salt over the skin.

Place the pork on a rack over a roasting tin. Roast for 30 minutes at Gas 7/220°C/425°F, then reduce the heat to Gas 5/190°C/375°F and roast for a further hour, until the crackling is golden-brown and the flesh is cooked through. Serve at once.

Tea Time Treats

Sarah's Seed Cake
Makes 1 cake

110 g (4 oz) poppy seeds
225 ml (8 fluid oz) milk
225 g (8 oz) butter
225 g (8 oz) light raw cane sugar
3 free-range eggs, separated
225 g (8oz) self-raising wholemeal flour

Preheat oven to Gas 4/180°C/350°F. Grease and line a 20 cm (8 in) cake tin.

Bring the poppy seeds to the boil in the milk, turn off the heat and leave them to soak for 25 minutes in the covered pan.

In a mixing bowl, cream the butter and sugar together until light and fluffy. Add the egg yolks, one at a time, and beat thoroughly. Fold the flour gently into the creamed mixture and stir in the seeds and milk. Whisk the egg whites until stiff and carefully incorporate into the mixture.

Spoon it into the prepared tin and bake for 1-1 ½ hours or until the centre is firm and the cake has stopped "singing". Let it stand for 10 minutes, then turn out to cool.

> "I also remember how exciting it was to go into Del Monico's, then the only Italian deli on Old Compton Street, and be able to buy ravioli, freshly made that day which you had to cook the same evening. I had only seen it in a tin before that! That was in the late 50s."
>
> *Sarah Edington*

A s both a food writer and a qualified Blue Badge guide, Sarah Edington has a keen interest in food and food history: "As guides you're encouraged to have a particular area of interest and my little corner is cooking. I've been thinking about my food experiences in London," says Sarah "and it occurred to me that I ate my first avocado here, probably smothered in mayonnaise and prawns, and also that I bought my first avocado here too, in Berwick Market which was just round the corner from my first job. I also remember how exciting it was to go into Del Monico's, then the only Italian deli on Old Compton Street, and be able to buy ravioli, freshly made that day which you had to cook the same evening. I had only seen it in a tin before that! That was in the late 1950s."

"This recipe was given to me about 12 years ago by a cook from Buckland Abbey, a National Trust property in deepest Devon. I have been making it to acclaim ever since! I like plain cakes and teabreads – I'm not a great gateaux person."

Helen's Teabread

Makes 2 loaves.

Dropping in at Helen Smith's home, friends are offered a cup of tea and a slice of home-made teabread. "I love drinking cups of tea," says Helen "and I don't like biscuits, but I do like a slice of teabread with butter." Helen's love of baking stems back to her childhood. "My mum always baked and she'd let me and my sisters help from when we were quite young. My parents would have friends round for tea on a Sunday," says Helen, "my mother would make scones and jelly and sandwiches. I can remember really looking forward to those teas." Today Helen particularly enjoys baking for and with her own children. "I make cakes with lots of fruit in them," she laughs, "because then I feel better about feeding my children cake."

175 g (6 oz) currants
175 g (6 oz) sultanas
100 g (3 ¹/₂ oz) Demerara sugar
100 g (3 ¹/₂ oz) light brown sugar
300 ml (¹/₂ pt) very strong tea, freshly-made
275 g (9 oz) self-raising flour
1 medium free-range egg
1 small eating apple, cored and finely chopped

The night before you want to bake the teabread, place the currants, sultanas, Demerara sugar and light brown sugar in a mixing bowl. Pour over the hot tea, cover and leave overnight.

Preheat the oven to Gas 2/150°C/300°F. Grease and line the bases of two 900 g (2 lb) loaf tins.

Stir the flour, egg and apple into the dried fruit mixture and mix well. Divide the mixture equally between the loaf tins, levelling out the top.

Bake for 1-1 ¹/₄ hours until risen and firm to touch. Test by inserting a skewer into the centre of each teabread; if it comes out clean then the teabread is cooked through. Cool on wire racks and serve sliced and buttered with a cup of tea.

"I make cakes
with lots of fruit
in them, because
then I feel better
about feeding my
children cake."

Helen Smith

Chelsea Buns
Makes 12 buns

Chelsea buns can be traced back to the 18th century, originating at the Bun House in Chelsea, a popular pastry house of the day. The Chelsea Bun House enjoyed the patronage of the royal House of Hanover and became known in particular for its rich Chelsea buns, flourishing into the 19th century. The buns themselves have a distinctive, squared-off shape and are notably sweet and sticky.

300 g (10 oz) plain white flour
pinch of salt
70 ml (2 ½ fl oz) milk
75 g (3 oz) butter
15 g (½ oz) dried yeast
55 g (2 oz) caster sugar
2 free-range eggs, beaten
55 g (2 oz) light brown sugar
55 g (2 oz) currants
1 tsp ground cinnamon
1 tsp ground mixed spice
runny honey, for glazing

Sift the flour and salt into a mixing bowl.

Heat the milk until lukewarm, then stir in 55 g (2 oz) butter and the yeast until the butter is dissolved. Stir in 55 g (2 oz) of caster sugar and the beaten eggs.

Pour the milk mixture into the flour and mix well until the mixture forms a sticky dough. Knead the dough on a lightly floured surface until smooth and elastic. Place the dough in an oiled bowl, cover with a damp cloth and set aside to rise for 1 hour.

Knock back the risen dough, return it to the bowl, cover and set aside to rise for 30 minutes.

Roll the dough out on a lightly floured board to form a large rectangle. Mix together the currants, light brown sugar, cinnamon and mixed spice. Melt the remaining butter and brush it generously over the dough. Sprinkle the currant mixture evenly over the dough. Carefully roll up the dough tightly lengthways, like a Swiss roll. Cut the dough roll into twelve evenly sized slices and place them, cut-side up, in a greased 20 cm (8 in) square tin. Cover and set aside in a warm place to rise for 30 minutes.

Preheat the oven to Gas 5/190°C/350°F. Bake the buns for 20-25 minutes, until risen and golden-brown. Brush with honey while hot, allow to cool slightly, then turn out and serve while warm.

Coffee Walnut Cake
Makes 1 cake

Truly a classic cake, often found at cake stalls because of its popularity. Coffee and walnuts go wonderfully well together.

175 g (6 oz) butter, softened
175 g (6 oz) caster sugar
3 medium free-range eggs, beaten
175 g (6 oz) self-raising flour, sifted
3 tbsp instant coffee, dissolved in 1 tbsp hot water
75 g (3 oz) walnut pieces

Icing:
75 g (3 oz) butter, softened
250 g (9 oz) icing sugar
1 tbsp instant coffee, dissolved in 1 tbsp hot water
8-12 walnut halves, to decorate

Preheat the oven to Gas 5/190°C/375°F.

In a mixing bowl, cream together the butter and caster sugar until thoroughly blended. Gradually mix in the beaten egg, adding a little flour if the mixture shows signs of curdling. Mix in the flour, coffee and walnut pieces.

Divide the mixture between two greased and lined 18 cm (7 in) cake tins. Bake the cakes in the centre of the oven for 20 minutes, until risen. Remove and cool on a wire rack.

Make the icing by mixing together the butter, icing sugar and dissolved instant coffee. Use the icing to sandwich and top the cake, decorating with walnut halves.

Maids of Honour Tarts

For a taste of history, head down to Newens Tea Rooms, alongside Kew Gardens at 288 Kew Road. Here, in these pleasantly traditional tea rooms, one can sit and enjoy a refreshing cup of tea and a Maid of Honour tart. Legend has it that these dainty almond curd tarts were a favourite with the Tudor monarch, King Henry VIII. Famous for his six wives, Henry was obviously a man of appetite and such was his fondness for these tarts that the recipe was reputedly kept secret, locked in a box in Richmond Palace.

John Newens, together with his wife Gillian, runs Newens Maids of Honour, a baking and tea shop business which has been passed down through his family since the 19th century.

Newens' splendid range of cakes, pies and quiches are all freshly baked on the premises. A customer sitting having tea remarks "It hasn't changed for years. The cakes are still the same and I've been coming for 40 years. It's the consistency that makes it so good."

The recipe for the Maids of Honour tarts remains a family secret to this day. "We still sell 200 a day on average," says John, "It's a sweet curd tart – everything you shouldn't eat in it!"

The Original Maids of Honour, 288 Kew Road, TW9

"My great-great grandfather worked at the original Maids of Honour shop in Richmond, then set up his own shop in 1850 in Richmond. In 1868 he took this place on Kew Road for his son Alfred," explains John.

"In those days most of our trade was bread and cake deliveries – we had 5 horse-drawn carts. Alfred died in 1927 and his son and daughter carried on running it up to and during the war. It was partially bombed during the war. Rationing was an issue too. I think they just opened for a few hours as they had so little to sell.

"I joined here in 1965; it was very busy then, teas were very popular – we'd do up to 200 teas then on a Saturday. We'd do roast lunch and a pudding – that was it. The waitress would come up to table and say 'Lamb today. So that's three lambs is it?' Now we offer a much bigger choice. My father started the steak pies. Now we do chicken and salmon pies too. You sell a lot more savoury things now than sweet things. Cakes used to be much more popular. In the 1950s people didn't know about cholesterol. If something works fairly well, there's no point in changing it too much."

John Newens

Imogen's Flapjacks
Makes 16

200 g (7 oz) margarine
175 g (6 oz) brown sugar
275-300 g (9-10 oz) porridge oats
pinch of ground ginger
1 handful of raisins
1 handful of chopped, stoned dates
2 big tbsp of golden syrup, warmed

Preheat the oven to Gas 4/180°C/350°F.

In a heavy-based saucepan, melt the margarine over a low heat, then add the sugar. Cook, stirring, until the sugar has melted. Meanwhile, gently warm the golden syrup by placing it on the hob whilst the oven pre-heats.

Add the oats, ginger, raisins, dates and warm golden syrup to the melted margarine and sugar and mix. The mixture should be thick and gloopy. If too runny, add more oats.

Transfer the mixture to a greased, 19 cm (7½ in), square cake tin and pat flat.

Bake for 25-30 minutes until the flapjacks look set and have stopped bubbling. "The marvellous thing about flapjacks is that they don't get upset if you open the oven door," observes Imogen. Allow to cool in the tin, then cut into 16 squares.

Imogen's Tip: To make the syrup easier to handle, warm the spoon under a hot running tap.

> *Every year I have a birthday tea party – I make flapjacks, chocolate, cakes, fruit cakes, biscuits. I love tea-pots and china – though actually I drink coffee!"*
>
> Imogen Smith

Actress Imogen Smith has fond childhood memories of eating and making flapjacks. "They were one of Grandma's specialities and then Mother made them too. Flapjacks were always part of tea-time at home; we used to help her make them. I like making them because they're very easy to make and you can bake other things alongside. Every year I have a birthday tea party – I make flapjacks, chocolate cakes, fruit cakes, biscuits. I love tea-pots and china – though actually I drink coffee!"

Afternoon Tea

The much-loved institution of afternoon tea England can be traced back to the 1800s and is popularly attributed to Anna, Duchess of Bedford. In order to sustain herself during the long period between lunch and her evening meal, the Duchess is said to have ordered her servants to send up a pot of tea and a little something to eat in the late afternoon. The custom of drinking tea and eating dainty sandwiches or cakes became very popular among aristocratic and fashionable circles and developed into a feminine, domestic ritual, graced by fine china and silver tea. In contrast to this leisurely afternoon repast, the more substantial early evening meal known as "High Tea" – offering savoury dishes alongside sweet baked items such as cakes or teabreads – was associated with the rural or urban working class.

Where to go

Many of London's most prestigious hotels offer elegant afternoon teas, complete with dainty sandwiches and freshly baked cakes and patisserie, albeit at a price. These are extremely popular, so advance booking is recommended. Vintage emporium Fortnum & Mason is a grand old name in tea-selling, while Shipp's Tearooms, the Tea Palace and the Wolseley all offer excellent afternoon teas.

Claridge's
55 Brook Street, W1
020 7409 6307

The Savoy
Strand, WC2
020 7836 4343

The Dorchester
53 Park Lane, W1
020 7629 8888

Shipps Tearooms
4 Park Street, SE1
020 7407 2692

Fortnum & Mason
181 Piccadilly, W1
020 7734 8040

Tea Palace
175 Westbourne Grove, W11
020 7727 2600

The Ritz
150 Piccadilly, W1
020 7493 8181

The Wolseley
160 Piccadilly, W1
020 7499 6996

A History of Tea

Today tea is regarded as a quintessentially British drink. Each day an estimated 165 million cups of tea are drunk in Britain. George Orwell, pondering aspects of Englishness, wrote in 1946 that "tea is one of the mainstays of civilization in this country", moving on to outline his firm personal convictions on how to make the "perfect" cup of tea. Indian tea, in Orwell's eyes, was essential; "Anyone who uses that comforting phrase 'a nice cup of tea' invariably means Indian tea." Orwell's ideal cuppa consisted of strong tea – six heaped teaspoons per quart – made with boiling water in a warmed china teapot, stirred in the pot and drunk from a breakfast cup, with milk added to the cup after the tea and without sugar; "Tea is meant to be bitter, just as beer is meant to be bitter. "

Originally, tea was an expensive, exotic luxury. Shipped in from China by the East India Company and heavily taxed it was a precious commodity, stored in specially-made, lockable tea caddies. An advertisement in a London newspaper in 1658 announced a "Chinese drink, called by the Chinese, Tcha, by other nations Tay, alias Tea", which was on sale at a coffee house in Sweetings Rents in the City. Tea's popularity in Britain can be traced back to the period of the Restoration, when Charles II became King. Charles' wife, Catherine of Braganza, the daughter of the King of Portugal, is credited with introducing the custom of drinking tea to the English royal court, making it a fashionable drink in aristocratic circles. In 1660 Samuel Pepys, characteristically keen to sample anything novel, recorded in his diary "I did send for a cup of tea (a China drink) of which I never had drank before."

Despite its high cost, tea became a popular and fashionable drink. 1679 saw the first London Tea Auction, held by the East India Company (which for a long time held the monopoly on importing tea) at its headquarters on Leadenhall Street. This trading event – which ceased only in 1998 – grew in importance and London became the centre of the international tea trade. Merchants catered to the demand for this new beverage. In 1706 the enterprising tea merchant Thomas Twining opened a tea shop on the Strand; today the shop is still there and the Twining family are still involved in the business. Fortnum and Mason, established in 1707, has long been well-known for its teas. Tea gardens, such as those at White Conduit House in Islington and Ranelagh Gardens in Chelsea, became popular places of entertainment.

While tea was finding a larger following, there was also much dispute over whether tea was a healthy drink or not. Dr Samuel Johnson, in defence of tea, cheerfully described himself as a "hardened and shameless tea-drinker, who has for many years diluted his meals with only the infusion of this fascinating plant." Such was the demand for tea and so heavily was it taxed that a huge and highly profitable black market in smuggled tea grew up in the 18th century. In 1784 the Prime Minister William Pitt the Younger dramatically cut the tax on tea from 119% to 12.5%, a move which reduced the demand for smuggled tea and made tea far more affordable.

The 19th century witnessed the rise of the clippers, fast, slender sailing ships built for speed, which made the long journey back from China around the Cape of Good Hope to bring cargoes of tea to London's docks.

Races between British and American clipper ships to bring back valuable cargoes caught the public imagination, with huge bets laid on the outcome. One famous race, which aroused immense excitement and interest, took place in 1866 with ten clippers speeding back to London from the Chinese port of Fouchow. The winner completed the race in 99 days, just 20 minutes ahead of its closest rival. The Cutty Sark, built in 1869 and currently under restoration, was one of the last of the clippers to be built. The opening of the Suez Canal in 1869 allowed steam ships viable access to the tea import market and put an end to the clipper races.

The 19th century also saw the East India Company lose its trading function and in 1834, it became an agent of the British government. Denied its profitable monopoly on China's tea trade, the company looked to its considerable interests in India and oversaw the rise of tea-cultivation in Assam, where indigenous tea plants had been found. Other regions of India were found to be suitable for tea-growing and by 1888 British tea imports from India exceeded those from China.

Tea was widely drunk, championed by the Temperance movement. In 1894 the first Lyons teashop opened on Piccadilly. Cheap, clean and efficient, with its waitresses nick-named "nippies" because of the speed with which they worked, Lyons went on to become a major chain.

Today tea-drinking is on the whole an everyday, domestic affair. Tea-bags, invented by a New York tea merchant around 1908, took off in Britain during the 1950s, in an age which valued convenience and speed. Today sales of tea-bags form an overwhelming 96% of the British tea market.

Classic Cream Tea
Makes 12 square scones or 8 round scones

Clotted cream is one of the glories of Britain's dairy culture – a traditional West Country delicacy made by slowly heating cream over a long period of time. Cream teas, popular in Devon and Cornwall, are also served at London's smart hotels. Eating freshly-baked scones, warm from the oven, is a true treat.

250 g (9 oz) self-raising flour
pinch of salt
1 tsp baking powder
50 g (2 oz) butter, diced
25 g (1 oz) sugar
1 medium free-range egg
125 ml (4 fl oz), buttermilk, or natural yoghurt, plus a little extra for glazing
1 tub of clotted cream, to serve
good-quality raspberry or strawberry jam, to serve

Preheat oven to Gas 7/220°C/425°F.

Sift the flour, salt and baking powder into a mixing bowl. Using your fingertips, rub in the butter until absorbed. Mix in the sugar.

Lightly whisk together the egg and buttermilk. Add to the flour mixture and fold in to form a soft, sticky dough.

On a lightly floured board, lightly roll out the dough to 2.5 cm (1 in) thickness. Using a sharp knife, cut into 12 evenly sized squares or, using a 15 cm (6 in) round cutter, into 8 rounds.

Place on a greased baking sheet. Brush with a little buttermilk or milk to glaze. Bake for 10-15 minutes until risen and golden. Serve warm from the oven.

Rose Fairy Cakes
Makes 12

Fairy cakes are a traditional tea-time favourite with grown-ups and children alike. Adding a little rose water gives them a delicious fragrance and perfumed flavour.

115 g (4 oz) butter, softened
115 g (4 oz) caster sugar
2 medium free-range eggs, lightly beaten
115 g (4 oz) self-raising flour
$1/_2$ tsp rose water
1-2 tbsp milk

Icing:
115 g (4 oz) icing sugar, sifted
1 tbsp hot water
1-2 drops of rose water
1 drop red food colouring (optional)
12 crystallised rose petals

Preheat the oven to Gas 4/180°C/350°F.

Using a wooden spoon, cream together the butter and sugar in a mixing bowl. Gradually mix in the beaten egg, adding a little flour if the mixture begins to curdle.

Sift in the flour and add the rose water and a tbsp of milk and mix together to form a soft cake mix, adding more milk if necessary. Spoon into 12 cup cake cases and bake on baking sheet for 15-20 minutes until risen and golden. Remove and cool on a wire rack.

Once the cakes are cool, prepare the icing. In a bowl mix together the icing sugar, hot water, rose water and food colouring until thoroughly mixed. Spread a little icing over the top of each fairy cake. Top each cake with a rose petal.

Lemon Curd Tarts
Makes 24

A delicious variation on classic jam tarts.

200 g (7 oz) plain flour
pinch of salt
1 tsp caster sugar
100 g (3 1/2 oz) butter, diced
1 free-range egg yolk
2-3 tbsp cold water, plus extra for brushing
lemon curd, for filling

In a food processor, pulse blend the flour, salt, sugar and butter until the mixture resembles crumbs. Add the egg yolk and cold water, blending until the mixture comes together to form a dough. Shape into a ball, wrap in clingfilm and chill in the refrigerator for 30 minutes.

Preheat the oven to Gas 6/200°C/400°F.

Finely roll out the pastry on a lightly floured surface. Cut out 24 pastry circles using an 8 cm (3 in) cutter. Press the pastry circles into two greased tart tins. Fill each pastry case with 1 heaped tsp of lemon curd. Brush the filling lightly with water and bake for 15 minutes until the pastry is golden. Carefully remove the tarts from the tins and cool on a wire rack.

Cinnamon Toast
Makes 2 slices

An old-fashioned treat – simple but very good.

15 g (1/2 oz) butter
1 tbsp Demerara sugar
1/2 tsp ground cinnamon
2 slices of bread

Mix together the butter, sugar and cinnamon until well-blended.

Toast the bread until browned on one side. Spread the cinnamon butter on the un-toasted side of the bread and grill until the butter has melted. Cut into fingers and serve at once.

"We called these biscuits 'krontze' – I don't know how to spell it. My mother got it from her Aunty Betty. It's a family recipe from my great-grandmother who came from Amsterdam. I remember the smell of them baking and the smell of cinnamon when they came out of the oven. There used to be trays of them and we had to keep our fingers off them; they're very tempting. My mother would say 'grocer biscuits' in a very disapproving voice. We never had grocer biscuits – everything was home-made."

Rosemary Jones

Rosemary's Biscuits

Makes about 36 biscuits

225 g (8 oz) butter, softened
150 g (5 oz) caster sugar
300 g (10 oz) plain flour
1 medium free-range egg
egg white, for brushing
cinnamon, for dusting

Cream together the butter and caster sugar until thoroughly mixed. Add the sifted flour and the egg and mix together until the mixture comes together to form a soft, sticky dough. Cover and chill for 30 minutes.

Preheat the oven to Gas 3/170°C/325°F.

Take a walnut-sized piece of the biscuit dough and roll in your palms to form a short, stubby tube. Coil the dough tube round into an ammonite shape and place on a greased baking sheet, spaced apart to allow room to spread. Repeat the process until all the dough has been shaped.

Brush the biscuits with egg white, then sprinkle with cinnamon. Bake for 15-20 minutes until pale gold in colour.

Charlotte's Lemon Sog Cake
Makes 1 cake

"I love this cake because it's the quickest, simplest cake recipe ever," says Charlotte Crow. "It's definitely the cake I bake more than any other. Great because you don't have to do any creaming, which is such a downer. I ate it as a child and I can remember that the cake would almost sink in the middle with a puddle of lemony syrup on top. It was Jackie, a great family friend of ours, who used to make it. Then she must have given the recipe to my mum and it became a family favourite of ours. My mum decided to cook it as a pudding, in a dinner party way, as well as a tea-time way. I think it was a recipe that I took away to university – a comforting, favourite thing to eat that friends really liked."

Charlotte serves her cake on pretty, old china plates, part of her collection of mass-produced and hand-painted 1930s china. "I like the colours and the shapes and the fact that these were used on a daily basis. I never wanted to collect them from antique shops – it's the joy of just finding one piece where no-one else has noticed it."

175 g (6 oz) butter
175 g (6 oz) Demerara sugar
175 g (6 oz) self-raising flour
2 free-range eggs, beaten
juice of a large lemon
50 g (2 oz) caster sugar

Decorative glazed lemon slices:
1 lemon, very finely sliced
2 tbsp caster sugar
2 tbsp water

The decorative glazed lemon slices are an optional touch and need to be made the night before the cake. Bring the caster sugar and water to the boil in a small pan "watching like a hawk to check that it doesn't start turning into toffee". Add the lemon and cook very gently for 3-5 minutes until the lemon slices are coated in a thick syrup. Remove from the heat and leave overnight in the syrup.

Preheat the oven to Gas 4/180°C/350°F.

Melt the butter in a saucepan. Over a low heat, stir in the Demerara sugar and flour, then take it off the heat. Stir in the beaten eggs, then turn into a 20 cm (8 in) cake tin and bake for 25-30 minutes until risen and set.

Remove the cake from the oven. Mix together the lemon juice and caster sugar and pour over the baked cake. Just before serving pat the glazed lemon slices dry, and place them on the centre of the cake.

The Story of Postcard Teas

Discreetly situated on a side-street, just off the hustle and bustle of Oxford Street, Tim D'Offay's tea shop Postcard Teas is an elegant, serene haven. The name, Postcard Teas, with its sense of snapshots of different places, is an appropriate one, reflecting Tim's personal knowledge of tea-producing countries as well as his, and his father's, penchant for collecting old postcards. Along one wall are the carefully chosen teas that Tim imports and sells while, at a long wooden table, customers can sit and taste them. Instead of the anonymity of buying on the open market, Tim cultivates relationships with tea plantations and tea makers in countries including India, Japan, Korea and Sri Lanka. His fascination with the tea-growing regions he visits is mirrored in his photographs of the estates and the people who work on them which hang on the walls of Postcard Tea's.

Ask Tim about a tea that he stocks – such as Goomtee's Second Flush from Darjeeling – and he'll tell you about the tea, the estate where it's grown and the people who grow and make it. "That's what I love about tea," explains Tim, "it's a combination of man and nature. You need to be a farmer, a scientist and an artist to make a great tea. If I find a good tea maker I work with them and buy directly. "The people I buy from know that I appreciate what they're capable of, their strong sense of tradition in what they're doing. They are businessmen but they're unlike the brokers. They're like farmers, so bound up in what they do; they have a huge responsibility for a lot of people."

Tim's special relationship with the tea estates means that he has been able to develop particular teas, including a unique Coffee Blossom tea. "The fun thing about working with small estates is that you're able to try things and experiment," says Tim. "I was visiting the Handunugoda Estate in Sri Lanka and came across a coffee plant on the estate in full bloom. It was so intensely scented that I thought why not try to use the flowers to scent tea leaves? I talked to Herman, the estate manager, and we sent samples back and forth; we've invented something."

Having, in his own words, "fallen in love with tea" ten years ago when he sampled a small, remarkably refreshing cup of tea without milk or sugar in Taipei, Tim's policy is to keep the prices of his tea tastings "deliberately low, to make them accessible". He takes pleasure from seeing the reactions of the customers when they taste a tea. "I enjoy personal relationships – with the growers, with the people who come to my shop. It's easy for me to talk about tea; I know how it's made, where it's come from."

That's what I love about tea, it's a combination of man and nature. You need to be a farmer, a scientist and an artist to make a great tea."

Tim D'Offay

Postcard Teas, 9 Dering Street, New Bond Street, W1S

Food for Friends

Steak with Celeriac Gratin

Serves 4

A piece of prime steak from a good butcher who goes to the trouble of sourcing his meat carefully and hanging it well makes a fantastic meal. Here griddled steak is paired with a rich, creamy celeriac gratin, with the celeriac adding a subtle, complex flavour to the dish.

4 pieces of prime rump steak
olive oil
1 garlic clove, peeled and scored
salt and freshly ground pepper
grain mustard, to serve

Celeriac gratin:
500 g (1 lb 2 oz) celeriac
500 g (1lb 2 oz) waxy potatoes
salt and freshly ground pepper
1 shallot, finely chopped
15 g (½ oz) butter, plus extra for dotting
1 tbsp plain flour
300 ml (½ pt) milk
1 bay leaf
300 ml (½ pt) double cream
freshly grated nutmeg

First prepare the celeriac gratin. Peel the celeriac and cut into very fine slices, placing the slices as you cut them in a bowl of water with a little lemon juice or vinegar added to prevent the celeriac from discolouring. Peel and very finely slice the potatoes.

Bring a large pan of salted water to the boil. Drain the celeriac slices and add them and the potato slices to the boiling water and blanch briefly; drain well.

Heat 15 g (½ oz) of butter in a heavy-based saucepan. Stir in the flour and cook, stirring, for 2-3 minutes. Gradually add the milk, stirring as you do so, and the bay leaf. Cook, stirring often, until the mixture thickens into a white sauce. Stir in the cream and season with salt, freshly ground pepper and a generous amount of freshly grated nutmeg.

Preheat the oven to Gas 5/190°C/350°F.

Generously butter a heavy-based, ovenproof dish. Layer in the blanched celeriac and potato slices, sprinkling over the shallot, dotting with butter and seasoning with salt and freshly ground pepper as you do so. Carefully pour over the white sauce and dot the top with a few more bits of butter. Bake for 1 hour until golden-brown.

Towards the end of the gratin's baking time, preheat two griddle pans on the hob over a high heat. Rub the steaks with olive oil and the scored garlic clove and season with salt and freshly ground pepper. Cook on the griddle pan until cooked to taste, turning over at least once during griddling.

Serve the steaks with the celeriac gratin hot from the oven and grain mustard on the side.

Paella
Serves 6

London's Spanish food shops, such as Garcia on Portobello Road, or Brindisa at Borough and Exmouth Markets provide the key ingredients for this classic Spanish rice dish: spicy, paprika-flavoured chorizo sausages, paella rice and saffron.

2 red peppers
1.2 ltr (2 pts) home-made chicken stock
4 tbsp olive oil
2 bay leaves
2 spicy, cooking chorizo sausages, chopped into chunks
4 free-range chicken breast fillets, chopped into large chunks
1 onion, peeled and chopped
4 garlic cloves, peeled and chopped
1 medium squid, cleaned, body chopped into rings, tentacles cut into short lengths
400 g (14 oz) paella rice
generous pinch of saffron threads, finely ground
150 ml (1/4 pt) dry white wine
salt and freshly ground pepper
freshly grated nutmeg
450 g (15 oz) cooked prawns, peeled
18 mussels, scrubbed under cold water, with any open ones discarded
a handful of flat-leafed parsley, chopped
lemon wedges, to serve

Roast the red peppers under a grill until charred on all sides. Wrap in a plastic bag (this makes them easier to peel), set aside to cool; peel and chop into strips.

Heat the stock in a saucepan, bringing it to a simmer. Heat the olive oil in a paella pan or large, heavy-based frying pan. Add the bay leaves, chorizo and chicken. Fry, stirring now and then, until the chorizo is lightly browned and the chicken is whitened on all sides. Add the onion, garlic and squid and fry, stirring now and then, until the onion is softened and the squid is opaque.

Mix in the rice, sprinkle over the saffron and pour over the white wine, allowing it to bubble for 2-3 minutes. Pour in around half the simmering stock and season with salt, freshly ground pepper and freshly grated nutmeg. Bring to the boil, then reduce the heat and cook for 10 minutes. Add the remaining stock, stir in the prawns and press the mussels into the rice and cook for a further 10-15 minutes until the stock has been absorbed, the mussels have opened and the rice is tender. Decorate with roasted red pepper strips, cover with a 'lid' of silver foil and set aside to rest for 5 minutes. Sprinkle with parsley and serve with lemon wedges.

Chicken Satay
Serves 4

Proper satay sauce, with its rich spicy nuttiness, is a world away from a dash of soy sauce stirred into peanut butter. The specialist ingredients – lemon grass, galingal, candlenuts and tamarind pulp – can be found in Chinatown or Thai food shops. Galingal is a brown-skinned rhizome which imparts a distinctive aroma to the dish. If you have difficulty finding galingal, ginger can be used as a substitute. Candlenuts are a hazlenut-sized oily nut which add texture to the sauce. If you have difficulty finding candlenuts raw macadamia nuts may be used. Marinating the meat overnight gives a depth of flavour. Satay tastes especially delicious when cooked over a barbecue, but is also good grilled.

500g chicken breast fillets
8 wooden skewers
1/2 cucumber

Marinade:
1 tsp cumin seeds
1 tsp fennel seeds
1 onion
2 garlic cloves
1 thumb-sized piece of galingal
2 stalks of lemon grass
1 tbsp ground coriander
1 tsp ground turmeric
1 tbsp sugar
1 tsp salt
1 tbsp sunflower or vegetable oil

Satay Sauce:
5 candlenuts (or raw macadamia nuts)
100 ml (3 1/2 fl oz) hot water
a walnut-sized piece of tamarind pulp
200 g (7 oz) roasted salted peanuts
1 onion
4 garlic cloves
1 thumb-sized piece of galingal
4 stalks of lemon grass
1 tsp ground turmeric
1 tsp chilli powder (optional)
75ml oil
300ml water
5 tbsp dark brown sugar

Cut the chicken breast fillets into small, evenly sized slices.

To make the marinade, dry-fry the cumin and fennel seeds until fragrant, then cool and finely grind. Peel and chop the onion, garlic and galingal. Peel the tough outer casing from each lemon grass stalk and finely chop the white bulbous part.

In a large bowl, mix together the chicken, cumin, fennel, onion, garlic, garlingal, lemon grass, coriander, turmeric, sugar, salt and oil. Cover and marinate overnight in the refrigerator. Set 8 wooden skewers to soak overnight in cold water.

To make the satay sauce, soak the candlenuts for 10 minutes in cold water; drain and finely grind. Meanwhile, pour the hot water over the tamarind, mix well and set aside for 15-20 minutes. Strain the tamarind water through a small sieve, pressing the pulp down to extract as much flavour as possible and reserve the strained water. Finely grind the peanuts and reserve. Peel and chop the onion, garlic and galingal. Peel the tough outer casing from each lemon grass stalk and finely chop the white bulbous part. Using a food processor, blend together the onion, garlic, galingal, lemon grass, candlenuts, turmeric and chilli powder into a paste.

Heat the oil in a wok or large, heavy-based saucepan. Add in the paste and fry for 5-10 minutes, stirring often, until fragrant. Add the tamarind water, water, ground peanuts and brown sugar, stirring well. Bring to the boil, then reduce the heat and simmer gently for 10 minutes. Set aside and serve warm or at room temperature.

To cook the satay, preheat your grill at its highest setting. Thread the chicken pieces onto the skewers, dividing evenly. Grill the satay until cooked through, around 10 minutes, turning often. Meanwhile, chop the cucumber into chunks.

Serve the chicken satay with the satay sauce and cucumber chunks.

Melissa's Crespelle Fiorentina
Serves 6

My food-loving Californian friend Melissa Keppel gave me this recipe years ago, having come across it while studying in Florence. This classic Florentine dish of spinach-stuffed pancakes is, to be honest, something of a time-consuming, labour of love. The result, however, repays the time and effort required, as it is a truly elegant and refined dish, which always goes down very well with guests.

Pancakes:
115 g (4 oz) plain flour
pinch of salt
1 free-range egg
300 ml (½ pt) milk
butter, for frying

Filling:
1 kg (2 ¼ lb) fresh spinach
salt and freshly ground pepper
500g (1 lb 2 oz) ricotta cheese
freshly grated nutmeg

To serve:
freshly grated Parmesan cheese, for
*   or sprinkling and serving*

Tomato sauce:
1 tbsp olive oil
1 garlic clove, peeled and chopped
1 onion, peeled and chopped
1 bay leaf
dash of Amontillado sherry (optional)
1 x 400 g (14 oz) can chopped tomatoes
salt and freshly ground pepper

White sauce:
25 g (1 oz) butter
2 tbsp plain flour
300 ml (½ pt) milk
salt and freshly ground pepper
freshly grated nutmeg

First, make the pancakes. Sift the flour and salt into a mixing bowl. Break the egg into the centre. Gradually whisk in the milk, forming a smooth batter. Heat a little butter in a 12 cm (5 in) heavy-based frying pan. Once the butter is foaming, pour in half a ladleful of the pancake batter. Tilt the pan, spreading the batter evenly and widely over the pan. Fry until set, loosen the edges with a spatula and flip the pancake over to briefly brown the other side. Set aside to cool. Repeat the process until all the batter has been used up.

Make the tomato sauce by heating the olive oil in a heavy-based saucepan. Add the garlic, onion and bay leaf and fry, stirring now and then, for 2-3 minutes until the onion has softened. Add the sherry, if using, and sizzle briefly. Mix in the tomatoes, season with salt and freshly ground pepper, bring to the boil and cook, stirring now and then, for 10-15 minutes. Remove the bay leaf and blend until smooth.

Make the white sauce by melting the butter in a heavy-based pan. Mix in the flour and cook, stirring, for 2-3 minutes. Gradually stir in the milk. Cook, stirring, until the mixture thickens into a white sauce. Season with salt, freshly ground pepper and freshly grated nutmeg. Stir the white sauce into the tomato sauce.

Prepare the filling. Rinse the spinach and place in a large pan. Cover and cook until the spinach is just cooked through. Season with salt and freshly ground pepper. Drain the spinach and squeeze out excess liquid. Roughly chop the cooked spinach.

In a bowl, mix together the ricotta and chopped spinach. Season generously with freshly ground pepper and freshly grated nutmeg.

Preheat the oven to Gas 5/190°C/375°F.

Top a pancake with a spoonful of the spinach and ricotta mixture. Using the back of a spoon, spread it evenly over the pancake. Roll up the pancake over the filling and cut the resulting pancake tube in half. Repeat the process until all the pancakes have been filled and cut in half.

Place the halved filled pancakes, spiral-side up, in a buttered ovenproof dish, large enough to hold them all side by side. Spoon over the sauce, filling the crevices between the filled pancakes. Sprinkle generously with grated Parmesan cheese.

Bake the pancakes for 30 minutes until golden-brown. Serve hot from the oven with grated Parmesan.

Polly's Roast Lamb Stuffed with Green Tapenade
Serves 4-6

100 g (3 ½ oz) green olives stuffed
   with anchovies (drained weight)
100 g (3 ½ oz) stoned green olives
3-4 anchovy fillets
2 garlic cloves, peeled and crushed
100 ml approx (3 ½ fl oz approx) olive oil
3-4 sprigs of rosemary
squeeze of lemon juice
salt and freshly ground pepper

Tapenade:
55g (2 oz) pine nuts
1-1.5kg boned loin of lamb (or boned breast
   or shoulder)
small glass of white wine
400 ml (14 fl oz) chicken stock

Start by making the tapenade. Place the drained olives in a food processor along with the anchovy fillets and garlic. Peel the garlic and crush into the processor. Pulse the processor, adding the olive oil slowly until you have a thick, coarse paste.

Take a small sprig of rosemary, separate the leaves from the stalk and chop the leaves finely. Add to the olive and anchovy paste, then stir in the lemon juice and season with black pepper to taste. Check for seasoning and leave to one side.

Toast the pine nuts in a small saucepan over a gentle heat until they are lightly browned all over. They will burn quickly so keep an eye on them. Once they are browned leave to cool slightly.

About 1 hour before you plan to eat, heat the oven to Gas 7/220°C/425°F. Lay the lamb onto a chopping board skin-side down. Generously spread the tapenade paste onto the meat, reserving about 1 tablespoon to use for the gravy. Once the lamb is coated with tapenade, sprinkle with the pine nuts, roll up the meat and tie securely with string. Don't worry if some of the tapenade oozes out of the sides. Squeeze the remaining rosemary sprigs under the string and season the outside of the meat well with salt and freshly ground pepper.

Place the meat in a heavy-based roasting tray and cook for 15 minutes before turning the oven down to Gas 3/170°C/325°F. Cook for a further 25-40 minutes, depending on whether you prefer your meat pink or well done. Once cooked remove from the oven and place the meat on a carving board to rest for 15-20 minutes.

While the meat is resting make the gravy. Place the roasting tray over a gentle-medium heat, add the white wine and bring to the boil. Scrape the bottom of the tray with a wooden spoon and stir until the wine has reduced to about half. Add the chicken stock and bring to a rapid boil. When the stock has reduced by half, stir in up to a tablespoon of the tapenade so that you have an intensely flavoured but light gravy.

Cut the lamb into thickish slices and serve with a small quantity of the gravy.

> "I really like meeting people and making connections – food is a way you can make a connection."
>
> *Polly Russell*

Polly Russell's appreciation of food and its associations with hospitality stems back to her childhood. "Both my parents are really great cooks," explains Polly. "During my childhood we'd often have people coming over for food. It was never fancy – but there'd be a big casserole simmering away because you wouldn't be sure who was coming round My Mum was part of that generation who were really into Claudia Roden, Madhur Jaffrey, Jane Grigson, Elizabeth David. I've got some of her cookbooks from those days, when people here were discovering new foods."

A year spent studying at Berkeley, California was a revelation. "This was the first time I saw farmers' markets. I saw ingredients I'd never seen before. I met people who were really interested in food – in real bread, great pizza, good ice cream."

Living in Louisiana was another seminal experience. "That was the first time I'd lived somewhere where everyone across the scale was interested in good food and eating. Everybody came together for gumbo, jambalaya, crayfish boil . . . It was never flash – there was food and music and dancing. You could get deep-fried oysters – 6 for \$1 at Happy Hour, with an ice-cold beer in a frozen glass – the best thing on earth." Polly gets great pleasure from cooking for her family and friends; "I really like meeting people and making connections – food is a way you can make a connection."

As a philosophy student in London he saw a Neal's Yard Dairy job advert asking "Do you like cheese?" and thought "that's the only thing I eat."

Dom Coyte

Dom Coyte is a man who loves cheese. As a philosophy student in London he saw a Neal's Yard Dairy job advert asking "Do you like cheese?" and thought "that's the only thing I eat." Working at Neal's Yard Dairy was a revelation; "the Lancashire, the Cheddar, the Cheshire – I couldn't believe they were so good. Until then, I'd always thought of Stilton as horrible and abrasive. At the Dairy it was smooth and mellow; I was bowled over by it. I got to understand how small cheese producers worked." Today Dom is a familiar figure on the Borough Cheese Company stall at Borough Market, selling Comté cheese, hand-selected and imported by the Company from the Franche-Comté region of France. "The flavour of Comté is fantastic. It's not a cheese that hits you between the eyes," Dom explains, "it's a slow-burning flavour that seems to keep going. We'll give out a sample, the person eats it, walks off, then slows down and comes back to buy a piece. It's a refined cheese, wonderful for cooking as it holds its flavour well when melted."

Borough Cheese Company, Borough Market, SE1

Dom Coyte's Leek and Comté Tarts
Makes 9

Shortcrust pastry:
240 g (8 ¹/₂ oz) plain flour
115 g (4 oz) butter, at room temperature
water, to mix

Filling:
25g (1 oz) butter
1 tsp olive oil
3 medium leeks, chopped into 1 cm (¹/₂ in) slices
100 g (3 ¹/₂ oz) smoked bacon, very finely sliced (optional)
150 ml (5 fl oz) double cream
freshly ground pepper
200 g (7 oz) Comté cheese, grated finely

Make the pastry by sifting the flour into a mixing bowl, chopping the butter into small cubes and rubbing it lightly into the flour. Add water and knead until it comes together into a ball of dough. Wrap in a damp cloth or clingfilm and leave in the fridge for 20 minutes.

Melt the oil and butter in a frying pan and add the leeks. Cover tightly and stew until soft, stirring now and then, for 15 minutes. Uncover and add the bacon strips, if using, and fry until the bacon is cooked.

Preheat the oven to Gas 7/220°C/425°F.

Grease a nine hole muffin tin with a little butter. Roll out the pastry and cut out 9 circles, large enough to line each muffin space, making sure that there is enough surplus to allow for the pastry to shrink in the oven.

Put a generous spoonful of leeks and bacon in each pastry case. Fill three-quarters full with cream, season each tart with a little black pepper, then top up with grated Comté.

Bake in the oven for 15-20 minutes until set and golden. Serve warm from the oven.

Game

The term "game" was traditionally applied to birds and animals that were hunted for their meat. Originally these were wild animals, but today certain birds and animals that are considered as game are reared rather than wild; venison, for example, can come from farmed deer as well as wild deer that have been hunted. Many game birds and animals can only be hunted during certain times of the year. The "Glorious Twelfth" of August, which sees grouse-hunting commence, is the traditional start of Britain's game season.

Game glossary

Grouse: is a game bird characterised by its dark flesh and distinctive herbal flavour. Season August 12-December 10.

Hare: the wild brown hare, related to the rabbit with gamey-flavoured flesh. Not sold between March 1-July 31.

Partridge: grey-legged partridges are indigenous to Britain while red-legged partridges were introduced from France. Both species have delicately-flavoured flesh. Season September 1-February 1.

Pheasant: a widely available game bird, traditionally sold in a brace (one male and one female). Season October 1-February 1.

Rabbit: available farmed or wild, the latter having more flavour.

Snipe: a small, long-billed bird, considered a delicacy. Season August 12-January 31.

Teal: a species of small, wild duck with a delicate flavour. Season September 1-January 31.

Venison: comes from both farmed and wild deer, the latter having a stronger, more gamey taste.

Woodcock: a small wading bird rarely available over the counter. Season October 1-January 31.

Wood pigeon: an inexpensive game bird. Available all year.

Where to eat game

Rules
35 Maiden Lane, WC2
020 7836 5314
London's oldest restaurant, founded in 1798, with game supplied from the owner's estate in Scotland.

St John
26 St John St, EC1
020 7251 0848
This elegantly austere, robustly carnivorous restaurant, has championed 'nose to tail' eating.

Where to buy game

Allen's
117 Mount Street, W1
020 7499 5831
A beautiful, old butchers in the heart of Mayfair, noted for the range and quality of its game.

Borough Market
Southwark Street, SE1
www.boroughmarket.org.uk
A number of businesses in and around Borough offer game, including Furness Fish & Game (015395 59544), Wyndham House Poultry (020 7403 4788) and West Country Venison, which specialises in fallow deer venison.

M. Moen & Sons
24 The Pavement, Clapham Common, SW4
020 7622 1624
A dapper butchers with an fine range of game.

Allen's, 117 Mount Street, W1

Susan's Monkfish Wrapped in Parma Ham with Spicy Sauce
Serves 4

2 monkfish tails, around 450 g (1 lb) in weight
salt and freshly ground pepper
6 slices of Parma ham
a little olive oil
mashed potato, to serve
wilted spinach, to serve

For the spicy sauce:
115 ml (4 fl oz) single cream
6 tbsp soy sauce
dash of white wine
2 tbsp West Indian chilli sauce
4 sprigs of tarragon
freshly ground pepper

Preheat the oven to Gas 4/180°C/350°F.

Season the monkfish tails with salt and freshly ground pepper, bearing in mind the saltiness of the Parma ham. Wrap the two monkfish tails, side by side, in the Parma ham to make one parcel.

Heat the olive oil in a heavy-based, roasting tray on the hob. Add the monkfish parcel and cook over a medium heat for 3-5 minutes on each side. Transfer the roasting tray to the oven and roast for a further 20-25 minutes, until cooked through.

Meanwhile, make the spicy sauce. Heat the cream in a heavy-based pan, then add the soy sauce and white wine. Cook, stirring, for a minute or two. Mix in the chilli sauce, then the tarragon sprigs and season with freshly ground pepper. Cook, stirring often, for 15 minutes until reduced and thickened.

Cut the roast monkfish into 8 slices and serve on hot dinner plates with the spicy sauce poured over the fish and with mash and spinach on the side.

Susan's Sashimi with Spicy Dressing

Serves 4

16 slices of yellowtail or bluefin tuna
coriander sprigs, to garnish

For the dressing:
50 ml (2 fl oz) soy sauce
115 ml (4 fl oz) freshly squeezed lime juice
4 garlic cloves, peeled and minced
2 tsp red chilli paste

First make the dressing by mixing together the soy sauce, lime juice, garlic and chilli paste. Cover and leave in the refrigerator for 5-10 minutes.

Arrange the sashimi on a large platter, pour over the dressing, garnish with coriander sprigs and serve at once.

Born in County Cork, Ireland, Susan Hackett has lived in London for several years, running her own hairdressing salon. Both her Mum and Dad were "wonderful cooks" says Susan. "I remember oysters, home-smoked eel, watching chicken liver pâté being made. They loved having people round and were very creative in what they cooked. I grew up seeing this as a normal thing." One of things Susan loves about living in London is the chance to find different foods: Indian, Thai, Chinese and Japanese. "I had sashimi and thought it was fantastic," she enthuses. Warmly hospitable, Susan loves having her friends round for meals and often serves fish, which she's particularly partial to. Susan buys the fish for her sashimi from Fuji Foods, a Japanese food shop at the foot of Muswell Hill. "It's a treat, for friends or for a birthday."

Mutton and Potato Curry
Serves 4-6

Mutton, once a staple meat in Britain, is now so little eaten that a Mutton Renaissance campaign has been launched to promote this distinctive, flavourful meat. At his stall at Borough Market, farmer Andrew Sharp, whose great-great uncle was Beatrix Potter's shepherd, is a proud and articulate advocate of the lamb and mutton from his hardy, nimble Herdwick sheep, reared in the hills of the Lake District. This recipe uses mutton in a traditional Malay-style curry, as its robust flavour stands up well to the spiced coconut milk gravy in which it is simmered.

75 ml (3 fl oz) hot water
1 walnut-sized piece of tamarind pulp
3 tbsp sunflower oil
2 onions, peeled and chopped
4 garlic cloves, peeled and chopped
a thumb-sized piece of fresh root ginger,
*   peeled and chopped*
500 g (1 lb 2 oz) diced mutton
1 x 400 ml (14 fl oz) can coconut milk
200 ml (7 fl oz) water
1 lemon grass stalk
salt
6 small new potatoes, halved

Curry powder:
1 tbsp coriander seeds
1 tbsp cumin seeds
1 tsp fennel seeds
1 cinnamon stick
6 cloves
6 black peppercorns
1/4 tsp finely grated nutmeg
1/2 tsp ground turmeric
1 tsp ground chilli

First prepare the curry powder. Dry-fry the coriander, cumin, fennel, cinnamon, cloves and peppercorns in a small frying pan, stirring, for 2-3 minutes until fragrant. Set aside to cool. Finely grind the dry-fried spices and stir in the turmeric and chilli. Add just enough cold water to form a paste.

While the spices are cooling, mix the hot water with the tamarind pulp, stirring together thoroughly. Set aside for 15 minutes, then strain, pressing down on the tamarind pulp to extract as much tamarind flavour as possible.

Heat the sunflower oil in a heavy-based casserole dish. Add the onion and fry gently, stirring often, for 5 minutes. Mix in the garlic and ginger and fry for a further 2-3 minutes, until fragrant. Thoroughly mix in the spice paste.

Add the mutton and coat well in the spice paste. Mix in the coconut milk, water and tamarind water, lemon grass and season with salt. Bring to the boil, cover, reduce the heat and simmer gently for 1 hour until the mutton is tender.

Add the halved new potatoes, bring to the boil, then reduce the heat, cover and simmer gently for a further 30 minutes, until the potatoes are soft. Serve with steamed rice and a green side-vegetable such as spinach cooked with garlic.

Lamb, Leek and Apricot Tagine

Serves 4

A simple, North African inspired tagine, especially good if made a day or so in advance to allow time for the flavours to develop. The dried apricots give a lovely sweetness to the dish. Serve it with buttery, steamed couscous or basmati rice.

1 tbsp sunflower oil
2 leeks, finely sliced
1 cinnamon stick
500 g (1 lb 2 oz) lamb neck fillet, sliced
½ tsp ground ginger
½ tsp ground cinnamon
pinch of saffron threads, ground
1 tbsp tomato purée
500 ml (18 fl oz) chicken or vegetable stock
salt and freshly ground pepper
115 g (4 oz) organic, unsulphured dried apricots

Heat the oil in a heavy-based casserole dish. Add the leeks and cinnamon stick and fry gently for 5 minutes. Add the lamb and fry until browned on all sides. Sprinkle over the ground ginger, ground cinnamon and saffron. Mix in the tomato purée and pour in the stock. Season with salt and freshly ground pepper.

Bring to the boil, cover, reduce the heat and simmer for 1 hour, until the lamb is tender. Add in the dried apricots and simmer for a further 30 minutes.

A Taste of Middle Eastern London

The diverse strands of Middle Eastern cuisine, identified by Egyptian food writer Claudia Roden as Persian, Arab, Ottoman Turkish and North African, can all be found in London. A focal point for the city's Middle Eastern community is the bustling stretch of Edgware Road, between Marble Arch and the Marylebone Flyover. Here, and in its side-streets, one finds bars doing a roaring trade in fresh fruit juices and shawarma, homely Iranian cafés and glamorous, glitzy Lebanese restaurants serving mezze and grilled meat. Here too is an array of Middle Eastern food shops, including Green Valley, a smart, spacious food retailer complete with its own bread oven at the back of the shop and a mouth-watering display of pistachio-dusted baklava in the window.

TURNIP PICKLES
£4.25/KG

Wild Boar and Prune Casserole

Serves 4

Borough Market and London's farmers' markets offer a chance to buy less familiar meats, including a wide range of furred and feathered game. Wild boar, with its rich, gamey flavour can be found at, among other places, Sillfield Farm's stall at Borough Market.

900 g (2 lb) diced wild boar
1 onion, peeled and chopped
1 carrot, chopped
1 celery stick, chopped
3-4 juniper berries, crushed
1 bay leaf
2 sprigs of thyme
500 ml (18 fl oz) red wine
2 tbsp olive oil
1 tbsp tomato purée
salt and freshly ground pepper
1 garlic clove, peeled and crushed
6 shallots, peeled
250 g (9 oz) ready-to-eat, pitted prunes

First, marinate the boar. Place the boar, onion, carrot, celery, juniper berries, bay leaf and thyme sprigs in a large bowl. Pour over the red wine and marinate overnight or for a good few hours in the refrigerator.

Drain the boar, reserving the red wine marinade, juniper berries and herbs, but discarding the onion, carrot and celery.

Preheat the oven to Gas 5/190°C/375°F.

Heat the olive oil in a heavy-based casserole dish. Fry the wild boar until browned on all sides. Mix in the tomato purée and add the reserved red wine, juniper berries and herbs from the marinade. Add the garlic and season well with salt and freshly ground pepper.

Bring to the boil, cover and cook in the oven for 1 hour. Add the shallots and prunes. Cover and cook in the oven for a further 30-40 minutes.

Pot-roast Chicken with Tarragon and Shallots
Serves 4

Choose the best chicken that you can find for this dish. It's very simple to cook, but the results are fantastically flavourful. I serve this simply with steamed basmati rice, French beans and buttered carrots.

12 shallots, peeled
1 x 1.4 kg (2 lb 14 oz) free-range, corn-fed chicken
25 g/1 oz butter
1 tbsp olive oil
100 ml Madeira wine
juice of 1 lemon
2 garlic cloves, peeled
4-6 sprigs of fresh tarragon
salt and freshly ground pepper

Preheat the oven to gas 5/190°C/375°F.

Blanch the shallots for 5 minutes in a pan of boiling water; drain.

Season the chicken with salt and freshly ground pepper. Heat the butter and olive oil in a large, heavy-based casserole dish. When the butter is frothing add the chicken and brown evenly on all sides.

Add the Madeira wine, lemon juice, garlic and tarragon sprigs. Place the shallots in the casserole dish around the chicken. Cover and cook in the oven for 1 hour 15 minutes, until cooked through. Remove the chicken to a serving plate and surround it with the shallots and whole garlic cloves (sucking each garlic clove from its skin is one of the best bits of this dish). Spoon the casserole juices into a bowl and serve them, as they are, as a gravy.

Steven's Coffee Chocolate Mousse Cake
Makes 1 cake

4 rounded dsp plus 1 tsp Union Hand-Roasted Revelation Blend or
  Organic Natural Spirit coffee
185 g (6 1/2 oz) self-raising flour
30 g (1 1/4 oz) Green and Black's cocoa powder
250 g (9 oz) unsalted butter
280 ml (9 1/2 fl oz) cherry brandy, cassis, or crème de framboise
95 g (3 1/3 oz) caster sugar
95 g (3 1/3 oz) dark cane sugar
3 x 100 g (3 1/2 oz) Green and Black's dark chocolate (85%), broken into pieces
2 large free-range eggs, lightly beaten
250 g (9 oz) fresh berries (such as raspberries, blueberries, blackberries or stoned cherries)
icing sugar, for sifting
Ben & Jerry's Cherry Garcia ice cream, to serve

Preheat the oven to Gas 4/180°C/350°F. Butter a 22 cm (9 in) spring-form cake tin and line with baking parchment.

Prepare the coffee by placing four rounded dessertspoons of Union Revelation coffee in an 8-cup cafetière. Let the kettle come off the boil for a few seconds, wet the grounds evenly then top up. Give it 4 minutes then plunge.

Sift together the flour and cocoa powder into a large mixing bowl. Put the butter, liqueur, sugars, chocolate and brewed coffee in a heavy saucepan and stir over a low heat until everything has melted and is rich and glossy.

Stir this mix into the sifted flour and cocoa powder. Beat until smooth, stir in a teaspoonful of Union Revelation ground coffee, add the eggs and continue beating. This gives a very runny mixture but the chocolate sets the mix during the baking.

Pour enough of the mixture into the prepared tin to cover the base of the tin, add the berries then pour the rest of the mix on top. Place into the oven and bake for 40-45 minutes until the top is firm and very slightly cracked.

Place the cake on a rack to cool slightly, carefully turn out, then sift icing sugar over the top. Serve with Ben & Jerry's Cherry Garcia ice cream.

> ## *Sometimes I'll have that craving – I've got to have some home-made cake!"*
>
> *Steven Macatonia*

Steven Macatonia, Roastmaster at Union Hand-Roasters, has something of a sweet tooth. When friends come round for dinner, he says "Everyone expects that I'll serve ice cream for dessert, because I'm such an ice cream addict, but I like to serve this cake as coffee and chocolate are a great combination. I find cooking relaxing and I do lots of baking, though you've got have time and be in the right mood. Sometimes I'll have that craving – I've got to have some home-made cake!"

The recipe is derived from Nigella Lawson's *How to Eat* cookbook. "I've increased the coffee intensity, using a full 8-cup cafetière of our Revelation Blend and stirring in a teaspoonful of ground coffee into the mix," explains Steven. "Revelation is our deepest roast, which I've dedicated to those who believe in dessert. Nigella Lawson recommends eating this cake when still warm at blood heat which I agree with, particularly with Ben & Jerry's ice cream. But on the rare occasions when there's been some left over, I store it overnight in the fridge where the frothiness compacts down becoming dense and deep, like truffle."

The Greengrocer's Story

The Clocktower Store in Crouch End hums quietly with activity – at the front ripe nectarines are being carefully arranged for display while customers stand with baskets, choosing from the colourful display of fresh fruit and vegetables on offer: picking a punnet of raspberries, selecting small new potatoes, adding bunches of green leafy spinach to their shopping.

The Clocktower Store, 52 The Broadway, N8

"My best friend's father set up the shop about 25 years ago. I worked here and took over it five years ago" says Chris Kyriacou. "I have an early start six days a week. I get up at 3.30am, get to New Spitalfields Market up at Leyton by 4.15am, spend four hours there buying and loading. I've got a big van and I fill it up every day. Get to the shop around 9am-9.30am, help the boys finish setting up here. I try to leave at around 3pm or 4 pm. I try to have a bit of a life as well. We've got a big fridge at the back where everything's stored. It's fresh every day. I buy a little more on Thursday and Friday for the weekend. The market's closed on Sunday. If I find something nice I'll get it, so today I got 40 boxes of peaches, 20 boxes of melons. I taste all the stuff. There are so many different suppliers in the market; there is a lot of rubbish sold. We get stuff from all over the world. But when it's English season I try to stock it – so at the moment we've got peas, broad beans, potatoes, spring onions. We did have English strawberries but it's been a wet summer so not good for soft fruit. It's self-service, so people can pick what they like. I don't eat as much fruit as you might think. My daughter loves lychees and I found some today in the Market, so I got some for her. It's lucky that I work with my wife so we see each other."

Chris Kyriacou

Naomi's Duck
Serves 4-6

1 duck
coarse fine salt
lots of powdered ginger

Gravy:
1 tbsp plain flour
red wine
good quality apple juice
liquid from a tin of petit pois (optional)

With a new razor blade, slash carefully through the skin and fat at 2.5 cm (1 in) intervals along the top and underneath of the duck. Slash under the wings and legs and ends – all the fatty bits! Try not to cut into the meat itself.

Rub the duck all over with coarse fine salt and lots of powdered ginger. Place on a rack on a roasting pan, breast down. Let the duck remain like this at room temperature for at least 2 hours. You can prepare this the day before and refrigerate overnight, in which case, make sure to bring the duck back to room temperature.

Preheat the oven to Gas 6/200°C/400°F.

Place the duck in the roasting tin in the oven and roast for 20 minutes. Reduce the oven temperature to Gas 3/170°C/325°F. Cook the duck, still breast down, for 1 hour 15 minutes.

Turn the oven up to Gas 6/200°C/400°F. Turn the duck over, breast side up, and roast for a further 20 minutes. Remove from the oven and leave to rest for 20-30 minutes.

Meanwhile, make the gravy. Pour off the duck fat from the roasting pan. Add the flour to the pan, stirring well to mix in all the duck residue. Add in the red wine and apple juice to the consistency you like and the liquid from the petit pois, if using.

Serve the duck with the gravy.

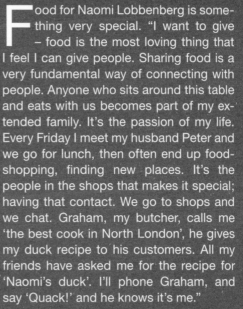

> *All my friends have asked me for the recipe for 'Naomi's duck'. I'll phone Graham, my butcher, and say 'Quack!' and he knows it's me."*
>
> Naomi Lobbenberg

Food for Naomi Lobbenberg is something very special. "I want to give – food is the most loving thing that I feel I can give people. Sharing food is a very fundamental way of connecting with people. Anyone who sits around this table and eats with us becomes part of my extended family. It's the passion of my life. Every Friday I meet my husband Peter and we go for lunch, then often end up food-shopping, finding new places. It's the people in the shops that makes it special; having that contact. We go to shops and we chat. Graham, my butcher, calls me 'the best cook in North London', he gives my duck recipe to his customers. All my friends have asked me for the recipe for 'Naomi's duck'. I'll phone Graham, and say 'Quack!' and he knows it's me."

261

Patricia's Home-made Ricotta

Makes 450 g (1 lb)

Patricia Michelson's passion for cheese led her to found La Fromagerie, her famous cheese shop, which now has two branches, one in Highbury and one in Marylebone. The cheese counters in both shops offer a discriminating selection of farmhouse cheeses from Britain, France, Ireland and Italy.

3 ltr (5 ¼ pt) organic full-fat milk
170 ml (6 fl oz) organic double cream
80 ml (3 fl oz) fresh lemon juice
a pinch of fine sea salt, optional

The cheese must be made in one session from start to finish – count on about 1 ½ hours, although much of this time is semi-unattended cooking. You should be in the kitchen, but you needn't be hovering over the stove. The recipe may seem daunting in its detail, but it is really quite easy. Because cheesemaking is unfamiliar to many, the instructions lead through the process step by step.

Stir together all the ingredients except the salt in a heavy saucepan with a non-reactive interior. Set the pan on a heat-diffusing pad over a medium-low heat. Cook for 40 minutes, or until the milk reaches 77°C/170°F on an instant-reading thermometer. Keep the heat at medium low. To keep the curd large, do not stir more than 3-4 times. If you lift it with the spatula, you will see sand-like particles of milk forming as the clear whey begins to separate from the curd. As the milk comes close to 77°C/170°F, the curds will be slightly large. When the temperature reaches 77°C/170°F turn the heat up to medium. Do not stir. Take 6-8 minutes to bring the mixture to 96°C/205°F at the centre of the pot. The liquid whey will be almost clear. By the time the cheese comes to 96°C/205°F the curd should mound on the spatula like a soft white custard. At this temperature the liquid will be on the verge of boiling, with the surface looking like mounds about to erupt. Turn off the heat and let the cheese stand for 10 minutes.

Line a colander with a double thickness of dampened muslin cheesecloth. Turn the mixture into it, and let it drain for 15 minutes or until the drained cheese is thick. Turn the cheese into a covered storage container, add the salt (optional), and refrigerate until needed. Use the whey for making muffins or feed to your cat or dog.

"Now we have access to fresh milk thanks to farmers' markets, we can make fresh cheese, like our grandmothers did. You can serve this ricotta as a savoury dish, with grated lemon or some finely chopped chilli, or baked, or use it to make a cheesecake, served with strawberries."

Patricia Michelson

La Fromagerie

Discreetly positioned down a secluded Marylebone side-street, Patricia Michelson's rustically elegant La Fromagerie is a food shop to be savoured. Carefully sourced, artisan cheeses from France, Italy, Britain and Ireland form the core of the shop, arrayed on shelves in a separate, temperature-controlled cheese room. Shoppers can also choose from fresh seasonal produce such as Amalfi lemons, pale pink Yorkshire rhubarb, quinces, charcuterie and fine oils or simply sit in the tasting café and sample dishes freshly made in the kitchen downstairs.

It was a small piece of Beaufort cheese which started Patricia on the journey that led to La Fromagerie's creation. While skiing in France in 1990, Patricia had a bad day coming down the mountain, getting lost in the snow but eventually managing to make her way down. "I was so tired and depressed," recalls Patricia, "and as I made my way through the village I passed a cheese shop – called La Fromagerie – and bought a little piece of Beaufort cheese with my last few francs. All that evening I kept thinking how amazing it was that something as simple as a piece of cheese can lift your spirits and make you feel good again." The next day Patricia tracked down the cheese-maker in the local market and asked if she could buy some of his cheese. "He offered to deliver it and when he came I found he'd brought a whole wheel, not just a piece of cheese; it cost a fortune! We put it in the car next to our children and drove home. What to do with the cheese was the question? I put it in my garden shed and starting inviting people round for cheese and wine parties."

Patricia enterprisingly set about importing more French cheeses and started a home-delivery service. "Cheese is something I'd always loved. I've always enjoyed the cheese course in restaurants when the waiter brings over the trolley and explains what's on it. The sense of theatre about it really appeals to me. I still use my cheese-tasting notes from those days; I always wanted people to know about the cheese they were tasting." Her next step was a stall at Camden Lock. "Ladies from Hampstead used to come down to buy their cheeses from me on a Saturday morning, before the market got busy." From there, Patricia opened her first shop in Highbury, "a lovely, little place, decorated with artefacts raided from my own home. It was an instant success. I was open six days a week and delivering at night." From there, Patricia expanded to a second, larger Highbury shop, which she still has to this day.

The move to Marylebone came about with an approach from Howard de Walden Estates. "Two men in suits came into the shop," recalls Patricia, "and asked 'How would you like to have a shop in Marylebone?' I loved the idea." Despite the sceptics who thought the shop would never work in a small side street La Fromagerie has gone from strength to strength. The shop's success has encouraged a farmers' market and organic butchers to establish themselves here and has helped put Moxon Street on the culinary map.

La Fromagerie, 2-4 Moxon Street, W1 & 30 Highbury Park, N5

Beef Pie
Serves 4

I have a great weakness for pies. This recipe combines a flavourful steak filling with a flaky puff pastry topping – irresistible. Pies have long been a characteristic aspect of British cuisine, popular traditional fillings included venison, game and steak. "The itinerant trade in pies is of the most ancient of the street callings of London," wrote Henry Mayhew in 1851, "The meat pies are made of beef or mutton; the fish pie of eels; the fruit of apples, currants, gooseberries, plums, damsons, cherries, raspberries, or rhubarb, according to the season – and occasionally of mince-meat." One classic English pie is the pork pie, traditionally made in Melton Mowbray in Leicestershire where it gained popularity as a handy picnic food with the local aristocratic hunts. A perennially popular comfort food, pies today are also positively fashionable, featuring on smart restaurant menus and found on market stalls and at good butchers.

2 tbsp olive oil
1 onion, peeled, halved and chopped into semi-circles
2 leeks, chopped
1 celery stick, chopped
2-3 sprigs of thyme
700 g (1 ½ lb) diced braising steak
generous glug of Madeira
1 tbsp tomato purée
300 ml (½ pt) good beef stock
few drops of Worcestershire sauce
salt and freshly ground pepper
4 carrots, peeled, halved lengthways and cut into 5 cm (2 in) pieces
4 tbsp chopped parsley
sprinkle of sugar
300 g (10 oz) puff pastry
milk, for glazing

Heat the olive oil in a casserole dish. Add the onion, leeks, celery and thyme and fry gently until softened and fragrant. Add the steak and fry until browned on all sides.

Pour over the Madeira and allow to bubble for 1-2 minutes. Mix in the tomato purée, then add the stock and Worcestershire sauce. Season with salt and freshly ground pepper and add the carrot, parsley and sugar. Bring to the boil, reduce the heat, cover and simmer for 1 hour, stirring now and then, until the meat is tender. Set aside to cool thoroughly.

Preheat the oven to Gas 6/200°C/400°F.

Fill a 1 ½ ltr (2 pt 14 fl oz) pie dish with the beef mixture. Finely roll out the puff pastry and use it to cover the dish with a pastry lid, cutting a slash in the centre. Brush lightly with milk to glaze it and bake for 30-40 minutes until the pastry is golden.

Mrs Elizabeth King's stall at Borough Market

The Story of Neal's Yard Dairy

Founded in 1979, at a time when British farmhouse cheeses were struggling to find a market, Neal's Yard Dairy has played a pivotal part in championing British farmhouse cheeses, introducing traditional cheeses such as clothbound Somerset Cheddars as well as new cheeses like Beensleigh Blue and Tymsboro to a larger audience. Randolph Hodgson's involvement with Neal's Yard Dairy goes back to its origins. In a small courtyard in Covent Garden – which, following the closure of the old Covent Garden Market was then a run-down, sleepy place – Nicholas Saunders set up Neal's Yard, a bakery and a wholefood warehouse and a dairy. "I was a food science student and Nicholas wanted someone to make Greek yoghurt, so I helped and then started to work there," explains Randolph. "Quite soon Nicholas decided to move on and I had a chance to take over the dairy, which at the time wasn't making any money. I had become fascinated by cheese and decided that as well as making our own we would get more cheeses. Hilary Charnley had sent us a sample of her Devon Garland – a lovely cheese – so I decided that I'd go and visit her. The idea that other people were out there making cheese too was inspiring. I visited Hilary and discovered that once you start driving around the country and talking to cheesemakers, you find other cheesemakers."

Randolph (then, in his own words, "a dishevelled, long-haired young man from London, driving an old, battered blue van")

continued tracking down cheesemakers, such as Caerphilly producer Chris Duckett, and stocking their cheeses. Visiting the cheesemakers directly gave Randolph a chance to learn more about the cheeses and how they were made and should be stored and ripened. "The thing that struck me was that we didn't know as much about the other cheeses that we were selling. We knew about the soft cheeses we were making, like Perroche, and so had more to say. Our whole style of selling came from that realisation."

From those early days and that long learning process, Randolph has developed Neal's Yard Dairy into a major cheese retailer and wholesaler, selling cheeses abroad as well as in the UK. Neal's Yard Dairy enjoys a close relationship with the cheesemakers whose cheeses it stocks. "The cheesemakers and I have a sense of camaraderie," explains Randolph, "because farmhouse cheese-making then was nearly extinct. Things are different now. We used to put 15 cheeses on our counters when we started, now there are nearly 100 cheeses that we'd be happy to sell."

Customers to Neal's Yard Dairy are always invited to sample the cheeses they're looking at. "It's all very well for us to be driving round the country making judgements on flavour," observes Randolph, "the real point is what the customer wants. Giving tastings means people can select on taste. People are used to trying cheeses in our shops now but originally it was an uphill struggle. People were worried they were going to be asked to have an opinion. We try and engage with people – the main aim is that the customer goes home with the cheese that they want and that they like."

Neal's Yard Dairy, 17 Shorts Garden, WC2

> *I wanted to stop cheese-buying being too pompous or intimidating. I can remember as a student being made to feel very out-of-place in a grand cheese-shop – it shouldn't be like that."*
>
> *Randolph Hodgson*
> *Neal's Yard Dairy*

A Trip to Neal's Yard Dairy

Neal's Yard Dairy's two retail shops are the public face of the company's retailing activities – the tip of the ice-berg, so to speak. Behind the scenes, Neal's Yard also run a large wholesale operation, storing and ripening a huge quantity of cheese under the railway arches in Bermondsey. Chris George of Neal's Yard Dairy explains why the site is perfect for cheese storage: "This is like a man-made cave; it's quite hard to find a natural cave in the centre of London, so this is the closest we can come to it. Above us it's all red brick, which makes it damp and humid in here. Most people store cheese in a fridge, but the fridge is too cold and too dry." The 70 artisanal cheeses stocked here vary enormously, from young, soft rind cheeses to hard-pressed blue cheeses several months old. Different atmospheres are required for the various cheeses at different stages of development, with four walk-in cooling rooms – one used to dry out young cheeses with too much moisture, the warmest and most humid for washed rind cheeses, the two others for bloomy rind cheeses – and a large hard cheese room. Constant attention is required: "The soft cheeses turned twice to three times a day," says Chris, "while the Stiltons are turned once a week – it's quite labour-intensive."

Storing and ripening the stock requires an understanding of the intricacies of how cheese is formed and ripens. Milk, naturally, is the starting point. "These are artisanal cheeses and we know the source of the milk," explains Chris. "It's a better guarantee of quality. Different breeds of cattle produce different milks. What you want is milk with a level of fats and proteins. The thing about cheese is that you can't make good cheese from bad milk. Salt's a very important ingredient in cheese-making," he adds, "it brings out the flavour and is a preserving agent and inhibits the starter cultures that you need but want to control."

Bacteria, however, are key to the transformative and ripening process. "Lots of great foods – cheese, bread, wine, need bacteria – the right sort," observes Chris. "Lots of English cheese-makers use Penicillum camemberti, but Geotrichum candidum, that's my favourite mould," Chris laughs, "How sad is that, having a favourite mould, but different moulds give you different flavours. Geotrichum can be tricky to get right but produces some wonderful complex flavours, while the B. linens bacteria creates flavours that are much earthier and meatier, like mushrooms and smoked bacon. The mould makes the cheese soft and runny; it's an integral part of the cheese. Lots of people when they see a mouldy cheese think 'yuk'. When we see mould here, especially a different mould, we think 'let's taste it'."

Neal's Yard work closely with the cheese-makers themselves, offering advice, feedback and the willingness to accept the variables that artisanal cheese-making throws up. "In the milk used for a cheese, minute variations will be amplified through time. If you have 1000 litres of milk and you muck it up, that's a lot of money. Even changing the mills for the curd can affect the cheese. When you take out all the variables, you get standardisation. We're willing to take a variation."

In the hard cheese room, Chris explains that "the rinds on these cheeses for the most part are protective; you're trying to seal moisture in, but not to suffocate it, we want to concentrate the flavour. Look at that, he enthuses, "this is such a characteristic of English cheeses – cloth-binding signals English cheese, so characteristic of British cheeses like Cheddar, Lancashire, Cheshire – very much the tradition." Neal's Yard stocks magnificent Cheddars, each about 50 lb in weight, hand-made the traditional way by Somerset Cheddar makers, using unpasteurised milk and animal rennet. The flavour and texture of the resulting cheese is very different from mass-produced Cheddar. "People are often really surprised when they try our Cheddars," observes Chris, "they have such a strong preconceived idea of Cheddar." Stored in this room, too, are the Colston Bassett Stiltons, made to Neal's Yard Dairy's specifications using an animal rennet. "We look for a creamy balanced Stilton," explains Chris, "you can overdo the penicillum roqueforti. It should be like a blue ice cream. This stuff has to be cut very carefully by hand – the more you handle it the tougher it gets. These are great cheeses. Stilton varies more than any other cheese. In the weeks before Christmas the first job at 5am in the morning is to try the Stiltons – dividing them into 'eat now', 'eat on Christmas Day' and 'eat on New Year's Day'."

Our priority is taste – that's the philosophy of the Dairy", says Chris. "In the shops the staff are always trying the cheese. Customers ask 'Don't you get told off for eating the cheese?' I say. 'We get told off it we DON'T eat the cheese.'"

Chris George
Neal's Yard Dairy

Celebrations

Naomi's Lamb and Apricots with Spiced Rice
(Serves 6-8)

Christmas and Passover in the Lobbenberg household are celebrated with much feasting a fact that will come to no surprise to those who know Naomi and Peter. Anna, their daughter, is closely involved in companionably helping Naomi with the preparation and cooking of these celebratory meals. This recipe, inspired by Claudia Roden, is one that Naomi serves for Passover.

4 Spanish onions, peeled and chopped
1 head of garlic, cloves peeled and chopped
olive oil
salt and freshly ground pepper
2 cinnamon sticks
1 large bunch of fresh coriander, chopped
splash of white wine
500g (1 lb 2 oz) unsulphured dried apricots
a strip of fresh orange zest
1 leg of lamb (with bone)

Spiced rice:
450 g (1 lb) basmati rice
salt
4-6 cardamom pods
1 tbsp fennel seeds
1 tbsp cumin seeds
3-4 cinnamon sticks
lots of butter

Spring vegetable broth:
600 ml (1 pt) Vegetable broth, to cover
1 jar of broad beans, drained
1 jar of white beans, drained
1 jar of small artichokes, drained
1 jar of extra fin petit pois
handful of finely chopped parsley
handful of finely chopped coriander
handful of finely chopped spring onions
handful of finely chopped mint

Slowly sauté the onion and garlic in olive oil in a large casserole dish until soft and fragrant. Season with salt and freshly ground pepper, break up the cinnamon sticks and add to the casserole, along with the coriander, a splash of white wine, the dried apricots and orange zest. Stew slowly for 20 minutes.

Meanwhile, brown the leg of lamb on all sides in plenty of olive oil in a large heavy frying pan. Season well with salt and freshly ground pepper. Place the lamb on top of the apricot mixture, cover with a lid or foil and bake for 4 hours.

To prepare the accompanying spiced rice, cook the basmati rice in lots of salted boiling water for 7 minutes; drain.

Heat the cardamom pods, fennel seeds, cumin seeds, coriander seeds and cinnamon pods in a heavy-based frying pan to release the perfume.

Layer the drained rice, assorted spices and plenty of butter in a heavy-based casserole dish. Cover the rice with a tea-towel, then cover the casserole. Bake at Gas 4/350°F/180°C for 30 minutes.

To make the spring vegetable broth, bring the vegetable stock to a rolling boil. Add the broad beans, white beans, artichokes and the petit pois (together with their liquid) and simmer briefly to heat through. Remove from direct heat and stir in the parsley, coriander, spring onion and mint.

Serve the roast lamb and apricots with the spiced rice and spring vegetable broth.

LOBBENGRUB

Syllabub Trifle
Serves 8-10

A much-loved, traditional English dessert, the trifle is a lovely way to round off a meal. There are many, many variations, but this recipe returns to its historic roots by using a tipsy syllabub as a topping.

4 trifle sponges
2 tbsp Amontillado sherry
2 passion fruit
300 g (10 oz) raspberries
2 ripe bananas
crystallised rose petals, to serve

Syllabub topping:
100 ml (3 1/2 fl oz) Amontillado sherry
2 tbsp brandy
zest and juice of 1 lemon
50 g (2 oz) caster sugar
300 ml (1/2 pt) double cream

Custard:
400 ml (14 fl oz) milk
4 free-range egg yolks
1 heaped tsp cornflour
100 g (3 1/2 oz) caster sugar
1/2 tsp vanilla extract

First make the syllabub. Place the sherry, brandy, lemon zest and juice and caster sugar in a bowl, stirring until the sugar has dissolved. Cover and refrigerate overnight. Transfer to a mixing bowl, add the cream and whisk until the cream becomes light and fluffy. Cover and chill until using.

Make the custard. In a heavy-based saucepan, bring the milk almost to the boil. Meanwhile, in a mixing bowl, whisk together the egg yolks, cornflour and caster sugar until pale and thickened. Gradually, stir in the hot milk, mixing together well.

Return the yolk mixture to the heavy-based pan and, over a very low heat, cook for around 5 minutes, stirring constantly, until the mixture thickens into a creamy-textured custard. Stir in the vanilla extract; allow to cool, cover and chill in the refrigerator.

To assemble the trifle, layer the trifle sponges in the base of a deep serving dish and sprinkle over the sherry. Slice the passion fruit in half and scoop out the flesh over the sponges. Top with the raspberries, then peel and slice the bananas and layer over the raspberries. Spoon over the chilled custard, then top with the chilled syllabub. Cover and chill until serving. Decorate with crystallised rose petals and serve.

Blinis
Serves 4-6

For a splendid meal try these small buckwheat pancakes, classically served with soured cream and caviar and accompanied by ice-cold vodka.

1 tsp sugar
300 ml (½ pt) hand-hot milk
1 tsp dried yeast
150 g (5 oz) plain white flour
75 g (3 oz) buckwheat flour
1 tsp salt
40 g (1 ½ oz) butter, melted
2 free-range eggs, separated

Suggested accompaniments:
smoked salmon with lemon wedges
soured cream topped with finely chopped chives or dill
smoked trout
caviar, salmon roe or lumpfish roe
beetroot salad
assorted pickled herrings
ice-cold vodka (such as Polish buffalo grass vodka), to serve

Mix the sugar into the hand-hot milk. Sprinkle the yeast over the milk, stir briefly and set aside to stand in a warm spot for 10-15 minutes until a frothy head forms.

Sift the white flour, buckwheat flour and salt into a warmed mixing bowl. Pour in the yeast mixture, add the egg yolks and whisk together to form a thick smooth batter. Stir in the melted butter. Cover and set aside for 1 hour.

Whisk the egg whites until stiff. Gently fold the stiff egg whites into the batter with a metal spoon.

Lightly oil a large frying pan or griddle pan and heat until very hot. Fry the blinis in batches, using a generous tablespoon of buckwheat batter for each one. Fry the blinis until small bubbles appear on the surface and the edges darken, then turn over and lightly brown the other side. Remove to a warmed plate and repeat the process until all the batter has been used up, making around 24 blinis. Serve at once with some or all of the suggested accompaniments.

Roast Goose with Quince and Apple Sauce
Serves 6

1 x 4.5 kg goose, with neck and giblets
1 head of garlic, sliced across
1 bunch of thyme
salt and freshly ground pepper
1 onion, peeled and chopped
1 carrot, chopped
1 bay leaf
a handful of parsley
1 celery stalk, chopped
1 glass of Madeira
1 tbsp red currant jelly

Quince and apple sauce:
1 quince
1 cooking apple
a squeeze of lemon juice
water
1-2 tbsp sugar

Preheat the oven to Gas 6/190°C/400°F.

Remove the neck and giblets from the goose and reserve them for the gravy stock. Place the halved garlic head and thyme inside the goose cavity. Lightly prick the skin of the goose all over with a fork. Season generously with salt and freshly ground pepper.

Place the goose on a rack over a deep roasting tray, cover with foil and roast in the oven for 3 hours. Every half hour or so, spoon off the goose fat that collects in the roasting tray. Remove the foil for the last half hour of roasting, basting the goose with its own fat. Transfer the roast goose to a warm serving plate, loosely cover with foil and let it rest in a warm place for 20-25 minutes.

While the goose is roasting, make the stock for the gravy. Place the goose neck and giblets in a pan with the onion, carrot, bay leaf, parsley and celery. Add 900 ml (1 $\frac{1}{2}$ pt) water, bring to the boil, skim off any scum, reduce the heat and simmer for 1 hour. Strain and use for the gravy.

To make the quince and apple sauce, peel, core and finely chop the fruit, placing the chopped quince in water acidulated with a squeeze of lemon juice to prevent it browning.

Place the chopped quince in a heavy-based pan with a splash of its lemon water. Cover and cook gently for 10 minutes, until soft enough to break up easily with a wooden spoon.

Meanwhile, peel and chop the cooking apple. Add it to the softened quince, along with another splash of water. Cover and cook for 10 minutes until the apple has softened. Beat together the quince and apple to form a purée. Mix in the sugar. Set aside to cool and serve at room temperature.

While the goose is resting, make the gravy. Heat the roasting tray on the stove and add a glass of Madeira, stirring well to scrape up all the roasting residues. Add the goose stock, stir in a tablespoon of red currant jelly and season with salt and freshly ground pepper.

Carve the goose and serve it, with the quince and apple sauce, gravy and potatoes roasted in goose fat.

Goose, the largest domestic fowl apart from turkey, was for a long time eaten on special feast days, including Michaelmas on September 29th and Christmas, but fell out of fashion. Today, thankfully, there's a resurgence of interest in eating goose, catered for by producers such as Seldom Seen Farm and Goodman's Geese. With its distinctively flavoured rich flesh, it is indeed a real treat. If you haven't cooked a goose before, the copious amounts of fat that come off it during roasting can be something of a shock. Simply spoon out the fat during the roasting process and set it aside, where as it cools it thickens and whitens. This treasure trove of fat is, as the French appreciate, a wonderful cooking medium. Store it in the fridge and use for cooking – roast potatoes cooked in goose fat are memorably good.

Seldom Seen Farm, Borough Market

Gastronomic Institutions

Fortnum & Mason

81 Piccadilly, London W1A
Tel: 020 7734 8040
Founded as a grocer's shop in 1707, this splendid emporium on Piccadilly continues to trade in style.

Paxton & Whitfield

93 Jermyn Street, London SW1Y
Tel: 020 7930 0259
A venerable cheesemongers, which can trace its history selling cheese to the gentry back to 1797.

Berry Bros & Rudd

3 St James's Street
St James's, London SW1A
Tel: 020 7396 9600
Britain's oldest wine and spirit merchant was founded in 1698 and it still trades from its original, atmospheric premises. Customers over the centuries have included the great and the good, such as Lord Byron, William Pitt and Louis Napoleon of France.

Allen & Co

117 Mount Street, Mayfair, W1K
Tel: 020 7499 5831
Founded in 1830 in the heart of Mayfair, Allen & Co is Britain's oldest butcher still operating on its original site. Complete with tiled walls, a magnificent wooden chopping block and knowledgeable, helpful staff, it is noted for its prime meat and poultry.

Books For Cooks

4 Blenheim Crescent, Notting Hill, W11
Tel: 020 7221 1992
Established in 1983, this much-loved specialist cookery bookshop in Notting Hill appetisingly features a huge range of food-related books as well as a testing kitchen, enabling customers to sample recipes.

Laila's Special Bread and Butter Pudding

Serves 8-10

I cook anything and everything," says Laila Nazira. "If I want traditional Gujurati food, I'll ask my sister to make it for me. My kids like my food and it's important to me to cook for my children. I rarely follow recipes from cookbooks; I use them for inspiration and also learn from my friends. I enjoy cooking and entertaining is my passion. I love cooking for lots of people." Laila's bread and butter pudding is her signature dish, much enjoyed by her family and friends and always requested for celebrations such as Christmas and New Year. "This is the first time I've shared this recipe with anyone," explains Laila, "my friends are really surprised, but I've decided to share it with the world."

1 large loaf thickly sliced white bread, preferably a couple of days old
unsalted spreadable butter, for spreading
225-250 g (8-9 oz) Demerara sugar
115-175 g (4-6 oz) currants
600 ml (1 pt) double cream
300 ml (½ pt) UHT longlife semi-skimmed milk
2 large free-range eggs
2 tbsp vanilla extract
½ tsp freshly grated or ground nutmeg
200 ml (7 fl oz) Bailey's original liqueur
fresh vanilla custard, to serve

Generously butter a 4 litre (7 pt) ovenproof dish. Lightly butter the bread slices on both sides, trim off the crusts and cut into triangles.

Place a layer of the bread triangles in the ovenproof dish, slightly overlapping them, then sprinkle with Demerara sugar and a scattering of currants. Repeat this process until all the bread has been used.

In a jug blender, blend together the double cream, milk, eggs, vanilla extract, 200 g (7 oz) Demerara sugar, nutmeg and Bailey's until the mixture looks frothy.

Pour the blended mixture slowly and gently over the bread, starting at the centre and making sure that the mixture goes down right to the bottom. Use a wide wooden spoon to press gently down on the top layer to make sure that it is well-covered by the mixture too. Set aside to soak for at least two hours.

Preheat the oven to Gas 4/180°C/325°F. Place the bread and butter pudding in the middle of the oven and reduce the oven temperature to Gas 2/150°C/300°F. Bake for 45 minutes to 1 hour until golden-brown. Check if the pudding is cooked through by poking a skewer in the centre; if it comes out clean, then the pudding is ready. Serve with fresh vanilla custard.

"This is the first time I've shared this recipe with anyone, my friends are really surprised, but I've decided to share it with the world."

Laila Nazira

Raspberry Pavlova
Serves 8

A scrumptious and attractive dessert, this is great for dinner parties as the meringue base can be made in advance (ideally overnight), with the pavlova quickly and easily assembled just before serving.

3 free-range egg whites
175 g (6 oz) caster sugar
1/2 tsp vanilla extract
300 ml (1/2 pt) double cream
2 passion fruit
250 g (9 oz) raspberries
8 physalis, husks peeled back (optional)

Preheat the oven to Gas 1/140°C/275°F.

Place the egg whites in a large, clean mixing bowl and whisk until stiff, ideally using an electric beater. Gradually fold in the caster sugar, whisking after each addition until the sugar is absorbed. Whisk in the vanilla extract.

Spread the meringue mixture into a circular shape on a baking sheet lined with baking parchment. Bake the meringue for 1 hour, then leave to cool in the oven, ideally overnight.

Assemble the pavlova just before serving. Whip the cream until fluffy. Spread it over the centre of the meringue circle, leaving a rim of meringue around the edges. Cut the passion fruit into half and scoop out the flesh over the cream. Top with raspberries, dot with physalis and serve.

Michael's Torta de Cenora
Serves 8

"In Portugal we use ingredients like sweet potatoes and beans in our cakes. A lot of Japanese cakes were introduced by the Portuguese," explains Michael. "The Portuguese love desserts with carrot."

500 g (1lb 2 oz) carrots, peeled and sliced
salt
4 free-range eggs separated
325 g (11 oz) caster sugar
1 orange, zest and juice
130 g (4 ½ oz) plain flour

Boil the carrots in salted water until extremely soft. Drain and rinse in cold water, then either mash thoroughly with a potato masher or purée with a hand blender.

Preheat the oven to Gas 4/180°C/350°F.

In a mixing bowl, beat the egg yolks and the caster sugar until the sugar has dissolved, but not until pale and fluffy. Mix in the orange zest and juice followed by the cold carrot purée and the flour.

In separate bowl, whisk the egg whites until they form soft peaks. Fold the whisked egg whites lightly into the carrot mixture.

Line a buttered Swiss roll tin with greaseproof paper; butter and lightly flour this too.

Spread the carrot mixture evenly in the tin and bake for about 12-15 minutes in the oven. Do not overcook; the top should still be quite moist.

Sprinkle caster sugar on a clean tea towel and turn the torte on to it. Roll it immediately and place it on a serving platter. Let it cool for about 2-3 hours. Serve as dessert with some whipped or clotted cream on the side or simply eat on its own.

N J's Courgette, Basil and Feta Soufflé
Serves 2

450 g (1 lb) courgettes
salt and freshly ground pepper
olive oil
75 g (3 oz) feta cheese
25 g (1 oz) basil leaves
zest of a lemon
good squeeze of lemon juice
salad of rocket, toasted hazelnuts and a little
* feta, dressed with lemon and oil, to serve*
warm bread (preferably home-baked) to serve

Béchamel:
55g (2 oz) butter
2 level tbsp plain flour
150 ml (¼ pt) milk
2 free-range egg yolks
3 free-range egg whites
salt and freshly ground pepper

Preheat the oven to Gas 4/180°C/350°F. Butter a 1.3 ltr (2 ¼ pt) soufflé dish and put it in the fridge.

Slice the courgettes on the bias and put them in a colander, salt them and put a weight on the top for an hour. After an hour, squeeze the courgettes in your hands to get rid of the excess moisture and put them in a heavy-bottomed pan over a low heat with a slick of olive oil and cook with the lid on until soft, about 30 minutes, stirring now and then to make sure they don't catch.

Put the cooked courgettes in a blender with the feta, basil, lemon zest and a good squeeze of lemon juice. Blend until you have a smooth purée.

Make the béchamel. Melt the butter in a thick-based saucepan, whisk in the flour, cook briefly and stir in the milk. Cook, stirring, until the mixture thickens. Remove the béchamel from the heat. Add the egg yolks, one by one, to the slightly cooled béchamel sauce, stirring in thoroughly.

In a large bowl, mix together the courgette purée and béchamel sauce. In a separate bowl, whisk the egg whites until peaky but not super-stiff.

Quickly fold the egg whites into the mixture in three parts with a metal spoon, being careful not to lose too much air.

Tip the whole thing into the soufflé dish and put it in centre of the oven with the utmost haste you can muster without burning yourself. Don't be tempted to take it out or open the oven door until after 25-30 minutes.

Serve at once with a salad of rocket, toasted hazelnuts and a little feta, dressed with lemon and oil, and warm bread, preferably home-baked.

> # "It's a romantic recipe, a dish for two."
>
> *N J Stephenson*

Taking "lovely fresh vegetables" and "really good ingredients" as her starting point, N J draws culinary inspiration from her collection of cookbooks from the 1960s and 1970s – "the ones with really Technicolor pictures" – and has a particular fondness for Robert Carrier. "There's a Robert Carrier recipe for onion soup with a cheese soufflé topping, it's really good, really rich," she enthuses. Soufflés are a dish N J enjoys cooking, appreciating their versatility. "I like the idea of making an effort when you cook and presenting your food as well as you can." This recipe is adapted from Elizabeth David's French Provincial Cooking. "It's a romantic recipe," says N J

> ## "
> *My idea of a meal
> would be bread,
> Parma ham, some
> olives, then two
> desserts!"*
>
> *Michael Salack*

I have to confess, I've got the sweetest tooth on earth," laughs Michael Salack. "My idea of a meal would be bread, Parma ham, some olives, then two desserts!" Michael's cookery reflects his Portuguese roots; "I lived in Portugal and we always had people coming round and family visiting; we were always cooking food. If you come to my house, I'm always feeding you." Michael's interest in food was inspired by his Portuguese Angolan mother's creative cooking. "My mother has a passion for cooking. During the 1960s she worked for Peter Sellers, Brian Epstein, Robert Carrier. As a kid I can remember hundreds of cakes," reminisces Michael. "I remember helping, beating the cream, whisking the egg whites, we were brought up around food. Our food at home was very real, not fancy, but I'd see what she'd do for catering – amazing things like a whole poached salmon, with spouts of three-coloured caviars coming out of its mouth and cucumber slices for scales."

Michael's Roulade de Frutas
Makes 1 roulade

Soft meringue:
4-5 free-range egg whites
1/2 tsp cream of tartar
a good squeeze of fresh lemon
1 tbsp of caster sugar per egg white used plus an extra one for the bowl
1 tbsp corn flour (or rice flour or plain flour)

Filling:
2-3 free-range egg yolks (you can use more if you are feeling extravagant)
2 tbsp white wine
2 heaped tbsp of caster sugar per egg yolk
1/2 tsp vanilla extract
pinch of fresh nutmeg
400 g (14 oz) any fruit of your choice (raspberries or
*   strawberries or peaches), fresh or canned*
1 x 250g tub of mascarpone cheese

Preheat the oven to Gas 3/170°C/325°F.

First make the soft meringue. With an electric mixer whisk the egg whites in a mixing bowl on a slow setting for 2-3 minutes, gradually increasing speed as you whisk in the cream of tartar and lemon juice, followed by the sugar a tablespoon at a time. Make sure that the sugar is completely whisked in. Once the egg whites are very firm and all the sugar has dissolved, whisk the flour in carefully.

Oil a Swiss roll tin and line it with baking or greaseproof paper which also needs to be oiled. Spread the meringue mixture evenly in the tin with a spatula. Bake in the oven for about 20 minutes. Do not overcook the meringue as it will be too firm to roll and may crumble. Once cooked turn the meringue onto a clean, damp tea towel, remove the greaseproof paper and allow it to cool down.

Meanwhile, prepare the filling. Whisk the egg yolks with the white wine in a bowl over hot water. Gradually whisk in the sugar. The yolks will increase in volume; this will take about 10 minutes. Once done, whisk in the vanilla essence and the nutmeg. Remove from the heat and continue to whisk the mixture with the bowl sitting in ice cold water. Leave to cool.

In a separate bowl whisk the mascarpone to soften it. Fold in the cooled egg yolk mixture to form a smooth creamy filling.

Wash and prepare the fresh fruit for the filling as needed; hulling and slicing strawberries and peeling and slicing peaches. Fold the fruit into the filling. Spread the filling over the cooled meringue and roll the meringue tightly using the tea towel. Keep for about an hour or two in the fridge still wrapped in the tea towel. Roll out on to a plate, slice and serve.

Henning's Indian Kofte with Coconut

Serves 4

"If you really want to make a delicious curry," explains Henning Marstrand, "you need to roast and grind your own spices. It's very easy – all you do is dry-roast them in a thick-based frying pan. Just be careful not to burn them or they will taste bitter; keep stirring them in the pan. When you have roasted them, let them cool and grind them up. I've got 50-60 spices in my kitchen cupboard; I go to Brick Lane to buy them. This is a recipe I've spent 15 years perfecting."

Kofte:
1 level tsp cumin seeds
4 level tsp coriander seeds
500 g (1 lb 2 oz) lean lamb mince
large pinch of salt
1 small to medium onion, chopped
2 garlic cloves, peeled and chopped
2.5 cm (1 in) piece of fresh root ginger, chopped
$\frac{1}{2}$ tsp chilli powder
olive oil, for frying
basmati rice, to serve
thick, natural yogurt, to serve

Kofte sauce:
1 level tsp brown cumin seeds
4 tsp coriander seeds
$\frac{1}{2}$ tsp black cumin seeds
2 black cardamoms (or 3 green cardamomsa)
3 whole cloves
8 cm (3 in) piece of cinnamon stick
1 medium-sized, medium-hot, fresh red chilli
1 x 400 g (14 oz) tin good quality, chopped
  plum tomatoes
$\frac{1}{2}$ cm ($\frac{1}{4}$ in) chunk of block creamed coconut
water
salt

First roast and grind the cumin and coriander seeds for the kofte. Put the lamb mince with a large pinch of salt into a mixing bowl. Add in the ground roasted cumin and coriander, onion, garlic, ginger and chilli and mix thoroughly with your hands. Some people add a little egg to the mince to bind it but it's not really needed. Now, with wet hands, take the mince mixture and shape it little balls, around 2.5 cm (1 in) in diameter. You should get around 20 balls from the mix.

Now prepare the spices for the sauce; fry and grind the brown cumin and coriander.

Heat a little oil in a large frying pan. Fry the kofte balls for 5-10 minutes on a medium heat until lightly browned and firm. Now add in the black cumin, black cardamom, cloves, cinnamon, ground cumin and coriander and chopped chilli. Fry, stirring, for a minute, then add the tin of chopped tomatoes. Fill the tomato tin half full of water and add that too. Stir so that everything blends together. Bring to the boil and then simmer on a low heat for half an hour. Check and stir occasionally. Add a little more water if the sauce reduces too much. Crumble the coconut cream into the sauce and stir in. Sprinkle with fresh coriander and serve with basmati rice and thick natural yoghurt.

Add more salt if desired.

A Taste of India

ondon's Asian communities are spread around the capital, with different communities often settling in particular parts of the city, hence Punjabi Southall, Gujurati Wembley, Bangladeshi Brick Lane and Tooting, home to a diverse Asian community with a large Tamil population.

These areas are the places to head to both for eating authentic Asian food and for shopping for Asian ingredients. Here, at remarkably reasonable prices, one can stock up with store-cupboard ingredients, from pulses and flours to spices and chutneys, to Asian vegetables, fruit and herbs. A particular delight are the sweet-fleshed Alphonso mangoes, which have a brief season from April to May.

In 1809, in a pioneering move, Sake Dean Mahomed opened Britain's first curry house, Dean Mahomed's Hindustani Coffee House at George Street in central London. Here he offered Indian dishes of the "highest perfection", planning to appeal to British people who had returned from India and had acquired a taste for Indian food. It was a bold and novel plan but failed to generate enough business and in 1812 he was declared bankrupt. Today, however, he is applauded as a culinary trail-blazer.

Now, around two centuries later, the British appetite for Indian food is enormous and chicken tikka masala is cited as a national dish. The concept of Indian food in Britain is inextricably linked to the idea of curries. The word "curry" is generally thought to have derived from the Tamil word "kaari". In India the word curry refers to a spiced sauce but here it is applied to a wide range of Indian dishes.

Whereas in 1960 there were only 500 Indian restaurants in Britain, there are now thought to be around 8,500. As a nation we spend £2.5 billion annually in Indian restaurants, as well as buying Indian ready meals from supermarkets and cooking Indian food at home. London is home to Veeraswamy, the oldest surviving Indian restaurant, opened in 1927 and popular with Edward VII and visiting maharajahs. What is most striking today about Britain's Indian restaurant scene, especially in London, is the range and variety of eateries one can find, from down-to-earth cafés for budget diners to elegant, Michelin-starred establishments offering sophisticated cuisine. The rich regional diversity of Indian cookery is also increasingly appreciated, so alongside the Punjabi-style tandoori restaurants – which for a long time was the archetypal Indian eaterie in the UK – are restaurants serving Gujarati, Keralan, Pakistani, Parsee and Sri Lankan cuisine.

Sophie's Doro Wott (Ethiopian Spiced Chicken Stew)
Serves 4-5

Traditionally, this dish is eaten with enjera, a spongy-textured, sour-ish Ethiopian flat bread made from the Ethiopian grain teff. "Teff is the smallest grain on earth," explains Sophie "it's name means lost' because if you drop it, forget it." This recipe calls for some specialist Ethiopian ingredients – berberre, spiced butter and enjera can all be purchased at Tobia, Sophie's restaurant in north London.

10-12 red onions, peeled and chopped
2-3 tbsp berberre (Ethiopian mild chilli powder)
1 tbsp crushed garlic and fresh root
  ginger, pounded together
3 tbsp flavoured clarified butter
600 ml (1 pt) hot water
1 small boiling chicken, cut into 12 pieces
salt
freshly squeezed juice of 2-3 lemons
12 free-range eggs, hard-boiled and shelled
cottage cheese, to serve
enjera, to serve

Flavoured clarified butter:
1 kg (2.2 lb) butter
1 tbsp crushed garlic and fresh root ginger,
  pounded together
1 tbsp powdered coriander
1 red onion, peeled and finely chopped

To make the flavoured clarified butter, melt the butter in a heavy-based saucepan. Add in the crushed garlic and ginger, coriander and onion and cook, stirring now and then, for 10-15 minutes. Remove and allow to cool.

To cook the doro wott, place the red onions in a large, earthenware pot, cover and cook over a medium heat, stirring often, until they get very dark. Add a little water, if necessary, but try not to add any water at all at this stage.

Once the onions are dark brown, stir in a little hot water and mix in the berberre and the garlic and ginger paste. Stirring as you do so, gradually add the hot water, a little at a time. Cover and simmer the wott (sauce) for 15-30 minutes, stirring often, until it thickens.

While the wott is simmering, wash the chicken pieces thoroughly and repeatedly and set aside to soak in cold water with salt and the freshly squeezed lemon juice.

Once the wott is thick and creamy, add the clarified butter. Once you add the butter, set it to simmer for another 20 minutes, stirring constantly.

Rinse the soaked chicken thoroughly, add it to the sauce, mixing well, cover and cook for around 30-40 minutes, until the chicken is cooked through. Add the hard-boiled eggs to the dish.

Serve with the cottage cheese on the side.

> *there's a lot of symbolism in Ethiopian cooking. Everything is round for sharing in Ethiopian food – there are no individual plates."*
>
> Sophie Sirak-Kebede

Just off the Finchley Road, above the Ethiopian Cultural Centre, restaurateur Sophie Sirak-Kebede presides over Tobia, the Ethiopian restaurant she started with her husband, greeting and serving her customers with traditional, courteous Ethiopian hospitality. Born and brought up in Ethiopia, Sophie first came to live in England when she was sent to boarding school here at the age of 15. "I used to take my chilli powder to add to the food," she laughs, "but one day Matron caught me and told me off. In Ethiopia a mother has to teach her daughter to cook, otherwise it reflects badly on the family. I had an interest. From tiny I was taught about Ethiopian culture. I cooked daily – I had to help after school." At Tobia, Sophie takes pride in offering the traditional dishes she learnt to cook as a child. Also on offer is Ethiopian coffee, made from freshly roasted coffee beans; "Ethiopian coffee is good for gossiping over as it takes 30 minutes to make," observes Sophie drily, adding "we drink coffee three times a day."

"For Doro Wott we cut the chicken into 12 pieces. In the past a girl would get a husband by how she cut the chicken and how the sauce was done. It's a dish for special occasions, like Christmas and Easter. Traditionally, it would have 12 eggs. Why 12? There are the 12 disciples. In the Coptic church the egg is eternal life – no beginning and no end – there's a lot of symbolism in Ethiopian cooking. Everything is round for sharing in Ethiopian food – there are no individual plates."

Desserts

Peter's Zwetschgenknödel (Plum Dumplings)
Serves 6-8

1 kg (2 ¼ lb) floury potatoes
2 free-range eggs
pinch of salt
around 300 g (10 oz) plain flour
20-30 zwetschgen plums
300 g (10 oz) butter
breadcrumbs (either fresh or the dried crumbs sold by Italian delis)
cinnamon sugar (1 tsp powdered cinnamon mixed with 50 g (2 oz) sugar) or sugar, to serve

Boil the potatoes in their jackets, then peel and mash them. Place the mashed potato in a mixing bowl, Mix in the eggs, a pinch of salt and add just enough flour to form a sticky dough.

Wrap each plum in a coating of the potato dough. Keep the dough fairly thin (about 5 mm or 1/5 in thick) and make sure to seal the dough tightly, otherwise the plum juices will leak out during cooking.

Bring a large saucepan of water to the boil. Add the dumplings and simmer them for 10-15 minutes, until they float to the surface. Carefully fish them out with a slotted spoon once they float.

Dry-fry the breadcrumbs in a heavy-based pan until golden-brown. Melt the butter in a separate pan and serve in a sauceboat or small jug.

Liberally sprinkle the dumplings with the fried breadcrumbs, melted butter and a little cinnamon sugar or sugar and serve at once.

Peter Lobbenberg is an adventurous and discriminating food shopper, who loves exploring London's food shops together with his wife Naomi. "We don't do pretentious," he says firmly. Green Lane's Turkish and Greek shops are a favourite, while "for fish we go to Steve Hatt's and for meat we go to Ginger Pig". Peter's Zwetschgenknodel, the recipe for which was handed down by his German mother, are legendary among his family. The plums for this recipe are zwetschgen plums, small blue "sweet-sour" plums, common on the continent but rather harder to find in London. "They're bigger than a damson, but not as big as a Victoria plum, about greengage-sized." Peter sometimes tracks them down at Marylebone Farmers' Market. If you can't find them, Peter says you could substitute mirabelles or greengages. It's the contrast of tastes and textures that's so good: the crispy breadcrumbs, the giving dough and the taste of the fruit, sweet and sour at the same time. My perfect food." He has been known to eat 20 at one sitting!

Rhubarb Ginger Fool

Serves 4-6

Fruit fools, made by combining raw or cooked fruit with whipped cream, are a very traditional British dish. Rhubarb and ginger go well together and this makes a simple but elegant dessert, particularly when made with forced "champagne" rhubarb.

400 g (14 oz) rhubarb
75-115 g (3-4 oz) granulated sugar
1 knob of stem ginger in syrup, finely chopped
150 ml (5 fl oz) double cream
2-3 tbsp natural yoghurt

Preheat the oven to Gas 4/180°C/350°F.

Trim off and discard any leaves on the rhubarb stalks as these are poisonous and cut the rhubarb stalks into short, evenly sized pieces.

Place the rhubarb, sugar and stem ginger in an ovenproof dish and cover tightly with foil. Bake for 25-30 minutes until the rhubarb is tender. Gently remove the rhubarb with a slotted spoon and set aside to cool.

In a large bowl, whisk the double cream until fluffy. Fold in the cooled rhubarb and the yoghurt. Cover and chill until serving.

Blood Orange Caramel

Serves 4-6

In late winter, one of the seasonal treats I really look forward to is the arrival of blood oranges in the shops. With their vivid red juice and subtle sweetness – with a hint of raspberry – they are delicious, both juiced or used in desserts. Here they are used to make a simple orange caramel.

6 blood oranges
150 ml (¹/₄ pt) water
115 g (4 oz) granulated sugar

Peel the blood oranges and cut horizontally into slices. Arrange the slices in a heat-proof serving dish.

Place the water and sugar in a small saucepan. Heat, stirring, until the sugar has dissolved. Bring to the boil and boil without stirring until the sugar syrup caramelises, turning a rich golden-brown colour. Carefully pour the liquid caramel over the orange slices. Set aside in a cold place for a few hours.

Pick-your-own Farms

For centuries much of the food that London consumed was grown or raised in farms around the edge of the city. Today Pick-your-own (PYO) farms on London's periphery offer city-dwelling Londoners the chance to enjoy the fun of foraging for fruit and vegetables in the open air. There is something quietly satisfying in picking a fruit or vegetable when it's ready to be harvested – the way a ripe raspberry comes off its stem in your fingers or an apple comes away in your hand.

Parkside Farm, which is walking distance from Cockfosters tube, is a family-run affair. The signs around the farm are in Turkish as well as in English and visiting the farm on a sunny summer's day one finds Turkish, Indian, Chinese, Polish and English families making their way round the farm, stopping en route to pick crimson raspberries or bright red strawberries, searching for courgettes among the large leaves, tugging beetroot and onions out of the soil and snapping off spinach leaves before making their way, laden with filled plastic bags and punnets, to have their pickings weighed.

Crockford Bridge Farm
New Haw Road
Addlestone, nr Weybridge
Surrrey KT15
01932-853 886

Garsons Farm
Winterdown Road
Esher
Surrey KT10
01372 464389
www.garsons.co.uk

Grays of Wokingham
Heathlands Road
Wokingham
Berks RG40
0118 9785 386
www.graysfarm.co.uk

Grove Farm
Ivinghoe
Leighton Buzzard
Beds LU7
012 96 668175
www.grovefarmpyo.co.uk

Parkside Farm
Hadley Road
Enfield
Middx EN2
020 8367 2035
www.parksidefarmpyo.co.uk

Spencers
Wickham Fruit Farm
Wickham St Pauls
Halstead
Essex CO9
01787 269476
www.spencerfarmshop.co.uk

Blackberry Lemon Sponge
Serves 4-6

Picking wild blackberries from the hedgerows is something I enjoyed as a child and still enjoy today. Even in a large city like London, one can find patches of brambles in the parks and commons to forage from.

115 g (4 oz) butter, softened
115 g (4 oz) caster sugar
2 medium free-range eggs
grated zest of 1 lemon
115 g (4 oz) self-raising flour, sifted
1 tbsp lemon juice
300 g (10 oz) fresh blackberries
cream or custard, to serve

Preheat the oven to Gas 4/180°C/350°F.

In a mixing bowl, cream together the butter and caster sugar until well-mixed. Beat in the eggs one at a time. Mix in the lemon zest. Fold in the flour and mix in the lemon juice.

Place the blackberries in the base of an 18 cm (7 in) ovenproof dish. Evenly spread over the lemon sponge mixture.

Bake for 45-50 minutes until golden-brown and set. Serve warm from the oven with cream or custard.

Apple Almond Crumble
Serves 4

Crumbles are a quintessentially English pudding. Adding ground nuts to the traditional crumble topping of flour, butter and sugar, is a simple way of adding flavour and texture.

4 Cox's apples
100 g (3 ¹/₂ oz) plain flour
100 g (3 ¹/₂ oz) ground almonds
100 g (3 ¹/₂ oz) butter, diced
100 g (3 ¹/₂ oz) caster sugar
double cream or custard, to serve

Preheat the oven to Gas 5/190°C/375°F.

Peel, core and chop the apples and place in an ovenproof dish.

To make the crumble topping, place the flour and ground almonds in a mixing bowl. Rub in the butter with your fingertips until the mixture resembles breadcrumbs. Stir in the caster sugar.

Evenly spread the crumble topping mixture over the apple, pressing down to form a smooth layer. Bake in the oven for 30-40 minutes until golden. Serve hot from the oven.

> *I want to combine ice and heat; the richness of the chocolate is set off well by the spiciness of the chilli."*
>
> *Simon Kiddell*

Manning Cool Chile's stall at Borough Market, Simon Kiddell buzzes with enthusiasm for genuine Mexican food, and he frequently travels to Mexico to experience more of the country and its diverse cuisine. Simon's passion for spicy food goes back to his childhood: "I've been fascinated by spicy food from an early age, first Indian, then Thai. I've been cooking since I was eight. I wanted more spice in my food and my Mum told me to add it myself." Back in London after travelling in India Simon met Dodie and discovered a "common interest" in chillies and started working for Cool Chile. On visiting Mexico he discovered the incredible markets there."Eight, nine, ten times the size of this," Simon enthuses, "with everything available. Sacks of chillies, stacks of corn husks, tropical fish, magic potions, Mexican candy… The Mexican street food, sold on street corners, is so unpretentious but so tasty."

Simon's recipe uses the Mexican habanero chilli, which he likes because "it's very hot but also incredibly fruity. It's one of the few chillies that doesn't change flavour substantially when dried. I want to combine ice and heat; the richness of the chocolate is set off well by the spiciness of the chilli."

Cool Chile Co., Borough Market, SE1

Simon's Chocolate and Habanero Ice Cream

Serves 4-6

200 g (7 oz) plain chocolate, finely chopped
300 ml (¹/₂ pt) milk
2 tsp diced habanero chilli
3 large free-range egg yolks
75 g (3 oz) caster sugar
200 ml (7 fl oz) double cream, well chilled
summer fruit, to serve

Put the chopped chocolate into a large bowl and set aside. Pour the milk into a medium-sized, heavy-based saucepan adding the habanero to the milk. Heat slowly, stirring frequently until the milk is too hot to touch. Remove from the heat and leave to infuse for about 15 minutes.

Put the egg yolks and sugar into a bowl and mix well. Add the milk, passing it through a sieve to remove the chilli. Rinse the pan, pour in the milk mixture and cook it over a low heat, stirring constantly, until the custard is thick enough to coat a wooden spoon. Don't let the custard boil or it will curdle.

When the custard is ready, pour it over the chocolate and stir until smooth. Let the chocolate chilli custard cool and then chill thoroughly.

Meanwhile, put a bowl and a whisk into the freezer or refrigerator to chill. When chilled pour the cream into the chilled bowl and whisk using the chilled whisk until the cream forms soft peaks. Stir in the chilled chocolate custard.

Pour the mixture into an ice cream maker to churn until frozen. If you don't have an ice cream maker, freeze the mixture in a shallow container, whisking 3 times during freezing to break down the ice crystals.

Serve with summer fruit.

A History of Ice Cream

For centuries ice cream was a luxury, reserved for royalty and aristocracy. The first recorded instance of ice cream being served in London was to King Charles II in 1672. During the 18th century, ices became very fashionable and a number of London confectioners were noted for their ices. One particularly successful confectionery was founded in Berkeley Square in 1769 by an Italian called Domenico Negri, who made and sold "all Sorts of Ice, Fruits and Creams in the best Italian manner".

It was the growth of commercial ice harvesting (that is, cutting huge quantities of ice from frozen lakes and rivers in other countries) in the early 19th century which made ice cream more affordable. Carlo Gatti (1817-78), an entrepreneurial Swiss-Italian immigrant to London, tapped into the new market for ice cream, setting up a stall near Charing Cross selling ice cream to passers-by, and also becoming an ice merchant. London's ice cream history has strong links to its Italian community, with Italian immigrants bringing their ice cream making skills with them. With many Italians working as itinerant ice cream salesmen throughout Britain, a popular nick-name for the street ice cream seller was the "hokey pokey man", an expression thought to derive from "ecco pocco", Italian for "here – a little". Ices were sold on glasses or "licks", which were then wiped clean and re-used.

The London Canal Museum
12-13 New Wharf Road,
London, N1 9RT
020 7713 0836
www.canalmuseum.org.uk
Housed in a 19th-century warehouse built to store ice imported from Norway by Carlo Gatti the museum tells the story of the ice trade and ice cream as well as exploring the history of London's canals.

Marine Ices, NW3

A much-loved North London ice cream institution is Marine Ices, an ice cream parlour and restaurant run by the Mansi family. Dante Mansi explains the family history: "My grandfather Gaetano Mansi came over in 1898 when he was 12 from Ravello in southern Italy – he was sent over here to make his living. First he worked for a family in Bermondsey who had an ice cream business, then, in 1908, he opened a "high-class fruiterer" in Drummond Street – my Dad used to tell me off for calling it a "greengrocer". He started making water ices from the fruit that was spoilt and discovered that they were very popular. In 1931 he moved here to 8 Haverstock Hill and set up Mansi's selling fresh fruit water ices and ice creams. This was our family home – that used to be the front room, and that was the garden. Over the years we've built into the garden, sideways, upwards. After the war Gaetano's son, Aldo, fitted the shop out like a ship with port-holes and changed the name from Mansi's to Marine Ices – we've got one last porthole left. Gaetano retired back to Ravello."

As Gaetano, Dante's brother, explains, Marine Ices make classic Italian-style gelati on the premises. "Our ice cream has less fat in it; it's lighter, not cloying. We don't use butter, we use cream. There's less dairy fat in our ice cream, so it melts quicker, but has stronger, intense flavours. We use natural flavours, real ingredients – pistachios, hazelnuts, coffee, lemons and melon. We've got subtle flavours like ricotta and pear. Our cassata is a classic and so is the pistachio."

"We're probably the last of the real ice cream parlours," observes Dante thoughtfully. "Our ice cream menu is probably longer than our restaurant menu! We get busy at nine in the evening, when people come for their ice cream after dinner."

> *We're probably the last of the real ice cream parlours," observes Dante thoughtfully. "Our ice cream menu is probably longer than our restaurant menu!"*
>
> *Dante Mansi*

Marine Ices' Knickerbocker Glory
Serves 1

Spoon some Melba sauce into a knickerbocker glory glass, top with a scoop of vanilla ice cream, spoon over a few pieces of chopped, skinned peach, a few chunks of fresh pineapple and a few pieces of banana. Spoon over more Melba sauce and chocolate sauce. Top with a scoop of vanilla ice cream and a scoop of strawberry ice cream. Decorate with whipped cream, a cherry and wafers and serve.

Marine Ices, 8 Haverstock Hill, NW3

If the word blancmange makes you shudder, and recall children's birthday parties, pink bunny moulds, Day-Glo trifles and school meals," says Cheryl Cohen of London Farmers' Markets, "perhaps it's time to think again." The fact that a blancmange is thickened with corn flour, rather than gelatine, gives it, in Cheryl's words "a pleasing, soft, yielding bite." Cheryl makes her blancmanges using "the glorious range of milk available at our farmers' markets – I use organic unpasteurised cow's milk from Lower Barn Farm in Suffolk and from Olive Farm in Somerset, but you could also use buffalo milk from Alham Wood Farm if you're worried about cholesterol, or goat's milk. Other farms with superb dairy products include Lincolnshire Poachers who have started to bring unpasteurised organic cow's milk to some markets and Douglas Partners from East Sussex who bring both pasteurised and unpasteurised milk to Blackheath farmers' market."

Cheryl's Blancmange
Serves 4

4 tbsp cornflour
600 ml (1 pt) milk
1 vanilla pod, slit lengthways
2 tbsp granulated sugar
roasted rhubarb, to serve

Alternative flavourings
cardamom and rosewater:
2 cardamom pods, crushed slightly
a few drops of rose water or 2 tsp rose syrup

Sloe gin:
2 tsp sloe gin
poached damsons, to serve

To make the blancmange, slacken the cornflour with a little of the milk. Gently warm the remaining milk with the vanilla pod. Set it aside for 5 minutes, to infuse.

Remove the vanilla pod and gently heat the milk once more. Just when it's about to come to a simmer – be very careful not to let it boil – stir in the cornflour mixture. Cook, stirring constantly, until the mixture thickens. Stir in the sugar. Pour the milk mixture into a wetted mould or individual moulds, cool and chill overnight until set.

To make the cardamom and rosewater blancmange, add the two cardamom pods instead of the vanilla pod to the milk, gently heat through and infuse for 5 minutes. Strain the milk, discarding the cardamom pods, and gently heat once more, making sure it doesn't come to the boil, and stir in the slackened cornflour as well as the rosewater or rose syrup. Proceed as above.

For a sloe gin blancmange, simply slacken the cornflour with a little of the milk. Gently warm the remaining milk and, when it's just at simmering point, stir in the cornflour mixture and the sloe gin. Proceed as above.

Teresa's Quince Tart
Serves 6-8

Pastry:
130 g(4 1/2 oz) unsalted butter, diced
250 g (9 oz) plain flour, sifted
1 tbsp icing sugar, sifted
1 free-range egg
1 free-range egg yolk
1 pinch salt

Filling:
500 g (1 lb 2 oz) ripe quinces
juice of 1/2 lemon
50 g (2 oz) sugar
1/2 tsp ground cinnamon

Cream:
1 free-range egg
60 g (2 1/2 oz) caster sugar
30 g (1 1/4 oz) plain flour
150 ml (5 fl oz) double cream
3 tbsp Marsala wine
icing sugar, for dusting
whipped cream, cream with yoghurt or
    mascarpone, to serve

First make the pastry. Place the butter, flour and icing sugar in a mixing bowl and mix together with your fingers until the texture is like fine crumbs. Add in the egg, egg yolk and salt and bring together to form a smooth dough. Knead lightly and mould into a ball, cover and refrigerate.

Preheat the oven to Gas 2/150°C/300°F.

Roll out the chilled pastry thinly and use it to line a 23 cm (9 in) tart tin.

To make the filling, peel and core the quince, being careful to get all the very hard, stringy bits out. Slice into evenly sized pieces, toss with lemon juice and steam for a few minutes to soften slightly. Toss the softened quince in the sugar and cinnamon.

Place the quince in the pastry shell and bake for around 20 minutes, until the pastry is pale golden.

Meanwhile, make the cream by whisking together the egg and caster sugar until thick and pale. Beat in the flour, then add the double cream and Marsala. Pour the cream mixture into the partly-baked pastry shell, return it to the oven and bake for a further 30-35 minutes until the custard has set.

Serve warm from the oven, with icing sugar sifted over and with whipped cream, cream with yoghurt or mascarpone on the side.

> *When I got my garden, the one thing I knew I wanted was a quince tree."*
>
> Teresa Checchia

Teresa Checchia's fondness for quinces stems from her childhood. 'Until I was six-years old, I was brought up in southern Philadelphia in America; my Dad's family were Italian Americans. The house we lived in had been his family's little house in the country, where you would go in the summer months when the city got too hot. Just a shack to start with, but over the years it was developed into a house. My Mum and Dad were great gardeners. Our garden was open – there were no fences between the houses. In the humid summer heat, the gardens ran riot. We had a very mature quince tree in the garden – I can remember these huge pumpkin plants growing up into the branches of the tree. It was such lush vegetation: pumpkins and watermelons. The food memories of my childhood are of pumpkin pie, proper Italian pizza from town, watermelon – my favourite fruit – and corn-on-the-cob, picked fresh from the garden. We never would have dreamt of eating something not freshly picked. There's something about the smell and texture of quince – the pear-y, apple-ly, lemony furriness of quince. When I hold a beautiful, fuzzy quince fruit in my hands, I almost want to nuzzle it. So when I got my garden, the one thing I knew I wanted was a quince tree. I've got a bumper crop this year, so I'll make quince jelly, jam and quince pie – like an American apple pie."

Queen of Puddings
Serves 4-6

Britain has a proud tradition of puddings and this is one of my favourites. The elements are simple – a baked bread custard, a layer of jam and a meringue topping – but the resulting dish is both elegant and extremely satisfying.

115 g (4 oz) fresh white breadcrumbs
2 free-range eggs, separated
a pinch of grated lemon zest
150 g (5 oz) vanilla or caster sugar
15 g (¹/₂ oz) butter
salt
600 ml (1 pt) milk
¹/₂ tsp vanilla extract
3-4 tbsp raspberry or strawberry jam
cream, to serve

Preheat the oven to Gas 3/170°C/325°F.

Place the breadcrumbs, egg yolks, lemon zest, 25 g (1 oz) of vanilla sugar, butter and ¹/₄ tsp of salt in a buttered baking dish.

Gently heat the milk to just below boiling point and pour over the breadcrumb mixture, stirring to mix in the egg yolks. Bake in the oven for 45 minutes to 1 hour until set.

Towards the end of the baking time, prepare the meringue topping. Whisk the egg whites with a pinch of salt in a mixing bowl until stiff. Fold in half the remaining vanilla sugar and whisk again until well mixed. Using a metal spoon, carefully fold in the remaining sugar and the vanilla extract.

Remove the baked bread custard from the oven and carefully spread over the jam. Spoon over the meringue topping to form an even layer. Return to the oven and bake at Gas 3/170°C/325°F for 15-20 minutes until set and lightly browned. Serve warm from the oven with cream.

St Clement's Cheesecake
Serves 8-10

I love cheesecakes, particularly baked ones. This one has a citrus flavour, inspired by the nursery rhyme "Oranges and lemons, say the bells of St Clements".

500 g (1 lb 2 oz) curd cheese
500 g (1 lb 2 oz) cream cheese
3 medium free-range eggs
100 g (3 1/2 oz) caster sugar
40 g (1 1/2 oz) plain flour
pinch of salt
1 tbsp lemon juice
1 tbsp orange juice
finely grated zest of 1 lemon
finely grated zest of 1 orange
100 g (3 1/2 oz) digestive biscuits
50 g (2 oz) ginger biscuits
60 g (2 1/2 oz) butter, melted
300 ml (1/2 pt) soured cream
1/2 tsp vanilla extract

Preheat the oven to Gas 4/180°C/350°F.

In a large mixing bowl, beat together the curd and cream cheeses until smooth. Beat in the eggs, sugar, flour, salt and lemon and orange juice and zest, mixing well.

Using a rolling pin or a food processor, crush the digestive biscuits and ginger biscuits into fine crumbs. Mix together with the melted butter and press evenly and firmly into the base of a 20 cm (8 in) spring-form cake tin.

Pour the cheese mixture into the cake tin over the biscuit base. Bake for 40 minutes, until just set. Beat together the soured cream and vanilla extract. Pour the flavoured soured cream over the baked cheesecake, gently spreading it out to form a shallow layer on top. Return the cheesecake to the oven and bake for a further 10 minutes.

Remove the cheesecake from the oven and allow to cool thoroughly, then refrigerate to chill before serving.

Hazelnut Plum Crumble

Serves 4-6

Hazelnut and plums combine to good effect in this pudding. Victoria plums, a traditional British variety which come into season in late summer, are particularly delicious.

100 g (3 ¹/₂ oz) butter, diced
100 g (3 ¹/₂ oz) plain flour
100 g (3 ¹/₂ oz) ground hazelnuts
100 g (3 ¹/₂ oz) Demerara sugar
700 g (1 ¹/₂ lb) ripe plums, pitted and quartered
cream or custard, to serve

Preheat the oven to Gas 5/190°C/375°F.

In a mixing bowl, rub the butter into the flour until the mixture resembles crumbs. Mix in the ground hazelnuts and the sugar.

Place the quartered plums in an ovenproof dish. Spread over the hazelnut mixture, pressing down firmly, to form the crumble topping.

Bake for 30-45 minutes until golden. Serve warm from the oven with cream or custard.

Tiramisu

Serves 6-8

A classic, wickedly rich dessert – widely found in London's Italian restaurants and always a crowd-pleaser.

4 free-range egg yolks
4 tbsp vanilla sugar
500 g (1 lb 2 oz) mascarpone cheese
300 ml (¹/₂ pt) strong, black coffee, cooled
2 tbsp brandy
20-24 Savoiardi biscuits or sponge fingers
50 g (2 oz) dark chocolate, grated
cocoa powder, for sprinkling

In a mixing bowl, whisk together the egg yolks and vanilla sugar until pale yellow and thickened. Gradually beat in the mascarpone.

In a shallow bowl, mix together the coffee and brandy. Dip half the Savoiardi biscuits into the coffee mixture and spread them in a layer in wide, shallow dish. Spread half the mascarpone cheese mixture evenly over the coffee-dipped biscuits. Sprinkle over half the grated chocolate. Repeat the process using the remaining Savoiardi biscuits, mascarpone and grated chocolate.

Cover and chill for at least 1 hour. Sprinkle with cocoa powder just before serving.

Baked Vanilla Rice Pudding
Serves 4

A classic British pudding that seems to be loved and loathed in equal measure. For me, it is a great comfort food. Ridiculously easy to make, long, slow cooking is the key to this recipe.

butter, for greasing
40 g (1 ½ oz) pudding rice
2 tbsp vanilla sugar
pinch of salt
600 ml (1 pt) full-fat milk
1 vanilla pod
good quality strawberry jam, to serve

Preheat the oven to Gas 1/140°C/275°F.

Generously butter a deep ovenproof dish. Place the pudding rice, sugar, salt and milk in the dish.

Slit open the vanilla pod lengthways, scraping out its black seeds into the milk in the dish. Add the scraped pod.

Bake for 3 ½-4 hours, so that a golden crust forms over the pudding. Serve warm from the oven with strawberry jam.

Lime and Rum Jelly
Serves 6

Tipsy jellies make great dinner party desserts. This one is inspired by the flavours of a classic Caribbean rum punch.

5 sheets of leaf gelatine (approx 8 g (¹/₃ oz) in weight)
200 ml (7 fl oz) freshly squeezed lime juice
150 g (5 oz) caster sugar
150 ml (5 fl oz) rum
a few drops of Angostura bitters
300 ml (¹/₂ pt) cold water

Soak the leaf gelatine in a bowl of cold water for 5 minutes. Drain and squeeze out excess moisture.

Place the lime juice, caster sugar and rum in a small pan and heat gently, stirring, until the sugar has melted. Stir in the Angostura bitters.

Spoon a little of the lime juice mixture into a small, heavy-based pan. Add the soaked gelatine and cook gently, over a very low heat, stirring, until the gelatine has melted. Add the remaining lime juice and mix well. Stir in the cold water and remove from direct heat.

Pour the mixture into 6 small dessert bowls, allow to cool and refrigerate overnight to set.

Mango Fool with Cardamom Wafers

Serves 6-8

A tropical fruit fool, inspired by luscious Alphonso mangoes.

Fool:
450 g (1 lb) canned Alphonso mango pulp
250 g (9 oz) mascarpone cheese
1 tsp Cointreau
150 ml (5 fl oz) whipping or double cream
2-3 ripe Alphonso or Kesar mangoes (if in season)

Cardamom wafers:
25 g (1 oz) butter
2 cardamom pods
1 free-range egg white
25 g (1 oz) plain white flour
50 g (2 oz) caster sugar

To make the mango fool, gently but thoroughly fold together the mango pulp and mascarpone cheese. Mix in the Cointreau. Whip the cream until stiff, then fold into the fool. Cover and chill for 2-3 hours.

Meanwhile, make the cardamom wafers. Preheat the oven to Gas 5/190°C/375°F.

Melt the butter and set aside to cool. Crack the cardamom pods, discard the husks and finely grind the fragrant black seeds.

In a bowl, whisk the egg white until stiff. Fold in the flour, ground cardamom, sugar and cooled butter. Place teaspoons of the mixture, spaced well apart, on a lined baking tray, making 16 wafers. Bake for 10 minutes until golden. Remove from the oven and cool on a wire rack.

Take each mango and cut off both 'cheeks', leaving the large, central stone. Peel the flesh off the cheeks and cut the flesh into strips.

Serve the mango fool with the fresh mango strips and cardamom wafers.

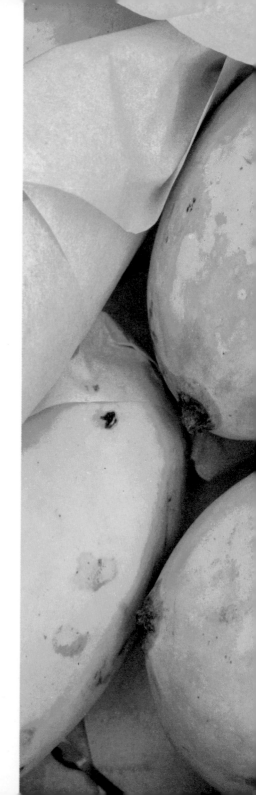

Gin and Lemon Jelly
Serves 6

Gin, the juniper-flavoured spirit originally from Holland, has a long association with London. By the first part of the 18th century, cheap gin had became the popular drink of London's poor with numerous gin-shops in the city selling drams of the spirit. In the late 1740s 20 million gallons of gin per year were being distilled in London alone. In 1751 the artist William Hogarth vividly depicted the social abuse caused by gin addiction in his famous print *Gin Lane*. Increased taxation and tighter control on distillation gradually reduced the consumption of gin. During the 19th century gin become an increasingly respectable tipple, a gentleman's drink. London gin was a more refined, less assertively flavoured gin that became popular, used as a mixer rather than drunk in its own right. The cocktail era saw gin receive a further new lease of life as a basis for many cocktails. Beefeater, founded in 1820, continues to distil London gin in the capital to this day. This simple recipe for a tangy gin-flavoured jelly makes a refreshing, grown-up dessert.

5 sheets of leaf gelatine (approx 8 g (1/3 oz) in weight)
200 ml (7 fl oz) freshly squeezed lemon juice
150 g (5 oz) caster sugar
150 ml (5 fl oz) gin
300 ml (1/2 pt) cold water

Soak the leaf gelatine in a bowl of cold water for 5 minutes. Drain and squeeze out excess moisture.

Place the lemon juice, caster sugar and gin in a small pan and heat gently, stirring, until the sugar has melted.

Spoon a little of the lemon juice mixture into a small, heavy-based pan. Add the soaked gelatine and cook gently over a very low heat, stirring, until the gelatine has melted. Add in the remaining lemon juice mixture and mix well. Stir in the cold water and remove from direct heat.

Pour the mixture into 6 small dessert bowls, allow to cool and refrigerate overnight to set.

A History of Chocolate

Chocolate arrived in London during the 17th century, following England's capture of Jamaica from the Spanish in 1655, which opened up access to cocoa from the island's plantations. The first record of its sale in London is a notice dated 1657 advertising that "In Bishopsgate Street, by Queen's Head Alley, at a Frenchman's house is an excellent West Indies drink called Chocolate to be sold". This novel and expensive drink, highly taxed on import, was a luxury, enjoyed by the aristocratic and wealthy and popular at the court of King Charles II. The diarist Samuel Pepys had a fondness for it, enthusing in his diaries, "drank my morning Chocollate, very good." The chocolate drink was made by scraping chocolate powder from a cake made from roasted, sweetened cocoa beans and adding liquid to the powder. Chocolate houses developed, many of them in the City and Mayfair, such as White's Chocolate House which opened on fashionable St James Street, in 1693, and which evolved into White's, the famous gentlemen's club. Confectioners, too, began to offer cakes and other confections made using chocolate, but chocolate remained a costly treat.

In the 19th century considerable progress was made in chocolate processing techniques. In Holland Coenraad J Van Houten made a major breakthrough in 1825, inventing a hydraulic chocolate press which separated cocoa butter from the cocoa mass. Following on from this invention, Francis Fry produced Britain's first eating chocolate in 1847, a mixture of cocoa liquor, sugar and cocoa butter and went on to become Britain's largest manufacturer of chocolate and cocoa. Taxes on imported cocoa were reduced by Gladstone in 1853, a move which helped make chocolate products more affordable. Terry's, developed from a confectionery founded in 1767, Cadbury's, which started making drinking chocolate in 1831, and Rowntree's, founded in 1862, were other major companies in the history of British chocolate.

Today, when mass-produced eating chocolate is cheap and widely available, chocolate's original mystique and glamour can be hard to understand. Across London, however, a handful of chocolatiers are producing exquisite hand-made chocolates, recreating it as a luxury.

CHOCOLATE SHOPS

L'Artisan du Chocolat
89 Lower Sloane Street
London, SW1
020 7824 8365
www.artisanduchocolat.com

William Curley
10 Paved Court
Richmond, TW9
020 8332 3002
www.williamcurley.co.uk

Melt
59 Ledbury Road
London, W11
020 7727 5030
www.meltchocolates.com

Rococo
321 King's Road
London, SW3
020 7352 5857
www.rococochocolates.com

Rococo
45 Marylebone High Street
London, W1
020 7935 7780
www.rococochocolates.com

Paul A. Young Fine Chocolates
33 Camden Passage
London, N1
020 7424 5750
www.payoung.net

The Chocolatier's Story

One of these chocolatiers is Paul Young, whose Islington-based chocolaterie opened in 2006 to much acclaim. "We're not a chocolate shop," explains Paul. "We make everything on the site. It's an artisan business. I look to Paris. They have chocolatiers there. You see the kitchens at the back of the shops where they make what they sell. I don't see why we can't do that over here. Everything is done by hand. We spend money on people not equipment. We don't use anything artificial – it's fresh herbs, fresh spices, fresh fruit. Our chocolates have a shelf life of only 5-7 days, so we make them every day and stay up at night if we have to. People have said it can't be done, that we can't go on making everything by hand, but we have and we will.

"I was a pastry chef and spent six years working for Marco Pierre White. As a pastry chef I worked with chocolate, so it was a natural, organic progression. If I didn't like it I wouldn't do it. I do like creating flavours – you always feel you need more time to develop more things. We've got 85 lines in the shop. I don't have favourites. People love our sea-salted chocolates and our Marmite ganache and chocolate brownies. We vary the chocolates according to the season – so in the summer we have elderflower and Pimms, in the autumn apples, pears and pumpkin and at Christmas cranberry, cinnamon, orange and nutmeg, all those things that people want at that time of year."

33 Camden Passage, N1

We spend money on good ingredients. I've roasted these hazelnuts myself, then peeled them all – it's the attention to detail. We make honest chocolates. If it's a raspberry chocolate then it's going to taste of fresh raspberries, not concentrate. It's about having a passion. You can't work with chocolate if you don't like it – the smell is too strong."

Paul Young

DIRECTORY

A Gold
42 Brushfield Street, E1
020 7247 2487

Algerian Coffee Stores
52 Old Compton Street, W1
020 7437 2480
www.algcoffee.co.uk

Allen & Co
117 Mount Street, Mayfair, W1
020 7499 5831

Angelucci
23b Frith Street, W1
020 7437 5889

Athenian Grocery
16A Moscow Road,
Bayswater, W2
020 7229 6280

Beetroot Deli
92 Fleet Road, NW3
020 7424 8544
www.beetrootdeli.co.uk

Berry Bros & Rudd
3 St James's Street, SW1A
020 7396 9600

Biggles
66 Marylebone Lane, W1
020 7935 7788
www.ebiggles.co.uk

Billingsgate Market
Trafalgar Way, E14
020 7987 1118

Books For Cooks
4 Blenheim Crescent, W11
020 7221 1992
www.booksforcooks.com

Borough Cheese Company
Borough Market, SE1
www.boroughcheesecompany.
com

Borough Market
Southwark Street, SE1
020 7407 1002
www.boroughmarket.org.uk

Brindisa
32 Exmouth Market, EC1
020 7713 1666

Brindisa
Floral Hall, Stoney Street, SE1
020 7407 1036
www.brindisa.com

Chelsea Physic Garden
66 Royal Hospital Road, SW3
020 7352 5646
www.chelseaphysicgarden.co.uk

Claridge's
55 Brook Street, W1
020 7409 6307

Clocktower Store
52 The Broadway, N8
020 8348 7845

Cookery School
15b Little Portland Street, W1
020 7631 4590
www.cookeryschool.co.uk

Cool Chile Co.
Borough Market, SE1
www.coolchile.co.uk

Crockford Bridge Farm
New Haw Road,
Addlestone, nr Weybridge,
Surrrey KT15
01932 853 886

Dorchester, The
53 Park Lane, W1
020 7629 8888

Dory's Café
3 St Alban's Road, EN5
020 8440 1954

F Cook
9 Broadway Market, E8
020 7254 6458

Flour Power City
Borough Market, SE1
www.flourpowercity.com

H Forman & Sons
Stour Road, Fish Island, E3
020 8221 3900
www.formans.co.uk

Fortnum & Mason
81 Piccadilly, W1A
020 7734 8040

Garden Museum, The
Lambeth Palace Road, SW1
020 7401 8865
www.museumgardenhistory.org

Garsons Farm
Winterdown Road,
Esher, Surrey, KT10
01372 464389
www.garsons.co.uk

Grays of Wokingham
Heathlands Road,
Wokingham, Berks, RG40
0118 9785 386
www.graysfarm.co.uk

Green Valley
36 Upper Berkeley St, W1H
020 7402 7385

Grove Farm
Ivinghoe, Leighton Buzzard,
Beds LU7
01296 668175
www.grovefarmpyo.co.uk

H R Higgins
79 Duke Street, W1
020 7629 3913
www.hrhiggins.co.uk

I Camisa & Son
61 Old Compton Street, W1
020 7437 7610

Kerala
15 Great Castle Street, W1
020 7580 2125

L'Artisan du Chocolat
89 Lower Sloane Street, SW1
020 7824 8365
www.artisanduchocolat.com

La Casalinga
64 St John's Wood High St, NW8
020 7722 5959

La Fromagerie
2-4 Moxon Street, W1
020 7935 0341

La Fromagerie
30 Highbury Park, N5
020 7359 7440
www.lafromagerie.co.uk

Leila's
17 Calvert Avenue, E2
020 7729 9789

C Lidgate
110 Holland Park Avenue, W11
020 7727 8243

Lina Stores
18 Brewer Street, W1
020 7437 6482

London Canal Museum
12-13 New Wharf Road, N1
020 7713 0836
www.canalmuseum.org.uk

London City Farms
www.farmgarden.org.uk

London Farmers' Markets
www.lfm.org.uk

M Moen & Sons
24 The Pavement, Clapham, SW4
020 7622 1624

Maison Bertaux
28 Greek Street, W1
020 7437 6007

Manzes
87 Tower Bridge Road, SE1
020 7407 2985
www.manze.co.uk

Maria's Market Café
Borough Market,
Southwark Street, SE1

Marine Ices
8 Haverstock Hill, NW3
020 7482 9003
www.marineices.co.uk

W Martyn
135 Muswell Hill Broadway, N10
020 88835642
www.wmartyn.co.uk

Melrose and Morgan
42 Gloucester Avenue, NW1
020 7722 0011
www.melroseandmorgan.com

Melt
59 Ledbury Road, W11
020 7727 5030
www.meltchocolates.com

Monmouth Coffee House
27 Monmouth Street, WC2
020 7370 3516

Monmouth Coffee House
2 Park Street, SE1
020 7645 3585
www.monmouthcoffee.co.uk

National Society of Allotments & Leisure Gardeners
www.nsalg.org.uk

Neal's Yard Dairy
17 Shorts Garden, WC2
020 7240 5700

Neal's Yard Dairy
6 Park Street, SE1
020 7645 3554
www.nealsyarddairy.co.uk

New Covent Garden Market
Nine Elms, SW8
020 7720 2211

Nordic Bakery
14 Golden Square, W1
020 3230 1077
www.nordicbakery.com

Original Maids of Honour
288 Kew Road, TW9
020 8940 2752
www.theoriginalmaidsofhonour.co.uk

Parkside Farm
Hadley Road, Enfield,
Middx, EN2
020 8367 2035
www.parksidefarmpyo.co.uk

Paul A Young Fine Chocolates
33 Camden Passage, N1
020 7424 5750
www.payoung.net

Paxton & Whitfield
93 Jermyn Street, SW1
020 7930 0259
www.paxtonandwhitfield.co.uk

E. Pellicci
332 Bethnal Green Road, E2
020 7739 4873

Platters
10 Halleswell Parade,
Finchley Road, NW11
020 8455 7345

Postcard Teas
9 Dering Street, W1S
020 7629 3654

Queen's Market
Green St (at corner with Queen
Road), E7

R H Fisheries
Barnet Market,
St Albans Road, Barnet, EN5

R.E.D.
300 Kentish Town Road, NW5
020 7482 7300

Ritz, The
150 Piccadilly, W1
020 7493 8181

Rococo
321 King's Road, SW3
020 7352 5857
www.rococochocolates.com

Rococo
45 Marylebone High Street, W1
020 7935 7780
www.rococochocolates.com

Royal Botanic Gardens
Kew, Richmond,
Surrey, TW9
020 8332 5655

Rules
35 Maiden Lane, WC2
020 7836 5314

St John
26 St John St, EC1
020 7251 0848

Savoy, The
Strand, WC2
020 7836 4343

Seldom Seen Farm
Billesdon,
Leicestershire, LE7 9FA
0116 259 6742
www.seldomseenfarm.co.uk

Shipps Tearooms
4 Park Street, SE1
020 7407 2692

Sillfield Farm
Endmoor, Kendal,
Cumbria, LA8 OHZ
015395 67609
www.sillfield.co.uk

Singapore Garden
83A Fairfax Road, WN6
020 7624 8233
www.singaporegarden.co.uk

Smithfield Market
Charterhouse St, E11
020 7332 3092

Spencers
Wickham Fruit Farm,
Wickham St Pauls, Halstead,
Essex, CO9
01787 269476
www.spencersfarmshop.co.uk

Steve Hatt
88-90 Essex Road, N1
020 7226 3963

Tea Palace
175 Westbourne Grove, W11
020 7727 2600

Tobia
First floor,
Ethiopian Community Centre
2A Lithos Road, NW3
020 7431 4213
www.tobiarestaurant.co.uk

Toff's
38 Muswell Hill Broadway, N10
020 8883 8656

Union Hand-Roasted
The New Roastery, Unit 2,
7a South Crescent, E16
020 7474 8990
www.unionroasted.com

W & F Fish Ltd
56-64 Crogsland Road, NW1
020 7485 6603

William Curley
10 Paved Court,
Richmond, TW9
020 8332 3002
www.williamcurley.co.uk

Wolseley, The
160 Piccadilly, W1
020 7499 6996

Wyndham House Poultry
3 Stoney Street, Southwark, SE1
020 7403 4788

KITCHENWARE SHOPS

Londoners who enjoy cooking are lucky enough to have access to a number of specialist kitchenware shops. These range from elegant shops with attractively displayed tableware and copper pans to professional chef's stores, crammed with covetable bits of kit from formidable knives to powerful food processors.

David Mellor
4 Sloane Square, W1
020 7730 4259
www.davidmellordesign.co.uk
Discriminating stock of kitchen design classics.

Denny's
55a Dean Street, W1
01372 377904
www.dennys.co.uk
Chef's ware and catering clothes.

Divertimenti
227-229 Brompton Road, SW3
020 7581 8065
www.divertimenti.co.uk
Delectable ceramics and kitchenware.

Divertimenti
33-34 Marylebone High Street, W1
020 7935 0689
www.divertimenti.co.uk

Gill Wing Cook Shop
190 Upper Street, N1
020 7226 5392
Wide-ranging kitchen ware.

Gill Wing Cook Shop
45 Park Road, N8
020 8348 3451

Kooks Unlimited
2-4 Elton Street
Richmond, TW10
020 8332 3030
Comprehensive cookware.

La Cuisiniere
81-83 and 90 Northcote Road, SW11
020 7223 4487
www.la-cuisiniere.co.uk
In-depth kitchen and cookware.

Leon Jaeggi
77 Shaftesbury Avenue, W1
020 7580 1974
Professional catering equipment.

Pages
121 Shaftesbury Avenue, W1
020 7240 4259
Professional catering equipment.

Richard Dare
93 Regent's Park Road, NW1
020 7722 9428
www.richarddare.com
Tasteful pans and tableware.

See Woo
19 Lisle St, WC2
020 7439 8325
Chinese woks and tableware.

FOODIE MARKETS

Berwick Street Market, W1
Berwick Street
(from Broadwick Street to Peter Street)
Open: Mon-Sat 9am-5pm
A traditional fruit and veg market with a great fish stall in the heart of Soho.

Brixton Market, SW9
Electric Avenue and Atlantic Road
Open: Mon-Sat 8am-5.30pm
A sprawling international food market.

Smithfield Market, EC1
Charter House Street
Open: Mon-Fri 4am-12noon
London's oldest wholesale meat market, which also welcomes individual customers.

Chapel Market, N1
Chapel Market
(between Liverpool Road and Baron Street)
Open: Tues-Sat 9am-6pm, Sun 9am-4pm
A great local food market offering good quality fruit and veg, fresh fish and several delicatessen stalls.

Church Street Market, NW8 & W2
Church Street (from Edgware Road to Lisson Grove)
Open: Tues-Sat 9am-5pm
This market is at its best on Saturdays when there is a good mix of quality food stalls.

Portobello Road Market, W11
Lonsdale Road to Lancaster Road
Open: Mon-Sat 8am-6.30pm, Thurs 8am-1pm
This market is best known for its antiques market, but the daily food market is one of the best in London.

Broadway Market, E8
London Fields
Open: Sat 9am-4.30pm
The food here is excellent with fresh bread and pastries, cheeses, organic meat and a good choice of fruit and veg.

Northcote Road Market, SW11
North end of Northcote Road
Open: Mon-Sat 9am-5pm, Wed 9am-1pm
A good local market with fresh produce, bread and deli foods available.

Borough Market, SE1
Southwark Street
Open: Fri 12noon-6pm, Sat 9am-4pm
London's largest and finest (see page 144).

Billingsgate Market, E14
North Quay of West India Dock, Isle of Dogs
Open: Tues-Sat 5am-8.30am
London's large scale fresh fish market and well worth a visit if you can manage to get up that early.

Ridley Road Market, E8
Ridley Road
Open: Mon-Sat 9am-5pm
A large market with food from all over the world.

Walthamstow Market, E17
Walthamstow Market
Open: Mon-Sat 9am-5pm
London's longest market with some very good food stalls. There is also a farmers' market here on Sunday (see Farmer's Markets opposite).

Whitechapel Market, E1
North side of Whitechapel Road
(from Vallance Road to Brady Street)
Open: Mon-Sat 8.30am-5.30pm, Thurs 8.30am-1pm
A vibrant market with lots of fresh produce.

FARMERS' MARKETS

London Farmers' Markets
www.lfm.org.uk

Acton W3
Public Square on Acton High Street/King Street
Open: Sat 9am-1pm

Blackheath SE3
Blackheath Rail Station Car Park,
2 Blackheath Village
Open: Sun 10am-2pm

Clapham SW4
Bonneville Primary School,
Bonneville Gardens
Open: Sun 10am-2pm

Ealing W13
Leeland Road, West Ealing
Open: Sat 9am-1pm

Islington N1
William Tyndale School,
Upper Street
Open: Sun 10am-2pm

Marylebone W1
Cramer Street Car Park,
Corner Moxon Street
(off Marylebone High Street)
Open: Sun 10am-2pm

Notting Hill W8
Car Park behind Waterstones
(access via Kensington Place)
Open: Sat 9am-1pm

Peckham SE15
Peckham Square, Peckham High St
Open: Sun 9.30am-1.30pm

Pimlico Road SW1
Orange Square, Corner of Pimlico Road
& Ebury Street
Open: Sat 9am-1pm

Queen's Park NW6
Salusbury Primary School, Salusbury Road
Open: Sun 10am-2pm

South Kensington SW7
Bute Street (just off Brompton Road)
Open: Sat 9am-1pm

Swiss Cottage NW3
Eton Avenue (opposite Hampstead Theatre)
Open: Wed 10am-4pm

Twickenham TW1
Holly Road Car Park (off King Street)
Open: Sat 9am-1pm

Walthamstow E17
Town Square by
Selbourne Walk Shopping Centre (off King Street)
Open: Sun 10am-2pm

Wimbledon SW19
Wimbledon Park High School, Havana Road
Open: Sat 9am-1pm

Growing Communities
www.growingcommunities.org

Stoke Newington Farmers' Market, N16
William Patten School,
Stoke Newington Church Street
Open: Sat 10am-2.30pm
London's only independent farmers' market which
is run by a local food initiative called Growing
Communities (see above).

BIBLIOGRAPHY

Ackroyd, Peter, *London the Biography*, Chatto & Windus, 2000

Clifford, Sue & King, Angela, *England in Particular*, Hodder & Stoughton, 2006

David, Elizabeth, *Harvest of the Cold Months*, Michael Joseph, 1994

Davidson, Alan, *The Oxford Companion to Food*, Oxford University Press, 1999

Fearnley-Whittingstall, Hugh, *The River Cottage Meat Book*, Hodder & Stoughton, 2004

Hibbert, Christopher, *London the Biography of a City*, Penguin Books, 1980

Hope, Annette, *Londoners' Larder*, Mainstream Publishing, 1990

Hsiung, Deh-ta, *The Chinese Kitchen*, Kyle Cathie, 1999

Humble, Nicola, *Culinary Pleasures*, Faber & Faber, 2005

Jayne-Staines, Sara, *Chocolate the Definitive Guide*, Grub Street, 1999

Mason, Laura, *Traditional Foods of Britain*, Prospect Books, 1999

Mayhew, Henry, edited by Quennell, Peter, *Mayhew's London*, Bracken Books, 1987

Liddell, Caroline and Weir, Robin, *Ices the Definitive Guide*, Grub Street, 1999

Merriman, Nick (Ed), *The Peopling of London*, Museum of London, 1994

Michelson, Patricia, *The Cheese Room*, Penguin Books, 2005

Norman, Jill, *The New Penguin Cookery Book*, Penguin, 2001

Panjabi, Camellia, *Fifty Great Curries of India*, Kyle Cathie Ltd, 1995

Picard, Liza, *Restoration London*, Phoenix, 1997

Richardson, John, *The Annals of London*, Cassell & Co, 2000

Roden, Claudia, *Coffee*, Penguin Books, 1981

Roden, Claudia, *The Food of Italy*, Chatto & Windus, 1989

So, Yan-kit, *Yan kit's Classic Chinese Cookbook*, Dorling Kindersley, 1989

Spencer, Colin, *British Food*, Grub Street, 2002

Trager, James, *The Food Chronology*, Aurum Press Ltd, 1996

Weinreb, Ben and Hibbert, Christopher (Ed), *The London Encyclopedia*, Papermac, 1987

INDEX